SELECTED LITERARY AND POLITICAL PAPERS AND ADDRESSES OF WOODROW WILSON

VOLUME ONE

COPYRIGHT BY PACH BROTHERS, N.Y.

Woodrow Wilson

SELECTED LITERARY AND POLITICAL PAPERS AND ADDRESSES OF WOODROW WILSON

IN THREE VOLUMES
VOLUME I

PUBLISHED BY ARRANGEMENT
WITH HARPER & BROTHERS

GROSSET & DUNLAP
PUBLISHERS   NEW YORK

CONTENTS

Written while Wilson was a senior at Princeton
and published in the *International Review,*
August, 1879, Vol. 6, pp. 146–163. It is a curious fact, recalled during the latter years of Wilson's life, that Henry Cabot Lodge was editor of
the *International Review* and thus became the
publisher of the future President's first article.

The one hundredth anniversary of the inauguration of George Washington. Address delivered
April 30, 1889 (place not given). From original manuscript in Mr. Wilson's handwriting:
in Mrs. Wilson's possession.

From *The Forum,* December, 1896, Vol. 22,
pp. 447–466. An oration delivered at the
Princeton Sesqui-centennial celebration, October
21, 1896.

From the *Atlantic Monthly,* March, 1897, Vol.
79, pp. 289–300. Walter H. Page was then
editor of the *Atlantic Monthly.*

Speech before the New England Society of New
York City, December 22, 1900. Proceedings
printed by William Green, New York, 1900, pp.
39–49.

Woodrow Wilson lived from 1856 to 1921. During most of his career he was greatly engaged, either in Princeton University or in public and national politics. He was a most thoughtful and incessant energy. He composed constant books and delivered innumerable addresses and orations.

The result is a mass of papers which could never be compressed into regular tomes.

Of his interesting efforts, by far the best and those volume contained MAN OF MAN, for which Ex- says "when Jefferson said 'Know the Man Comes to himself". They reveal the rich variety of his work and interests. In addition to giving a vivid picture of his conceptions of the fundamental, they contain much of the point of view—his view, his story—the point of view, which he expressed in his longer historical works, such as his "History of the American People", "Division and Reunion", and "George Washington", published while he was living at Princeton. They give a view of that most interesting phase of his life, before he turned from literature and education to public. In a literary sense they are the best of Wilson.

They, therefore, have been presented in this set complete.

PREFACE

1

WOODROW WILSON lived from 1856 to 1924. During most of those years he was actively engaged, either in Princeton University or in state and national politics. He was a man of fertile mind and incessant energy. He wrote articles and books, and delivered innumerable addresses and orations.

The result is a mass of papers which could never be compressed into popular form.

Of his literary efforts, by far the best are those volumes entitled "An Old Master, and Other Essays", "Mere Literature", and "When a Man Comes to Himself". They reveal the wide variety of his intellectual interests. In addition to giving a vivid picture of his conception of the humanities, they contain much of his point of view toward history—the point of view which he expressed in his longer historical works, such as his "History of the American People", "Division and Reunion" and "George Washington", published while he was living at Princeton. They give a view of that most interesting phase of his life before he turned from literature and education to politics. In a literary sense, they are the best of Wilson.

They, therefore, have been included in this set complete.

Where Wilson's political activities are concerned, these present volumes aim to present only the more important and self-revealing of his personal and political papers and addresses, and to present in succinct form a picture of the natural evolution of his ideals.

They contain Mr. Wilson's early literary articles, political papers and addresses, as well as the more interesting of the articles and speeches he delivered while Professor of Jurisprudence at Princeton, and later as President of that University. These papers are significant,—because Wilson's struggle at Princeton was a forerunner of his later larger struggle. They show clearly his steady intellectual growth. Practically all the theories on government and society which he later elaborated into political proposals, are evident in these papers, many of them written while he was still in his forties and before he became Governor of New Jersey.

Practically all the important documents of his later political career, are contained herein—those on the Tariff, the Federal Reserve, the Panama Canal Act, the Mobile speech in which he outlined his policy towards South America, and the more important addresses delivered before America entered the World War.

Of his War papers, only the most vital are included in this selection. It has not been thought necessary to include the actual Covenant of the League of Nations, which he was so largely instrumental in creating, nor the long list of popular speeches which he delivered in favor of the United

States joining the League.   These are well known
and available in many other forms, and add little
of vital consequence to the picture of Woodrow Wilson's ideas on that subject which the papers in these
volumes present.

   To the student who desires to make a more complete study of the subject, the Public Papers of
Woodrow Wilson, edited by Ray Stannard Baker and
William E. Dodd, and published by Harper & Bro.,
are recommended.   The papers in this set are largely
drawn from that source, and this present edition
would have been impossible had it not been for the
courtesy of their editors.   Any complete view of
Wilson should include a perusal of those volumes.

IDA M. TARBELL.

INTRODUCTION

WOODROW WILSON was born in Staunton, Virginia, on December 28, 1856. His family moved to Augusta, Georgia, the next year and, consequently, the early youth of the later President was spent in the beautiful old Southern town in the midst of the cotton belt. After the civil war Dr. Joseph Ruggles Wilson, the father, moved to Columbia, South Carolina, to become professor of theology in the school made famous by James H. Thornwell, one of the greatest preachers of his time. But Columbia and Augusta were different only in the intensity of their devotion to the cause of the South in the war between the sections.

The schools that give Wilson his early training were conducted by masters engaged for their learning in the classics and paid out of the pockets of the patrons. Wilson was never in a public school. But the principal instructor of young Woodrow was Doctor Wilson himself, a master of English form and diction, as one notes from the sermons that have come down to us. Out of this environment of the old and broken South, of influential Presbyterian preachers and pedagogues of the old style, young Wilson was sent to Davidson College, North Carolina, literally a school of the prophets for the Pres-

byterian Church of the South, in the autumn of
1874. There he remained the better part of a year.
In September, 1875, he went to Princeton, where
he received the regular four years' college course of
the time, mainly classical in its content.

From Princeton he went to the University of Virginia to "take law" under the greatest of all Southern teachers of that subject, Dr. John B. Minor.
There Wilson finished his formal legal training and
in 1882 he began the practice of his profession in
Atlanta. Already the young man had shown his
interest in and fitness for public life, and to so impatient a youth law seemed tedious and slow. He
abandoned the profession and renewed his studies at
the new Johns Hopkins University in the autumn of
1882. During the succeeding eight years he was a
student and a teacher, occupying positions in the
faculties of Johns Hopkins, Bryn Mawr, and Wes-
leyan universities. In September, 1890, he became
Professor of Jurisprudence in Princeton. There he
and his wife, Ellen Axson, of Savannah, Georgia, a
woman of similar Southern charm and background
as her husband, made their home for the next
twenty years, a remarkable home, simple, hospitable,
and a center of intellectual and social interests where
all the connections were ever at ease. From 1890
to 1910, Wilson remained at Princeton, first as a
professor and then as president and professor for
eight years; and two years as Governor of New Jersey brought him to the Presidency on March 4, 1913.
These years of keen and active intellectual life made

Mr. Wilson known to the country; they were the years
of his great apprenticeship.

The output of these preparatory years was a body
of literary material of great interest to any student
of American history and institutions.   A popular
history of the United States and a life of George
Washington   were   the   most   important,   perhaps,
though his little manual, *Division and Reunion,* was
of great value in the way of better interpretation of
the national conflict about slavery.   There were other
books—*Congressional Government, The State, Mere
Literature, An Old Master and Other Essays,* and
Constitutional Government in the United States—
which attest the *industry* and *range of interest* of
their author, and a vast flow of articles and addresses
not now accessible to the public.

When scanned carefully these papers illustrate admirably the growth of Woodrow Wilson as a thinker
and indicate the range and character of his major
interests.   In one of the earliest statements we note
a strong characteristic of the man:

It is not my purpose to represent any particular interest;
no man with his senses about him would recommend perfect
freedom of trade; protection is nothing more than a bounty
and bounties enable manufacturers to build up interests; [that
may have been permissible in times of war] but now that
peace has come, the South will insist upon having the fruits
of peace.

There was in this no dogmatic adherence to a doctrine, notwithstanding he and his section were identified with the ideal and the interest of free trade.

Of similar tendency was his advocacy of a closer relation between the Executive and Congress in the national government. He was one of the first of American publicists to point out the weakness of the system of checks and balances so perfectly illustrated in the conduct of Congress and Presidents. His first article that secured a wide reading began very much as a similar study of our government might begin to-day:

Our patriotism seems of late to have been exchanging its wonted tone of confident hope for one of desponding solicitude. Anxiety about the future of our institutions seems to be daily becoming stronger in the minds of thoughtful Americans. . . . Both State and National legislatures are looked upon with nervous suspicion, and we hail an adjournment of congress as a temporary immunity from danger.

In both of the statements from which the above quotations are taken there appears the strong note of interest in public questions. Of similar but more historic importance is the following striking summing up of the career and personality of Grover Cleveland, whom Wilson knew rather intimately and admired greatly:

We need not pretend to know what history shall say of Mr. Cleveland; we need not pretend that we can draw any common judgment of the man from the confused cries that now ring everywhere from friend and foe. We know only that he has played a great part; that his greatness is authenticated by the passion of love and hatred he has stirred up; that no such great personality has appeared in our politics since Lincoln; and that, either greater or less, his personality is his own, unique in the varied history of our government. He has made policies and altered parties after the fashion of an earlier age in our history, and the men who assess his fame in the future will be no partisans, but men who love candor, courage, honesty, strength, unshaken capacity, and high purpose such as his.

These quotations show the direction of Wilson's thought during the whole of his life, but as he rose to greater influence in the administration and guidance of Princeton, he tended to abandon political themes for education, education, to be sure, as a means of a better social and political order. When, therefore, the old college which he had known as a student was formally converted into a university and he was asked to take part in the proceedings, he made elaborate preparations and spoke to a vast audience on October 21, 1896, an audience of distinguished alumni and friends of the new university:

I have had sight of the perfect place of learning in my thought: a free place, and a various, where no man can be and not know with how great a destiny knowledge had come into the world—itself a little world; but not perplexed, living with a singleness of aim not known without; the home of sagacious men, hard-headed and with a will to know, debaters of the world's questions every day and used to the rough ways of democracy; and yet a place removed—calm science seated there, recluse, ascetic like a nun, not knowing that the world passes, not caring, if the truth but come in answer to her prayer; and Literature, walking within her open doors, in quiet chambers, with men of olden time, storied walls about her, and calm voices infinitely sweet; a place where ideals are kept in heart in an air they can breathe; but no fool's paradise. A place where to hear the truth about the past and hold debate about the affairs of the present, with knowledge and without passion; like the world in having all men's life at heart, a place for men and all that concerns them; but unlike the world in its self-possession, its thorough way of talk, its care to know more than the moment brings to light; slow to take excitement, its air pure and wholesome with a breath of faith; every eye within it bright in the clear day and quick to look toward heaven for the confirmation of its hope. Who shall show us the way to this place?

This was the ideal, an ideal college life, devotion to learning and the public interest, never realized anywhere on earth. But Wilson was nothing if not an idealist. As the years passed at Princeton and the professor of jurisprudence came to be recognized by his fellows, and by the trustees as well, as the foremost teacher of his subject perhaps in the country, there was an instant demand that he be made president to succeed Doctor Patton, who retired in June, 1902. Wilson was chosen and forthwith he began the campaign of education that made Princeton a subject of discussion wherever educators were assembled. He began his fateful career as president of Princeton University with zeal and energy. Before the end of December, 1902, he had formulated his first measure of reform. It was the tutorial system:

Gentlemen, if we could get a body of such tutors at Princeton we could transform the place from a place where there are youngsters doing tasks to a place where there are men doing thinking, men who are conversing about the things of thought, men who are eager and interested in the things of thought.

Seven short years followed. Wilson gathered millions of dollars for his new ventures in education; he set up the preceptorial system and more than doubled the number of instructors; and finally he sought to bring all the classmen and the clubs that were based on ideas of social separateness into common association. On this hard proposition of democracy and co-operation he failed. Slowly the students learned to resist him. Then some professors resented his growing prestige and sweeping control of all the life of the place. And finally the alumni reached a state of divided allegiance which threatened his sources of financial supplies. But before 1910 his influence and his career at Princeton had become known throughout the country. Other teachers and leaders in the field of education were profoundly influenced, albeit little official sympathy was expressed. The bearings of his work were tending more and more toward social and political issues; and it was clear that he was reapproaching his earlier realm of thought—politics.

In plain realization of this tendency of his life he said at the University of North Carolina on the occasion of the celebration of the anniversary of the birth of Robert E. Lee:

This man was not great because he was born of a soldier and bred in a school of soldiers, but because, of whomsoever he may have been born, howsoever he was bred, he was a man who saw his duty, who conceived it in high terms, and who spent himself, not upon his own ambitions, but in the duty that lay before him. . . . Now, what does it mean that General Lee is accepted as a national hero? It means simply this delightful thing, that there are no sections in this country any more; that we are a nation and are proud of all the great heroes whom the great processes of our national life have elevated into conspicuous places of fame. . . . I spoke just now in disparagement of the vocation of an orator. I wish there were some great orator who could go about and make men drunk with this spirit of self-sacrifice. I wish there were some man whose tongue might every day carry abroad the golden accents of that creative age in which we were born a nation; accents which would ring like tones of reassurance around the whole circle of the globe, so that America might again have the distinction of showing men the way, the certain way, of achievement and of confident hope.

In these last lines one readily notes the prophecy of his own future. That some one might again show the way, the way of achievement and of hope. Had he not closed his famous address to his Princeton friends in 1896 with this fond hope as applied to the realm of education? Now it is the way of the whole world upon which the true orator and leader of men would cast his helpful light. He was hardly through with the task in North Carolina and the South before we find him in Chicago on the occasion of the celebration of the hundredth anniversary of the birth of Abraham Lincoln, declaring before a distinguished Northern audience:

The most valuable thing about Mr. Lincoln was that in the midst of the strain of war, in the midst of the crash of arms, he could sit quietly in his room and enjoy a book that led his thoughts off from everything American; could wander in fields of dreams, while every other man was hot with the immediate contest. Always set your faith in a man who can withdraw himself, because only the man who can withdraw himself can see the stage; only the man who can withdraw himself can see affairs as they are.

And so the lesson of this day is faith in the common product of the nation; the lesson of this day is [that] the future as well as the past leadership of men, wise men, has come from the people. We should not be Americans deserving to call ourselves the fellow-countrymen of Lincoln if we did not feel the compulsion that his example lays upon us—the compulsion not to heed him merely but to look to our own duty, to live every day as if that were the day upon which America was to be reborn and remade.

In these addresses he is not so much the historian as he had been in his earlier writings; he is no longer the leader of a reform movement in an American university. He is making his appeal to men everywhere to remake their country and vaguely conscious of that destiny which beckons him first to the Governorship of New Jersey, then to the Presidency of the United States, and finally to that greater stage of the modern world, Paris, whence he was to return a broken, if not a disillusioned, man. In the midst of these growing interests he never ceased to take an active part in the religious problems and development of the country, as the following excerpt from one of his most famous speeches shows:

"I hope that the last thing I will ever be capable of will be casting a shadow on the church, and yet the churches—the Protestant churches, at least—have dissociated themselves from the people. They serve the classes, not the masses. They serve certain visible, uplifted strata and ignore the men whose need is dire."

Already he was interested in all the greater things

that were to come before him as President, interested
in and vaguely conscious of the causes and events
that were to make of his life one of the climaxes and
one of the tragedies of modern history.

II

The period of Mr. Wilson's leadership of the
United States was that of 1913 to 1917—a time when
the country was taking stock of its heritage and
its ideals. At this time Wilson formulated and put
into practice his progressive program, the most democratic and the most comprehensive of all the pro-
grams ever offered the country by any single leader.

It was a time of great stress, of violent prejudices,
like that of 1801 and 1861, and the President felt
every day of his life the press of danger, of opposition, and the risk of blunder. No other President
has ever been watched more closely; and only one
other has ever parried attack more successfully. An
anxious time for anxious souls: all the liberal and
imaginative and even dreamy men and women of
the country were looking with intense excitement and
praying with evident emotion for the "delicate" man
in the White House. And Wilson's words in speech
and messages throughout the four years reveal his
sense of anxiety and responsibility—responsibility
to the masses of "unknown men" and above all to
History, which he imagined would deal honestly, if
severely, with his record. One sees excellent evidence
of this in the first inaugural, worthy to be compared
with the two or three great inaugurals of his prede-
cessors in office:

We have built up a great system of government which has
stood through a long age as in many respects a model for
those who seek to set liberty upon foundations that will en-
dure against fortuitous change, against storm and accident.
Our life contains every great thing, and contains it in rich
abundance.

But the evil has come with the good, and much fine gold
has been corroded. With riches has come inexcusable waste.
We have squandered a great part of what we might have
used and have not stopped to conserve the exceeding bounty
of nature . . . scorning to be careful, shamefully prodigal
as well as admirably efficient. We have been proud of our
industrial achievements, but we have not hitherto stopped
. . . to count the human cost, the cost of lives snuffed out,
of energies overtaxed and broken, the fearful physical and
spiritual cost to the men and women and children upon whom
the dead weight and burden of it all has fallen pitilessly the
years through. The groans and agony of it all. . . . The
great Government we loved has too often been made use of
for private and selfish purposes, and those who used it had
forgotten the people.

There one feels the spirit and solemn tone of the
new leader. An honest, brooding, prophetic spirit
elevated in that fateful year to the highest position
to which one can be elevated in the United States, a
leader resolute of will and moved by a passion that
now and then led him close to the abyss of blunder.

III

Then burst the Great War upon the world, Wilson
sitting by the bedside of his dying wife, one of the
truest of women and noblest of wives. The brooding pedagogue of Princeton; cast out of the house

of his fellows by the very ideals that sent him to Washington, of necessity turned his thought upon ancient Europe, in one of those devastating grapples for life and supremacy that have now and then shaken the whole world. It was an embittered conflict as terrible as the Napoleonic wars. What would the United States, peopled by many races, immensely rich but screened by the Atlantic, have to do in such a conflict; and how would the frail philosopher interpret and guide the will of his complex and uneasy country? It was as critical a period as American history has known since Lincoln won his second election.

The program of the new democracy was hardly half enacted when the European war broke. The United States was dividing sharply and, as we think, preparing to defeat the President and make of his idealism a worthless abortion. But Germany let loose the dogs of war and two weeks afterward the President uttered the words which made him bitter enemies everywhere his name was spoken:

The people of the United States are drawn from many nations, and chiefly from the nations now at war. . . . Some will wish one nation, others another, to succeed in the momentous struggle. It will be easy to excite passion and difficult to allay it. . . . I venture, therefore, my fellow countrymen, to speak a solemn word of warning. . . . The United States must be neutral in fact as well as in name during these days that are to try men's souls. We must be impartial in thought as well as in action, must put a curb upon our sentiments as well as upon every transaction.

Was there ever such neutrality? Perhaps only

when Washington proclaimed neutrality in 1793.
But men had forgotten Washington and the French
Revolution. The reformer of a young and unruly
nation was now set both to making new or remaking
old laws while he must seek to keep warring elements and hostile instincts calm.

A year had hardly passed before Wilson was compelled to issue a warning to Imperial Germany that
seemed to anger every German in the United States.
A few days after the *Lusitania* was sunk he wrote
to the German Emperor:

In view of recent acts of the German authorities in viola-
tion of American rights on the high seas which culminated in
the torpedoing and sinking of the British steamship *Lusitania*,
on May 7, 1915, by which over one hundred American citizens
lost their lives, it is clearly wise and desirable that the Government of the United States and the Imperial German Government should come to a clear and full understanding as to the
grave situation which has resulted. . . . Expressions of regret
and offers of reparation in case of the destruction of neutral
ships sunk by mistake . . . can not justify or excuse a practice, the natural and necessary effect of which is to subject
neutral nations and neutral persons to new and immeasurable
risks.

The Imperial German Government will not expect the Government of the United States to omit any word or any act
necessary to the performance of its sacred duty of maintaining
the rights of the United States and its citizens and of safe-
guarding their free exercise and enjoyment.

It was a solemn warning to the imperialists of
Germany then entering upon what they thought
would be the last campaign of the war. Wilson
doubtless made less impression upon them than

the earnestness of his character ought to have commanded. He was ridiculed at home as "the schoolmaster," the leaders of Berlin taking him to be an ambitious amateur in the great game of "high politics." There followed a series of notes between Wilson and the Kaiser in which the President's passion for peace was seen to be strongly modified by his love of justice, perhaps the fighting blood of his Covenanter ancestors. The Allies did not like the notes, and in the United States opinion was sharply divided. But the historian reads them today with increasing admiration. The notes served to uncover the spirit and purposes of the German imperialists, and that seems to have been one of their major purposes.

IV

In December, 1915, the President made up his mind that the dangers of war were so imminent that he undertook the preparedness campaign which began in New York on the 27th of that month and ended at St. Louis, February 3, 1916, in a statement that looked clearly like belligerency:

You have either got to make the men of this Nation in sufficient number ready to defend the Nation against initial disaster, or you have got to take the risk of initial disaster. Think of the cruelty, think of the stupidity of putting raw levies of inexperienced men into the modern field of battle! We are not asking for armies; we are asking for a trained citizenship. . . . Have you ever let your imagination dwell upon the enormous stretch of coast from the Canal to Alaska—

from the Canal to the northern corner of Maine? There is no
other navy in the world that has to cover so great an area
of defense as the American Navy, and it ought, in my judgment, to be incomparably the most adequate navy in the world.

That sounded like German army and British navy
talk. But it guarded most carefully against any inference as to which side of the great conflict interested him most. From Wilson's return to Washington the next day till after election, preparations were
making for a possible entrance into the war—and
Congress lagged, very many of its members growing
resentful, willing to have all Americans abandon
the ocean entirely rather than risk a conflict.

In this state of opinion Wilson held a secret conference with a few leaders of Congress, presented
to them the likelihood of American participation in
the war. These leaders, we are now well informed,
grew angry, threatened to denounce the President
and carry the issue of war or peace to the country
in the coming election. Under these circumstances
Wilson bore his part in the House negotiations of
that summer, managed to hold Ambassador Page
in peaceful leash, and secured for himself renomi-
nation to the Presidency on a platform which "fea-
tured" the slogan, "He kept us out of war."

For a man so honest, high toned, and resolute the
position was most embarrassing. His speeches show
him constantly edging toward the position taken at
Cincinnati:

There had been growing up in Europe a mutual suspicion . . . an interlacing of alliances and understandings, a

complex web of intrigue and spying, that presently was sure
to entangle the whole of the family of mankind on that side
of the water in its meshes. Now revive that after this war
is over and sooner or later you will have just such another
war, and this is the last war of the kind or of any other
kind that involves the world that the United States can keep
out of. I say that because I believe that the business of
neutrality is over; not because I want it to be over but . . .
because the position of neutrals . . . becomes intolerable.
. . . We must have a society of nations. . . . The nations of
the world must get together and say: "nobody can hereafter
be neutral as respects the disturbance of the world's
peace. . . ."

His conduct of the campaign, in spite of embarrassments and most delicate foreign situations, was
masterly and its record is both honorable and distinguished.

V

Although the election gave the President a vast
popular majority and the new lease of office seemed
to be more than a mere vote of confidence, his leadership was by no means conceded by the great of the
country. No President since Lincoln has ever been
hated and feared so deeply. But in December he
endeavored to bring the warring parties into a peace
conference. He failed because Europe would not
listen, but, still hopeful of peace for the United
States, he turned to the Senate on January 22, 1917,
and after asserting that the implication of the assurances given by both groups of nations was that
"it must be a peace without victory" and that "only
a peace between equals can last," he said:

I would fain believe that I am speaking for the silent mass of mankind. . . . I am proposing . . . that the nations should with one accord adopt the doctrine of President Monroe as the doctrine of the world: that no nation should seek to extend its polity over any other nation or people, but that every people should be left free to determine its own polity, its own way of development, unhindered, unthreatened, unafraid, the little along with the great and powerful. . . . I am proposing government by the consent of the governed; that freedom of the seas which . . . representatives of the United States have urged . . . and that moderation of armaments which makes of armies and navies a power for order merely, not an instrument of aggression. . . .

This speech included ideas broached and discussed by Wilson in private conversation during the preceding twelve months, ideas which he touched upon in most of his preparedness and electoral campaigns. They were ideas that had been instinct, even agitated, in all early American history; they were the ideas which underlay the Wilson democracy, but they were not entirely acceptable either to the Senate or the angry constituencies behind Eastern public men and newspapers. Whatever Wilson did was certain to meet with violent opposition, but it was clear to all that war with Germany was hastening.

It was but a short step from the failure of the appeal to all the warring powers in December and the deeply prophetic appeal to the Senate of January 22d to the calling of Congress in extra session to consider at last the issue that had been thrust before the country by the *Lusitania* incident. The inaugural address of March 1917 presaged war; April saw the solemn declaration. The mobilization which followed, guided by the firm hand of the President, was upon a scale as vast and orderly as it was unprecedented. Four million men were called to the colors, munition plants were built to arm, and ships to transport them. Billions of dollars were raised to finance these stupendous operations. Following the vanguard of the American forces which were landed in France in June, 1917, nearly two million men were transported across three thousand miles of submarine-infested ocean. The tide of a deadlocked war was turned, and victory for the Allied arms assured. It was such an exhibition of gigantic power, utilized with coöperative skill and swift effectiveness, as the world had never seen before.

The recession and demobilization which followed the Armistice of November, 1918, was as striking in its way as the creation of the army had been, for it was wholly without disorder, and within four months after the close of hostilities the country had practically returned to normal conditions.

While these vast administrative processes were under way, the President, as the undisputed spokesman of the Allied and Associated Powers, became the dominating force in world diplomacy. He defined the objects for which America was entering the war, lifted the entire struggle to a new plane of moral purpose, and conducted with masterly skill the complicated negotiations with the enemy powers which led up to the Armistice. He laid down the accepted bases of the peace, the corner stone of which was to be a new world organization, a League of Nations.

The months that followed the Armistice of November, 1918, were rich in the essence of great and swift-moving drama. Breaking the century-old precedents of his office, the President set sail for Europe to join in the making of the peace. He was received by the people like some emperor turned savior; he declared again his ideals, again set forth his principles—but with ominous clouds of doubt and opposition beginning to gather. He entered the councils at Paris, bore a vital part in reconstituting the nations of the world, and by the exercise of sheer personal power secured the immediate adoption of the Covenant of a world League of Nations. He returned to his own country to find his support crumbling away from behind him. A nation saved from danger and raised to a new preëminence was turning swiftly from the visions its leader had inspired to the flesh pots of a new prosperity. A bitter struggle with the Senate over the ratification of the treaty continued for months. The tide which had been flowing so long and so powerfully with the Covenanter had now turned against him. He continued to fight the harder. In September, 1919, he made his great final appeal to the people for a renewal of their support. He had never for a moment lost faith in the people. If he could explain his purpose to the people they would compel the Senate to act! He had warnings enough of impaired physical vigor; he had been told that any such campaign would result disastrously. Nevertheless he went forward. He delivered forty addresses in twenty-two days, he traveled six thousand miles; a feat as amazing intellectually as it was physically. But the best that he had, all that he had, was not enough. The forces arrayed against him, his own physical limitations among them, were too strong. The worn Covenanter broke down before his appeal was concluded and there followed the sad return to Washington, the grim and tragic later years, and death on the winter day in 1924 with the street outside crowded with people kneeling in prayer.

RAY STANNARD BAKER.

WILLIAM E. DODD.

CABINET GOVERNMENT IN THE UNITED STATES

WRITTEN WHILE WILSON WAS A SENIOR AT PRINCETON AND PUBLISHED IN THE "INTERNATIONAL REVIEW," AUGUST, 1879, VOL. VI, PP. 46-163. IT IS A CURIOUS FACT, RECALLED DURING THE LATER YEARS OF WIL-SON'S LIFE, THAT HENRY CABOT LODGE WAS EDITOR OF THE "INTERNATIONAL REVIEW" AND THUS BECAME THE PUBLISHER OF THE FUTURE PRESIDENT'S FIRST ARTICLE.

OUR patriotism seems of late to have been exchanging its wonted tone of confident hope for one of desponding solicitude. Anxiety about the future of our institutions seems to be daily becoming stronger in the minds of thoughtful Americans. A feeling of uneasiness is undoubtedly prevalent, sometimes taking the shape of a fear that grave, perhaps radical, defects in our mode of government are militating against our liberty and prosperity. A marked and alarming decline in statesmanship, a rule of levity and folly instead of wisdom and sober forethought in legislation, threaten to shake our trust not only in the men by whom our national policy is controlled, but also in the very principles upon which our Government rests. Both State and National legislatures are looked upon with nervous suspicion, and we hail an adjournment of Congress as a temporary immunity from danger. In casting about for the chief cause of the admitted evil, many persons have convinced themselves that it is to be found in the principle of universal suffrage. When Dr. Woolsey, in his admirable work on Political Science, speaks with despondency of the influence of this principle upon our political life, he simply gives clear expression to misgivings which he shares with a growing minority of his countrymen. We must, it is said, purge the constituencies of their ignorant elements, if we would have high-minded, able, worthy representatives. We see adventurers, who in times of revolution and confusion were suffered to climb to high and responsible places, still holding positions of trust; we perceive that our institutions, when once thrown out of gear, seem to possess no power of self-readjustment,—and we hasten to cast discredit upon that principle the establishment of which has been regarded as America's greatest claim to political honor,—the right of every man to a voice in the Government under which he lives. The existence of such sentiments is in itself an instructive fact. But while it is indisputably true that universal suffrage is a constant element of weakness, and exposes us to many dangers which we might otherwise escape, its operation does not suffice alone to explain existing evils. Those who make this the scapegoat of all our national grievances have made too superficial an analysis of the abuses about which they so loudly complain.

What is the real cause of this solicitude and doubt? It is, in our opinion, to be found in the absorption of all power by a legislature which is practically irresponsible for its acts. But even this would not necessarily be harmful, were it not for the addition of a despotic principle which it is my present purpose to consider.

At its highest development, *representative* government is that form which best enables a free people to govern themselves. The main object of a representative assembly, therefore, should be the discussion of public business. They should legislate as if in the presence of the whole country, because they come under the closest scrutiny and fullest criticism of all the representatives of the country speaking in open and free debate. Only in such an assembly, only in such an atmosphere of publicity, only by means of such a vast investigating machine, can the different sections of a great country learn each other's feelings and interests. It is not enough that the general course of legislation is known to all. Unless during its progress it is subjected to a thorough, even a tediously prolonged, process of public sifting, to the free comment of friend and foe alike, to the ordeal of battle among those upon whose vote its fate depends, an act of open legislation may have its real intent and scope completely concealed by its friends and undiscovered by its enemies, and it may be as fatally mischievous as the darkest measures of an oligarchy or a despot. Nothing can be more obvious than the fact that the very life of free, popular institutions is dependent upon their breathing the bracing air of thorough, exhaustive, and open discussions, or that select Congressional committees, whose proceedings must from their very nature be secret, are, as means of legislation, dangerous and unwholesome. Parliaments are forces for freedom; for "talk is persuasion, persuasion is force, the one force which can sway freemen to deeds such as those which have made England what she is," or our English stock what it is.

Congress is a deliberative body in which there is little real deliberation; a legislature which legislates with no real discussion of its business. Our Government is practically carried on by irresponsible committees. Too few Americans take the trouble to inform themselves as to the methods of Congressional management; and, as a consequence, not many have perceived that almost *absolute* power has fallen into the hands of men whose irresponsibility prevents the regulation of their conduct by the people from whom they derive their authority. The most important, most powerful man in the government of the United States in time of peace is the Speaker of the House of Representatives. Instead of being merely an executive officer, whose principal duties are those immediately connected with the administration of the rules of order, he is a potent party chief, the only chief of any real potency,—and must of necessity be so. He must be the strongest and shrewdest member of his party in the lower House; for almost all the real business of that House is transacted by committees whose members are his nominees. Unless the rules of the House be suspended by a special two-thirds vote, every bill introduced must be referred, without debate, to the proper Standing Committee, with whom rests the privilege of embodying it, or any part of it, in their reports, or of rejecting it

altogether. The House very seldom takes any direct
action upon any measures introduced by individual
members; its votes and discussions are almost entirely confined to committee reports and committee
dictation. The whole attitude of business depends
upon forty-seven Standing Committees. Even the
discussions upon their directive reports are merely
nominal,—liberal forms, at most. Take, as an example of the workings of the systems, the functions
and privileges of the Committee of Ways and Means.
To it is intrusted the financial policy of the country;
its chairman is, in reality, our Chancellor of the
Exchequer. With the aid of his colleagues he determines the course of legislation upon finance; in
English political phrase, he draws up the *budget*.
All the momentous questions connected with our
finance are debated in the private sessions of this
committee, and there only. For, when the budget
is submitted to the House for its consideration, only
a very limited time is allowed for its discussion; and,
besides the member of the committee to whom its
introduction is intrusted, no one is permitted to speak
save those to whom he through courtesy yields the
floor, and who must have made arrangements beforehand with the Speaker to be recognized. Where,
then, is there room for thorough discussion,—for discussion of any kind? If carried, the provisions of
the budget must be put into operation by the Secretary of the Treasury, who may be directly opposed to
the principles which it embodies. If lost, no one
save Congress itself is responsible for the consequent
embarrassment into which the nation is brought,—

and Congress as a body is not readily punishable.

It must at once be evident to every thinking man that a policy thus regulated cannot be other than vacillating, uncertain, devoid of plan or consistency. This is certainly a phase of representative government peculiar to ourselves. And yet its development was most natural and apparently necessary. It is hardly possible for a body of several hundred men, without official or authoritative leaders, to determine upon any line of action without interminable wrangling and delays injurious to the interests under their care. Left to their own resources, they would be as helpless as any other mass meeting. Without leaders having authority to guide their deliberations and give a definite direction to the movement of legislation; and, moreover, with none of that sense of responsibility which constantly rests upon those whose duty it is to work out to a successful issue the policies which they themselves originate, yet with full power to dictate policies which others must carry into execution,—a recognition of the need of some sort of leadership, and of a division of labor, led to the formation of these Standing Committees, to which are intrusted the shaping of the national policy in the several departments of administration, as well as the prerogatives of the initiative in legislation and leadership in debate. When theoretically viewed, this is an ingenious and apparently harmless device, but one which, in practice, subverts that most fundamental of all the principles of a free State,—the right of the people to a potential voice in their own government. Great measures of legislation are discussed

and determined, not conspicuously in public session
of the people's representatives, but in the unapproachable privacy of committee rooms.

But what less imperfect means of representative
government can we find without stepping beyond the
bounds of a true republicanism? Certainly none
other than those which were rejected by the Constitutional Convention. When the Convention of 1787,
upon the submission of the report of the Committee
of Detail, came to consider the respective duties and
privileges of the legislative and executive departments, and the relations which these two branches of
the Government should sustain towards each other.
many serious questions presented themselves for solution. One of the gravest of these was, whether or
not the interests of the public service would be fur-
thered by *allowing some of the higher officers of State
to occupy seats in the legislature.* The propriety and
practical advantage of such a course were obviously
suggested by a similar arrangement under the British Constitution, to which our political fathers often
and wisely looked for useful hints. But since the
spheres of the several departments were in the end
defined with all the clearness, strictness, and care
possible to a written instrument, the opinion prevailed among the members of the Convention that it
would be unadvisable to establish any such connection between the Executive and Congress. They
thought, in their own fervor of patriotism and intensity of respect for written law, that paper barriers
would prove sufficient to prevent the encroachments
of any one department upon the prerogatives of any

other; that these vaguely broad laws—or principles
of law—would be capable of securing and maintaining the harmonious and mutually helpful co-operation of the several branches; that the exhibition of
these general views of government would be adequate
to the stupendous task of preventing the legislature
from rising to the predominance of influence, which,
nevertheless, constantly lay within its reach. But, in
spite of constitutional barriers, the legislature has
become the imperial power of the State, as it must
of necessity become under every representative system; and experience of the consequences of a complete
separation of the legislative and executive branches
long since led that able and sagacious commentator
upon the Constitution, Chief-Justice Story, to re-
mark that, "if it would not have been safe to trust
the heads of departments, as representatives, to the
choice of the people, as their constituents, it would
have been at least some gain to have allowed them
seats, like territorial delegates, in the House of Representatives, where they might freely debate without
a title to vote." In short, the framers of the Constitution, in endeavoring to act in accordance with
the principle of Montesquieu's celebrated and unquestionably just political maxim,—that the legislative, executive, and judicial departments of a free
State should be *separate,*—made their separation so
complete as to amount to *isolation.* To the methods
of representative government which have sprung
from these provisions of the Constitution, by which
the Convention thought so carefully to guard and
limit the powers of the legislature, we must look for

an explanation, in a large measure, of the evils over which we now find ourselves lamenting.

What, then, is Cabinet government? What is the change proposed? Simply to give to the heads of the Executive departments—the members of the Cabinet —seats in Congress, with the privilege of the initiative in legislation and some part of the unbounded privileges now commanded by the Standing Committees. But the advocates of such a change—and they are now not a few—deceive themselves when they maintain that it would not necessarily involve the principle of ministerial responsibility,—that is, the resignation of the Cabinet upon the defeat of any important part of their plans. For, if Cabinet officers sit in Congress as official representatives of the Executive, this principle of responsibility must of necessity come sooner or later to be recognized. Experience would soon demonstrate the practical impossibility of their holding their seats, and continuing to represent the Administration, after they had found themselves unable to gain the consent of a majority to their policy. Their functions would be peculiar. They would constitute a link between the legislative and executive branches of the general Government, and, as representatives of the Executive, must hold the right of the initiative in legislation. Otherwise their position would be an anomalous one indeed. There would be little danger and evident propriety in extending to them the first right of introducing measures relative to the administration of the several departments; and they could possess such a right without denying the fullest privileges to other

members. But, whether granted this initiative or
not, the head of each department would undoubtedly
find it necessary to take a decided and open stand for
or against every measure bearing upon the affairs of
his department, by whomsoever introduced. No high-
spirited man would long remain in an office in the
business of which he was not permitted to pursue a
policy which tallied with his own principles and convictions. If defeated by both Houses, he would naturally resign; and not many years would pass before
resignation upon defeat would have become an established precedent,—and resignation upon defeat is the
essence of responsible government. In arguing,
therefore, for the admission of Cabinet officers into
the legislature, we are logically brought to favor *responsible Cabinet government* in the United States.

But, to give the President the right to choose
whomsoever he pleases as his constitutional advisers,
after having constituted Cabinet officers *ex officio*
members of Congress, would be to empower him to
appoint a limited number of representatives, and
would thus be plainly at variance with republican
principles. The highest order of responsible government could, then, be established in the United States
only by laying upon the President the necessity of
selecting his Cabinet from among the number of representatives already chosen by the people, or by the
legislatures of the States.

Such a change in our legislative system would not
be so radical as it might at first appear: it would
certainly be very far from revolutionary. Under our
present system we suffer all the inconveniences, are

hampered by all that is defective in the machinery, of responsible government, without securing any of the many benefits which would follow upon its complete establishment. Cabinet officers are now appointed only with the consent of the Senate. Such powers as a Cabinet with responsible leadership must possess are now divided among the forty-seven Standing Committees, whose prerogatives of irresponsible leadership savor of despotism, because exercised for the most part within the secret precincts of a committee room, and not under the eyes of the whole House, and thus of the whole country. These committees, too, as has been said, rule without any of that freedom of public debate which is essential to the liberties of the people. Their measures are too often mere partisan measures, and are hurried through the forms of voting by a party majority whose interest it is that all serious opposition, all debate that might develop obstructive antagonism, should be suppressed. Under the conditions of Cabinet government, however, full and free debates are sure to take place. For what are these conditions? According as their policy stands or falls, the ministers themselves stand or fall; to the party which supports them each discussion involves a trial of strength with their opponents; upon it depends the amount of their success as a party; while to the opposition the triumph of ministerial plans means still further exclusion from office, their overthrow, accession to power. To each member of the assembly every debate offers an opportunity for placing himself, by able argument, in a position to command a place in

any future Cabinet that may be formed from the
ranks of his own party; each speech goes to the building up (or the tearing down) of his political fortunes.
There is, therefore, an absolute certainty that every
phase of every subject will be drawn carefully and
vigorously, will be dwelt upon with minuteness, will
be viewed from every possible standpoint. The legislative, holding full power of final decision, would
find itself in immediate contact with the executive
and its policy. Nor would there be room for factious
government or factious opposition. Plainly, ministers must found their policies, an opposition must
found its attacks, upon well-considered principles;
for in this open sifting of debate, when every feature
of every measure, even to the motives which
prompted it, is the subject of outspoken discussion
and keen scrutiny, no chicanery, no party craft, no
questionable principles can long hide themselves.
Party trickery, legislative jobbery, are deprived of
the very air they breathe,—the air of secrecy, of concealment. The public is still surprised whenever they
find that dishonest legislation has been allowed to
pass unchallenged. Why surprised? As things are,
measures are determined in the interests of corporations, and the suffering people know almost nothing
of them until their evil tendencies crop out in actual
execution. Under lobby pressure from interested
parties, they have been cunningly concocted in the
closest sessions of partisan committees, and, by the
all-powerful aid of party machinery, have been hurried through the stages of legislation without debate;
so that even Press correspondents are often as igno-

rant of the real nature of such special measures as the outside public. Any searching debate of such questions would at once have brought the public eye upon them, and how could they then have stood? Lifting the lid of concealment must have been the discovery to all concerned of their unsavory character. Light would have killed them.

We are thus again brought into the presence of the cardinal fact of this discussion,—that debate is the essential function of a popular representative body. In the severe, distinct, and sharp enunciation of underlying principles, the unsparing examination and telling criticism of opposite positions, the careful, painstaking unravelling of all the issues involved, which are incident to the free discussion of questions of public policy we see the best, the only effective, means of educating public opinion. Can any one suppose for one moment that, in the late heated and confused discussions of the Bland silver bill, the Western papers would have had any color of justification in claiming that the Resumption Act of 1875 was passed secretly and without the knowledge of the people, if we had then had responsible government? Although this all-important matter was before the country for more than a year; was considered by two Congresses, recommended by more than one Congressional committee; was printed and circulated for the perusal of the people; was much spoken of, though little understood by the Press at the time,—the general mass of our population knew little or nothing about it, for it elicited almost no statesmanlike comment upon the floor of Congress,

was exposed to none of the analysis of earnest debate. What, however, would have been its history
under a well-ordered Cabinet government? It would
have been introduced—if introduced at all—to the
House by the Secretary of the Treasury as a part of
the financial policy of the Administration, supported
by the authority and sanction of the entire Cabinet.
At once it would have been critically scanned by the
leaders of the opposition; at each reading of the bill,
and especially in Committee of the Whole, its weak
points would have been mercilessly assailed, and its
strong features urged in defence; attacks upon its
principle by the opposition would have been met by
an unequivocal avowal of "soft money" principles
from the majority; and, defended by men anxious
to win honors in support of the ministry, it would
have been dissected by all those who were at issue
with the financial doctrines of the majority, discussed
and rediscussed until all its essential, all its accidental features, and all its remotest tendencies had
been dinned into the public ear, so that no man in
the nation could have pretended ignorance of its
meaning and object. The educational influence of
such discussions is two-fold, and operates in two di-
rections,—upon the members of the legislature themselves, and upon the people whom they represent.
Thus do the merits of the two systems—Committee
government and government by a responsible Cabinet—hinge upon this matter of a full and free discussion of all subjects of legislation; upon the
principle stated by Mr. Bagehot, that "free government is self-government,—a government of the people

by the people.'' It is perhaps safe to say, that the Government which secures the most thorough discussions of public interests,—whose administration most nearly conforms to the opinions of the governed,— is the freest and the best. And certainly, when judged by this principle, government by irresponsible Standing Committees can bear no comparison with government by means of a responsible ministry; for, as we have seen,—and as others besides Senator Hoar have shown,—its essential feature is a vicious suppression of debate.

Only a single glance is necessary to discover how utterly Committee government must fail to give effect to public opinion. In the first place, the exclusion of debate prevents the intelligent formation of opinion on the part of the nation at large; in the second place, public opinion, when once formed, finds it impossible to exercise any immediate control over the action of its representatives. There is no one in Congress to speak for the nation. Congress is a conglomeration of inharmonious elements; a collection of men representing each his neighborhood, each his local interest; an alarmingly large proportion of its legislation is "special"; all of it is at best only a limping compromise between the conflicting interests of the innumerable localities represented. There is no guiding or harmonizing power. Are the people in favor of a particular policy,—what means have they of forcing it upon the sovereign legislature at Washington? None but the most imperfect. If they return representatives who favor it (and this is the most they can do), these representatives being under no directing power will find a mutual agreement impracticable among so many, and will finally settle upon some policy which satisfies nobody, removes no difficulty, and makes little definite or valuable provision for the future. They must, indeed, be content with whatever measure the appropriate committee chances to introduce. Responsible ministries, on the other hand, form the policy of their parties; the strength of their party is at their command; the course of legislation turns upon the acceptance or rejection by the Houses of definite and consistent plans upon which they determine. In forming its judgment of their policy, the nation knows whereof it is judging; and, with biennial Congresses, it may soon decide whether any given policy shall stand or fall. The question would then no longer be, What representatives shall we choose to represent our chances in this haphazard game of legislation? but, What plans of national administration shall we sanction? Would not party programmes mean something then? Could they be constructed only to deceive and bewilder?

But, above and beyond all this, a responsible Cabinet constitutes a link between the executive and legislative departments of the Government which experience declares in the clearest tones to be absolutely necessary in a well-regulated, well-proportioned body politic. None can so well judge of the perfections or imperfections of a law as those who have to administer it. Look, for example, at the important matter of taxation. The only legitimate object of taxation is the support of Government; and who can so well determine the requisite revenue as those who conduct the Government? Who can so well choose feasible means of taxation, available sources of revenue, as those who have to meet the practical difficulties of tax-collection? And what surer guarantee against exorbitant estimates and unwise taxation than the necessity of full explanation and defence before the whole House? The same principles, of course, apply to all legislation upon matters connected with any of the Executive departments.

Thus, then, not only can Cabinet ministers meet the needs of their departments more adequately and understandingly, and conduct their administration better than can irresponsible committees, but they are also less liable to misuse their powers. Responsible ministers must secure from the House and Senate an intelligent, thorough, and practical treatment of their affairs; must vindicate their principles in open battle on the floor of Congress. The public is thus enabled to exercise a direct scrutiny over the workings of the Executive departments, to keep all their operations under a constant stream of daylight. Ministers could do nothing under the shadow of darkness; committees do all in the dark. It can easily be seen how constantly ministers would be plied with questions about the conduct of public affairs, and how necessary it would be for them to satisfy their questioners if they did not wish to fall under suspicion, distrust, and obloquy.

But, while the people would thus be able to defend themselves through their representatives against malfeasance or inefficiency in the management of their

business, the heads of the departments would also
have every opportunity to defend their administration of the people's affairs against unjust censure or
crippling legislation. Corruption in office would
court concealment in vain; vicious trifling with the
administration of public business by irresponsible
persons would meet with a steady and effective check.
The ground would be clear for a manly and candid
defence of ministerial methods; wild schemes of legislation would meet with a cold repulse from ministerial authority. The salutary effect of such a change
would most conspicuously appear in the increased effectiveness of our now crumbling civil, military, and
naval services; for we should no longer be cursed
with tardy, insufficient, and misapplied appropriations. The ministers of War, of the Navy, of the
Interior, would be able to submit their estimates in
person, and to procure speedy and regular appropriations; and half the abuses at present connected with
appropriative legislation would necessarily disappear
with the present committee system. Appropriations
now, though often inadequate, are much oftener
wasteful and fraudulent. Under responsible government, every appropriation asked by an Executive
chief, as well as the reasons by which he backed his
request, would be subjected to the same merciless
sifting process of debate as would characterize the
consideration of other questions. Always having
their responsible agents thus before them, the people
would at once know how much they were spending,
and for what it was spent.

When we come to speak of the probable influence

of responsible Cabinet government upon the development of statesmanship and the renewal of the now
perishing growth of statesmanlike qualities, we come
upon a vital interest of the whole question. Will it
bring with it worthy successors of Hamilton and
Webster? Will it replace a leadership of trickery
and cunning device by one of ability and moral
strength? If it will not, why advocate it? If it will,
how gladly and eagerly and imperatively ought we to
demand it! The most despotic of Governments under
the control of wise statesmen is preferable to the
freest ruled by demagogues. Now, there are few
more common, and perhaps few more reasonable,
beliefs than that at all times, among the millions of
population who constitute the body of this great nation, there is here and there to be found a man with
all the genius, all the deep and strong patriotism, all
the moral vigor, and all the ripeness of knowledge
and variety of acquisition which gave power and lasting fame to the greater statesmen of our past history.
We bewail and even wonder at the fact that these
men do not find their way into public life, to claim
power and leadership in the service of their country.
We naturally ascribe their absence to the repugnance
which superior minds must feel for the intrigues, the
glaring publicity, and the air of unscrupulousness
and even dishonesty which are the characteristics, or
at least the environments, of political life. In our
disappointment and vexation that they do not, even
at the most distressing sacrifice of their personal convenience and peace, devote themselves to the study
and practice of statecraft, we turn for comfort to

reread history's lesson,—that many countries find
their greatest statesmen in times of extraordinary
crisis or rapid transition and progress; the intervals
of slow growth and uninteresting everyday administration of the government being noted only for the
elevation of mediocrity, or at most of shrewd cunning, to high administrative places. We take cold
consolation from the hope that times of peril—which
sometimes seem close enough at hand—will not find
us without strong leaders worthy of the most implicit
confidence. Thus we are enabled to arrive at the
comfortable and fear-quieting conclusion that it is
from no fault of ours, certainly from no defects in
our forms of government, that we are ruled by scheming, incompetent, political tradesmen, whose aims and
ambitions are merely personal, instead of by broad-
minded, masterful statesmen, whose sympathies and
purposes are patriotic and national.

To supply the conditions of statesmanship is, we
conclude, beyond our power; for the causes of its
decline and the means necessary to its development
are beyond our ken. Let us take a new departure.
Let us, drawing light from every source within the
range of our knowledge, make a little independent
analysis of the conditions of statesmanship, with a
view to ascertaining whether or not it is in reality
true that we cannot contribute to its development, or
even perchance give it a perennial growth among us.
We learn from a critical survey of the past, that, so
far as political affairs are concerned, great critical
epochs are the man-making epochs of history, that
revolutionary influences are man-making influences.

And why? If this be the law, it must have some
adequate reason underlying it; and we seem to find
the reason a very plain and conspicuous one. Crises
give birth and a new growth to statesmanship because
they are peculiarly periods of action, in which talents
find the widest and the freest scope. They are periods
not only of action, but also of unusual opportunity
for gaining leadership and a controlling and guiding
influence. It is opportunity for transcendent influence, therefore, which calls into active public life
a nation's greater minds,—minds which might otherwise remain absorbed in the smaller affairs of private
life. And we thus come upon the principle,—a principle which will appear the more incontrovertible the
more it is looked into and tested,—that governmental
forms will call to the work of administration able
minds and strong hearts constantly or infrequently,
according as they do or do not afford them at all times
an opportunity of gaining and retaining a commanding authority and an undisputed leadership in the
nation's councils. Now it certainly needs no argument to prove that government by supreme committees, whose members are appointed at the caprice of
an irresponsible party chief, by seniority, because of
reputation gained in entirely different fields, or because of partisan shrewdness, is not favorable to a
full and strong development of statesmanship. Certain it is that statesmanship has been steadily dying
out in the United States since that stupendous crisis
during which its government felt the first throbs of
life. In the government of the United States there
is no place found for the leadership of men of real

ability. Why, then, complain that we have no leaders? The President can seldom make himself recognized as a leader; he is merely the executor of the sovereign legislative will; his Cabinet officers are little more than chief clerks, or superintendents, in the Executive departments, who advise the President as to matters in most of which he has no power of action independently of the concurrence of the Senate. The most ambitious representative can rise no higher than the chairmanship of the Committee of Ways and Means, or the Speakership of the House. The cardinal feature of Cabinet government, on the other hand, is responsible leadership,—the leadership and authority of a small body of men who have won the foremost places in their party by a display of administrative talents, by evidence of high ability upon the floor of Congress in the stormy play of debate. None but the ablest can become leaders and masters in this keen tournament in which arguments are the weapons, and the people the judges. Clearly defined, definitely directed policies arouse bold and concerted opposition; and leaders of oppositions become in time leaders of Cabinets. Such a recognized leadership it is that is necessary to the development of statesmanship under popular, republican institutions; for only such leadership can make politics seem worthy of cultivation to men of high mind and aim.

And if party success in Congress—the ruling body of the nation—depends upon power in debate, skill and prescience in policy, successful defence of or attacks upon ruling ministries, how ill can contending parties spare their men of ability from Congress!

To keep men of the strongest mental and moral fibre in Congress would become a party necessity. Party triumph would then be a matter of might in debate, not of supremacy in subterfuge. The two great national parties—and upon the existence of two great parties, with clashings and mutual jealousies and watchings, depends the health of free political institutions—are dying for want of unifying and vitalizing principles. Without leaders, they are also without policies, without aims. With leaders there must be followers, there must be parties. And with leaders whose leadership was earned in an open war of principle against principle, by the triumph of one opinion over all opposing opinions, parties must from the necessities of the case have definite policies. Platforms, then, must mean something. Broken promises will then end in broken power. A Cabinet without a policy that is finding effect in progressive legislation is, in a country of frequent elections, inviting its own defeat. Or is there, on the other hand, a determined, aggressive opposition? Then the ministry have a right to ask them what they would do under similar circumstances, were the reins of government to fall to them. And if the opposition are then silent, they cannot reasonably expect the country to intrust the government to them. Witness the situation of the Liberal party in England during the late serious crisis in Eastern affairs. Not daring to propose any policy,—having indeed, because of the disintegration of the party, no policy to propose,—their numerical weakness became a moral weakness, and the nation's ear was turned away from them. Eight words con-

tain the sum of the present degradation of our political parties: *No leaders, no principles; no principles, no parties.* Congressional leadership is divided
infinitesimally; and with divided leadership there can
be no great party units. Drill in debate, by giving
scope to talents, invites talents; raises up a race of
men habituated to the methods of public business,
skilled parliamentary chiefs. And, more than this,
it creates a much-to-be-desired class who early make
attendance upon public affairs the business of their
lives, devoting to the service of their country all their
better years. Surely the management of a nation's
business will, in a well-ordered society, be as properly
a matter of life-long training as the conduct of private
affairs.

These are but meagre and insufficient outlines of
some of the results which would follow upon the establishment of responsible Cabinet government in the
United States. Its establishment has not wanted
more or less outspoken advocacy from others; nor,
of course, have there been lacking those who are
ready to urge real or imaginary objections against
it, and proclaim it an exotic unfit to thrive in American soil. It has certainly, in common with all other
political systems, grave difficulties and real evils connected with it. Difficulties and evils are inseparable
from every human scheme of government; and, in
making their choice, a people can do no more than
adopt that form which affords the largest measure of
real liberty, whose machinery is least imperfect, and
which is almost susceptible to the control of their
sovereign will.

Few, however, have discovered the real defects of such a responsible government as that which I now advocate. It is said, for instance, that it would render the President a mere figurehead, with none of that stability of official tenure, or that traditional dignity, which is necessary to such figureheads. Would the President's power be curtailed, then, if his Cabinet ministers simply took the place of the Standing Committees? Would it not rather be enlarged? He would then be in fact, and not merely in name, the head of the Government. Without the consent of the Senate, he now exercises no sovereign functions that would be taken from him by a responsible Cabinet.

The apparently necessary existence of a partisan Executive presents itself to many as a fatal objection to the establishment of the forms of responsible Cabinet government in this country. The President must continue to represent a political party, and must continue to be anxious to surround himself with Cabinet officers who shall always substantially agree with him on all political questions. It must be admitted that the introduction of the principle of ministerial responsibility might, on this account, become at times productive of mischief unless the tenure of the presidential office were made more permanent than it now is. Whether or not the presidential term should, under such a change of conditions, be lengthened would be one of several practical questions which would attend the adoption of a system of this sort. But it must be remembered that such a state of things as now exists, when we find the Executive

to be of one party and the majority of Congress to
be of the opposite party, is the exception, by no means
the rule. Moreover we must constantly keep before
our minds the fact that the choice now lies between
this responsible Cabinet government and the rule of
irresponsible committees which actually exists. It
is not hard to believe that most presidents would
find no greater inconvenience, experience no greater
unpleasantness, in being at the head of a Cabinet
composed of political opponents than in presiding,
as they must now occasionally do, over a Cabinet of
political friends who are compelled to act in all matters of importance according to the dictation of
Standing Committees which are ruled by the opposite
party. In the former case, the President may, by
the exercise of whatever personal influence he possesses, affect the action of the Cabinet, and, through
them, the action of the Houses; in the latter he is
absolutely helpless. Even now it might prove practically impossible for a President to gain from a
hostile majority in the Senate a confirmation of his
appointment of a strongly partisan Cabinet drawn
from his own party. The President must now moreover, acting through his Cabinet, simply do the bidding of the committees in directing the business of
the departments. With a responsible Cabinet—even
though that Cabinet were of the opposite party—he
might, if a man of ability, exercise great power over
the conduct of public affairs; if not a man of ability,
but a *mere* partisan, he would in any case be impotent. From these considerations it would appear
that government by Cabinet ministers who represent

the majority in Congress is no more incompatible with a partisan Executive than is government by committees representing such a majority. Indeed, a partisan President might well prefer legislation through a hostile body at whose deliberations he might himself be present, and whose course he might influence, to legislation through hostile committees over whom he could have no manner of control, direct or indirect. And such conditions would be exceptional.

But the encroachment of the legislative upon the executive is deemed the capital evil of our Government in its later phases; and it is asked, Would not the power of Congress be still more dangerously enlarged, and these encroachments made easier and surer, by thus making its relations with the Executive closer? By no means. The several parts of a perfect mechanism must actually interlace and be in strong union in order mutually to support and check each other. Here again permanent, dictating committees are the only alternative. On the one hand, we have committees directing policies for whose miscarriage they are not responsible; on the other, we have a ministry asking for legislation for whose results they are responsible. In both cases there is full power and authority on the part of the legislature to determine all the main lines of administration: there is no more real control of Executive acts in the one case than in the other; but there is an all-important difference in the character of the agents employed. When carrying out measures thrust upon them by committees, administrative officers can throw off all sense of responsibility; and the committees are safe from punishment, safe even from censure, whatever the issue. But in administering laws which have passed under the influence of their own open advocacy, ministers must shoulder the responsibilities and face the consequences. We should not, then, be giving Congress powers or opportunities of encroachment which it does not now possess, but should, on the contrary, be holding its powers in constant and effective check by putting over it responsible leaders. A complete separation of the executive and legislative is not in accord with the true spirit of those essentially English institutions of which our Government is a characteristic offshoot. The Executive is in constant need of legislative co-operation; the legislative must be aided by an Executive who is in a position intelligently and vigorously to execute its acts. There must needs be, therefore, as a binding link between them, some body which has no power to coerce the one and is interested in maintaining the independent effectiveness of the other. Such a link is the responsible Cabinet.

Again, it is objected that we should be cursed with that instability of government which results from a rapid succession of ministries, a frequent shifting of power from the hands of one party to the hands of another. This is not necessarily more likely to occur under the system of responsibility than now. We should be less exposed to such fluctuations of power than is the English government. The elective system which regulates the choice of United States Senators prevents more than one third of the seats becoming vacant at once, and this third only once every two years. The political complexion of the Senate can be changed by a succession of elections.

But against such a responsible system the alarm-bell of *centralization* is again sounded, and all those who dread seeing too much authority, too complete control, placed within the reach of the central Government sternly set their faces against any such change. They deceive themselves. There could be no more despotic authority wielded under the forms of free government than our national Congress now exercises. It is a despotism which uses its power with all the caprice, all the scorn for settled policy, all the wild unrestraint which mark the methods of other tyrants as hateful to freedom.

Few of us are ready to suggest a remedy for the evils all deplore. We hope that our system is self-adjusting, and will not need our corrective interference. This is a vain hope! It is no small part of wisdom to know how long an evil ought to be tolerated, to see when the time has come for the people, from whom springs all authority, to speak its doom or prescribe its remedy. If that time be allowed to slip unrecognized, our dangers may overwhelm us, our political maladies may prove incurable.

MAKE HASTE SLOWLY [1]

THE ONE HUNDREDTH ANNIVERSARY OF THE INAUGURA-
TION OF GEORGE WASHINGTON, ADDRESS DELIVERED
APRIL 30, 1889, AT (PLACE NOT GIVEN). FROM ORIGI-
NAL MANUSCRIPT IN MR. WILSON'S HANDWRITING, IN
MRS. WILSON'S POSSESSION.

PRECEDENCE belongs to-day as of right to
thoughts of thanksgiving and joy. To have
kept our national government from destruction or
decay for one hundred years were itself justification
for gratification and pride. But we have done more
than that. We are more—much more—than a preserved nation: we are a strengthened, elevated, matured nation. We have triumphed over difficulties,
not by steadfastness merely but by progress also. We
have had that best evidence of health, namely growth.
Vastly better, greater, more worthy, whether for
strength, for unity, or for achievement are the Re-
United States than were the merely *United* States.
We have done more than kept faith with the deeds
of our Fathers: we have kept faith with their spirit
also. We cannot doubt that in building together a
compact and confident nation out of the somewhat
disagreeing elements which they handled, with
courage and in hope but not without doubt and mis-
giving, we have returned them their own with usury.

[1] Title supplied by editors.

Their thirteen talents, coined in various mints, bearing no single or standard value, have become in our hands thirty-eight talents, made up of coins bearing all the same image and superscription, emblems of liberty and nationality.

We may boast, too,—if boasting may have a place—that we have led the modern movement of Politics: that it is at our hands that popular liberty has received its most absolute test and its highest confirmation. Never before we gave them scope of empire had the principles of democratic government received more than a narrow local application. Snug Swiss cantons, buttressed by Nature against the disturbances of European politics; mediæval cities forcibly holding the feudal world a while at arm's length; Rome straining her city constitution to the point of breaking by imposing upon it the weight of an Empire's affairs; the republics of Greece ruling territories ridiculously small when compared with the power and the abiding influence of the peoples whom they sustained—none of these afford any precedent for this continental rule of the people, so familiar to us now, but which we have astonished the world by successfully establishing. Our success has been on the scale of our geography: democracies there had been before and confederacies not a few; but never a democracy of sixty millions of people, never a federal state as large and as whole as a continent.

But these great things, which have unquestionably put us at the front of the world's politics, have not been accomplished by those elements of thought and character which make for pride and self-gratulation.

It is significant of the forces that have made us what
we are that we celebrate to-day not only the establishment of a government but also the inauguration
of a man.[1] But Washington, it seems to me, though
high-statured even beyond the other giants of his
day, bore in his mien and stature the marks of the
race to which he belonged. In him we may discern
the "brief chronicle and abstract" of a time and a
nation. His courageous calmness in seasons of political crisis; his solemn sense of public duty; his
steady aptitude for affairs; his hold upon men of
various and diverse natures; his capacity for persuasive counsel; his boldness without dash, and
power without display—do we not see in these things
the perfect epitome of what the slow processes of
English national history had proved themselves
capable of producing in the way of manhood and
character? Washington was neither an accident nor
a miracle. Neither chance nor a special Providence
need be assumed to account for him. It was God,
indeed, who gave him to us; but God had been preparing him ever since English constitutional history
began. He was of the same breed with Hampden
and Pym and Cromwell. Burke and Chatham both
recognized him as a brother so soon as they saw
opened before them the credentials of his deeds. He

---

[1] You know by heart, of course, Mr. Lowell's fine lines, of 1876:
> "Virginia gave us this imperial man
> Cast in the massive mould
> Of those high-statured ages old
> Which into grander forms our mortal metal ran.
>
> . . . .
>
> Mother of States and undiminished men,
> Thou gavest us a Country giving him."

was of such heroic stuff as God had for centuries been so graciously and so lavishly weaving into the character of our race.

Do you recall that striking story of one of the opening incidents of the Constitutional Convention related by Gouverneur Morris, an eye-witness of scenes? "Of the delegates," he says, "some were for halfway measures, for fear of displeasing the people; others were anxious and doubting. Just before there were enough to form a quorum, Washington, standing self-collected in the midst of them, his countenance more than usually solemn, his eye seeming to look into futurity, said:—'It is too probable that no plan we propose will be adopted. Perhaps another dreadful conflict is to be sustained. If, to please the people, we offer what we ourselves disapprove, how can we afterwards defend our course? Let us raise a standard to which the wise and honest can repair; the event is in the hands of God.'" That is an utterance, not of statesmanship merely, but of character as well: and do we not understand that character; do we not thrill at its expression? It strikes to the quick of our sensibilities because we are of the same race and derivation that this man was of.

I press this point because it seems to me the point of chief instruction and inspiration, the best point, of to-day's suggestion. There is no strength in mere self-gratulation: there is no hope in being sure. Enlightened endeavour is the law of progress: a stouthearted dissatisfaction with what has been done, a clear-sighted understanding of what there remains to do, an undaunted spirit to undertake and achieve it.

I fear that we are becoming a little prone as a nation to mistake the real nature of our success. It does not lie in the forms but in the essence of our institutions. We are not great in popular government because we invented written constitutions: for we did not invent them. We are not successful because we put into our constitution new devices whereby to moderate the disorders or facilitate the better influences of politics: for we originated no devices. We are great because of what we perfected and fulfilled, not because of anything that we discovered: and it is only by extending such lines of development as can be clearly traced backwards through the normal evolutions of politics in the past that we can make further permanent advances. We did not break with the past: we understood and obeyed it, rather. The most thorough way of understanding ourselves lies through an intimate acquaintance with the long processes of our breeding. There are no individual discoveries to be made in politics as there are in astronomy or biology or physics; society grows as a whole, and as a whole grows into knowledge of itself. Society is an organism, which does not develop by the cunning leadership of a single member so much as by a slow maturing and an all-round adjustment, though led at last into self-consciousness and self-command by those who best divine the laws of its growth.

So long were we compelled to centre our thoughts in national politics upon the interpretation of our written standards—so short is the period during which we have been excused from looking exclusively

into our constitutions for the sanction and substance
of our national life, that it is open to question
whether we have even yet accepted the fact that the
real foundations of political life in the United States
are to be found elsewhere than in our legal documents.

Our politics and our character were derived from a

> "land that freemen till
> That sober-suited Freedom chose,
> The land where, girt with friends or foes,
> A man may speak the thing he will;
>
> "A land of settled government,
> A land of just and old renown,
> Where freedom broadens slowly down
> From precedent to precedent:
>
> "Where faction seldom gathers head,
> But by degrees to fulness wrought,
> The strength of some diffusive thought
> Hath time and space to work and spread."

We have been strong and successful—and shall be—
just in proportion to our fidelity to this so great
heritage of political manliness. It is no light thing
to have such traditions behind us: liberty is not
something that can be laid away in a document, a
completed work. It is an organic principle, a principle of life, renewing and being renewed. Democratic institutions are never done—they are, like the
living tissue, always a-making. It is a strenuous
thing this of living the life of a free people: and we
cannot escape the burden of our inheritance.

But this burden is light: the only grievous burden
is to be held back from liberty by a heritage of subjection. Those of you who have followed the course
of events in France and who share with all lovers of
liberty the anxiety caused by the present posture of
her affairs will know whence my best illustration will
be drawn. You know how straight M. Monod has
pointed his finger at his country's trouble in what he
says in the current (the April) number of the *Con-
temporary Review.* "France," he says, "is suffering mainly from moral instability and disease of the
imagination, the result of a too sudden rupture with
her own traditions." "After every revolution," he
adds,—and he is right,—"and in spite of 17 changes
of constitution in a single century, she always rights
herself, and knows no pause in her intellectual and
industrial activity, nor any decline in her material
force." This is indeed true. In her habit of being
prosperous France is established; in her habit of
making her wit tell in literature and in art she is
well grounded; but the habit of being free she as yet
most imperfectly possesses. That habit, instead of
having something like a thousand years of steady
practice in it with her as with us, has but the uneven
exertions of a brief hundred years of feverish change.
She is acquiring it: but it would be a miracle could
she adopt it, as one would put on a garment. We
only make ourselves contemptible when we despise
France because she has failed at the miracle: we only
make ourselves ridiculous when we pity her; she
deserves sympathy and she will achieve success: we
cannot do better than learn a lesson from her.

The profitable thing for us to remember is, that, though the saving habit in politics may be acquired by wisdom and sober, steadfast endeavour, which are very rare, it may be lost by folly, which is very common. Evidently wisdom and endeavour have had rare good opportunities in America during the century that is past: wisdom is not difficult where resources are unbounded; endeavour is not arduous where there is exceeding rich reward. But the century which *begins* to-day will doubtless make a very different distribution of its favours among us. It is easier to be new than to be old—far lighter work to be pioneers needing mere muscle and physical courage, than patiently and resolutely to face the problems of a crowded and perplexed civilization. It was easier to drive out an army of English troops than it will be to assimilate a heterogeneous horde of immigrants. It required less self-possession to establish our governments than it will require to maintain them: the principles on which they should be constructed to meet our needs in the beginning were much plainer to see than are the principles upon which they must be modified to meet the needs of the present and future.

For us this is the centennial year of Washington's inauguration; but for Europe it is the centennial year of the French Revolution. One hundred years ago we gained, and Europe lost, self-command, self-possession. But since then we have been steadily receiving into our midst and to full participation in our national life the very people whom their home politics have familiarized with revolution: our own equable blood we have suffered to receive into it the most feverish blood of the restless old world. We are facing an ever-increasing difficulty of self-possession with ever deteriorating materials: for your only reliable stuff in this strain of politics is Character.

Think! Our task is to be

> "A nation yet, the rulers and the ruled—
> Some sense of duty, something of a faith,
> Some reverence for the laws ourselves have made,
> Some patient force to change them when we will,
> Some civic manhood firm against the crowd."

And our material? "Minds cast in every mould of race, minds inheriting every bias of environment, warped by the histories of a score of different nations, warmed or chilled, closed or expanded by almost every climate of the globe!"

This is not the place or the occasion for the discussion of policies: we are here only to renew our vows at the altar of Liberty, only to look ourselves in the face, to examine and know ourselves,—to confess ourselves to God and ask of him succour and guidance. It behooves us once and again to stand face to face with our ideals, to renew our enthusiasms, to reckon again our duties, to take fresh views of our aims and fresh courage for their pursuit. To-day we should stand close to the thought and close to the hearts of those who gave our nation life. The tasks of the future are not to be less but greater than the tasks of the past: it is our part to improve even the giant breed of which we came—to return to the high-statured ages: to weld our people together in a patri-

otism as pure, a wisdom as elevated, a virtue as sound
as those of the greater generation whom to-day we
hold in special and grateful remembrance—a nation
knowing

> "Its duties,—prompt to move, but firm to wait,—
> Knowing, things rashly sought are rarely found:
> That, for the functions of an ancient State—
> Strong by her charters, free because imbound,
> Servant of Providence, not slave of Fate—
> Perilous is sweeping change, all chance unsound."

PRINCETON IN THE NATION'S SERVICE

FROM "THE FORUM," DECEMBER, 1896, VOL. XXII, PP. 447-466. AN ORATION DELIVERED AT THE PRINCETON SESQUI-CENTENNIAL CELEBRATION, OCTOBER 21, 1896.

PRINCETON pauses to look back upon her past, not as an old man grown reminiscent, but as a prudent man still in his youth and lusty prime and at the threshold of new tasks, who would remind himself of his origin and lineage, recall the pledges of his youth, and assess as at a turning in his life the duties of his station.

· We look back only a little way to our birth; but the brief space is quick with movement and incident enough to crowd a great tract of time. Turn back only one hundred and fifty years, and you are deep within quiet colony times, before the French and Indian War, or thought of separation from England. But a great war is at hand. Influences restrained and local presently spread themselves at large upon the continent, and the whole scene is altered. The brief plot runs with a strange force and haste:—First, a quiet group of peaceful colonies, very placid and commonplace and dull, to all seeming, in their patient working out of a slow development; then, of a sudden, a hot fire of revolution, a quick release of power, as if of forces long pent up, but set free at last in the generous heat of the new day; the mighty processes of a great migration, the vast spaces of a waiting continent filled almost suddenly with hosts bred in the spirit of conquest; a constant making and renewing of governments, a tremendous growth, a perilous expansion. Such days of youth and nation-making must surely count double the slower days of maturity and calculated change, as the spring counts double the sober fruitage of the summer.

Princeton College was founded upon the very eve of the stirring changes which put this drama on the stage,—not to breed politicians, but to give young men such training as, it might be hoped, would fit them handsomely for the pulpit and for the grave duties of citizens and neighbors. A small group of Presbyterian ministers took the initiative in its foundation. They acted without ecclesiastical authority, as if under obligation to society rather than to the church. They had no more vision of what was to come upon the country than their fellow-colonists had; they knew only that the pulpits of the middle and southern colonies lacked properly equipped men and all the youth in those parts ready means of access to the higher sort of schooling. They thought the discipline at Yale a little less than liberal, and the training offered as a substitute in some quarters elsewhere a good deal less than thorough. They wanted "a seminary of true religion and good literature" which should be after their own model and among their own people. It was not a sectarian school they wished. They were acting as citizens, not as clergymen, and the charter they obtained said never a word about creed or doctrine; but they gave religion the

first place in their programme, which belonged to it
of right, and the formation of their college they con-
fided to the Rev. Jonathan Dickinson, one of their
own number, and a man of such mastery as they
could trust.

Their school was first of all merely a little group
of students gathered about Mr. Dickinson in Eliza-
bethtown. Its master died the very year his labors
began; and it was necessary to induce the Rev. Aaron
Burr, one of the trustees, to take the college under his
own charge at Newark. It was the charm and power
of that memorable young pastor and teacher which
carried it forward to a final establishment. Within
ten years many friends had been made, substantial
sums of money secured, a new and more liberal charter obtained, and a permanent home found at Princeton. And then its second president died, while still
in his prime, and the succession was handed on to
other leaders of like quality.

It was the men, rather than their measures, as
usual, that had made the college vital from the first
and put it in a sure way to succeed. The charter was
liberal and very broad ideas determined the policy
of the young school. There were laymen upon its
board of trustees, as well as clergymen—not all Pres-
byterians, but all lovers of progress and men known
in the colony: no one was more thoroughly the friend
of the new venture than Governor Belcher, the representative of the crown. But the life of the college
was in the men who administered it and spoke in its
class-rooms,—a notable line of thinkers and orators.
There were not many men more regarded in debate

or in counsel in that day than Jonathan Dickinson;
and Aaron Burr was such a man as others turn to
and follow with an admiration and trust they might
be at a loss to explain, so instinctive is it and inevitable—a man with a touch of sweet majesty in
his presence, and a grace and spirit in his manner
which more than made amends for his small and
slender figure; the unmistakable fire of eloquence in
him when he spoke and the fine quality of sincerity.
Piety seemed with him only a crowning grace.

For a few brief weeks after Burr was dead
Jonathan Edwards, whom all the world knows, was
president in his stead; but death came quickly and
left the college only his name. Another orator succeeded him, Samuel Davies, brought out of Virginia,
famous out of all proportion to his years, you might
think, until you heard him speak, and knew the
charm, the utterance, and the character that made
him great. He, too, was presently taken by the quick
way of death, though the college had had him but a
little while; and Samuel Finley had presided in his
stead, with a wise sagacity and quiet gift of leadership, for all too short a time, and was gone, when
John Witherspoon came to reign in the little academic
kingdom for twenty-six years. It was by that time
the year 1768; Mr. Dickinson had drawn that little
group of students about him under the first charter
only twenty-one years ago; the college had been
firmly seated in Princeton only those twelve years
in which it had seen Burr and Edwards and Davies
and Finley die, and had found it not a little hard
to live so long in the face of its losses and the uneasy

movements of the time. It had been brought to
Princeton in the very midst of the French and Indian
War, when the country was in doubt who should
possess the continent. The deep excitement of the
Stamp act agitation had come, with all its sinister
threats of embroilment and disaffection, while yet it
was in its infancy and first effort to live. It was
impossible it should obtain proper endowment or any
right and equable development in such a season. It
ought by every ordinary rule of life to have been
quite snuffed out in the thick and troubled air of the
time. New Jersey did not, like Virginia and Massachusetts, easily form her purpose in that day of
anxious doubt. She was mixed of many warring elements, as New York also was, and suffered a tur-
bulence of spirit that did not very kindly breed "true
religion and good literature."

But your thorough Presbyterian is not subject to
the ordinary laws of life,—is of too stubborn a fibre,
too unrelaxing a purpose, to suffer mere inconvenience to bring defeat. Difficulty bred effort, rather;
and Dr. Witherspoon found an institution ready to
his hand that had come already in that quickening
time to a sort of crude maturity. It was no small
proof of its self-possession and self-knowledge that
those who watched over it had chosen that very time
of crisis to put a man like John Witherspoon at the
head of its administration, a man so compounded of
statesman and scholar, Calvinist, Scotsman, and
orator, that it must ever be a sore puzzle where to
place or rank him,—whether among great divines,
great teachers, or great statesmen. He seems to be

all these, and to defy classification, so big is he, so various, so prodigal of gifts. His vitality entered like a tonic into the college, kept it alive in that time of peril,—made it as individual and inextinguishable a force as he himself was, alike in scholarship and in public affairs.

It has never been natural, it has seldom been possible, in this country for learning to seek a place apart and hold aloof from affairs. It is only when society is old, long settled to its ways, confident in habit, and without self-questionings upon any vital point of conduct, that study can effect seclusion and despise the passing interests of the day. America has never yet had a season of leisured quiet in which students could seek a life apart without sharp rigors of conscience, or college instructors easily forget that they were training citizens as well as drilling pupils; and Princeton is not likely to forget that sharp schooling of her youth, when she first learned the lesson of public service. She shall not easily get John Witherspoon out of her constitution.

It was a piece of providential good fortune that brought such a man to Princeton at such a time. He was a man of the sort other men follow and take counsel of gladly, as if they found in him the full expression of what is best in themselves. Not because he was always wise; but because he showed always so fine an ardor for whatever was worth while and of the better part of man's spirit; because he uttered his thought with an inevitable glow of eloquence; because of his irresistible charm and individual power. The lively wit of the man, besides, struck

always upon the matter of his thought like a ray of
light, compelling men to receive what he said or else
seem themselves opaque and laughable. A certain
straightforward vigor in his way of saying things
gave his style an almost irresistible power of entering into men's convictions. A hearty honesty showed
itself in all that he did and won men's allegiance
upon the instant. They loved him even when they
had the hardihood to disagree with him.

He came to the college in 1768, and ruled it till
he died, in 1794. In the very middle of his term as
head of the college the Revolution came, to draw
men's minds imperatively off from everything but
war and politics, and he returned with all the force
and frankness of his nature to the public tasks of the
great struggle; assisted in the making of a new Constitution for the State; became her spokesman in the
Continental Congress; would have pressed her on, if
he could, to utter a declaration of independence of
her own before the Congress had acted; voted for and
signed the great Declaration with hearty good will
when it came; acted for the country in matters alike
of war and of finance; stood forth in the sight of all
the people a great advocate and orator, deeming himself forward in the service of God when most engaged
in the service of men and of liberty. There were
but broken sessions of the college meanwhile. Each
army in its turn drove out the little group of students
who clung to the place. The college building became
now a military hospital and again a barracks for the
troops,—for a little while, upon a memorable day in
1777, a sort of stronghold. New Jersey's open coun-

ties became for a time the Revolutionary battle-
ground and field of manœuvre. Swept through from
end to end by the rush of armies, the State seemed
the chief seat of the war, and Princeton a central
point of strategy. The dramatic winter of 1776-77
no Princeton man could ever forget, lived he never
so long,—that winter which saw a year of despair
turned suddenly into a year of hope. In July there
had been bonfires and boisterous rejoicings in the
college yard and in the village street at the news of
the Declaration of Independence,—for, though the
rest of the country might doubt and stand timid for
a little to see the bold thing done, Dr. Witherspoon's
pupils were in spirits to know the fight was to be
fought to a finish. Then suddenly the end had
seemed to come. Before the year was out Washington
was in the place beaten and in full retreat, only
three thousand men at his back, abandoned by his
generals, deserted by his troops, hardly daring to
stop till he had put the unbridged Delaware between
himself and his enemy. The British came close at
his heels and the town was their until Washington
came back again, the third day of the new year, early
in the morning, and gave his view halloo yonder on
the hill, as if he were in the hunting field again.
Then there was fighting in the very streets, and
cannon planted against the walls of Old North herself. 'Twas not likely any Princeton man would
forget those days, when the whole face of the war
was changed and New Jersey was shaken of the burden of the fighting.

There was almost always something doing at the

place when the soldiers were out, for the strenuous
Scotsman who had the college at his heart never left
it for long at a time, for all he was so intent upon
the public business. It was haphazard and piecemeal
work, no doubt, but there were the spirit and the
resolution of the Revolution itself in what was done—
the spirit of Witherspoon. It was not as if some one
else had been master. Dr. Witherspoon could have
pupils at will. He was so much else besides schoolmaster and preceptor, was so great a figure in the
people's eye, went about so like an accepted leader,
generously lending a great character to a great cause,
that he could bid men act and know that they would
heed him.

The time, as well as his own genius, enabled him
to put a distinctive stamp upon his pupils. There
was close contact between master and pupils in that
day of beginnings. There were not often more than
a hundred students in attendance at the college, and
the president, for at any rate half their course, was
himself their chief instructor. There were two or
three tutors to whom the instruction of the lower
classes was entrusted; Mr. Houston was professor of
mathematics and natural philosophy and Dr. Smith
professor of moral philosophy and divinity, but the
president set the pace. It was he who gave range
and spirit to the course of study. He lectured upon
taste and style, as well as upon abstract questions of
philosophy, and upon politics as a science of government and of public duty, as little to be forgotten as
religion itself in any well-considered plan of life.
He had found the college ready to serve such purpose

when he came, because of the stamp Burr and Davies and Finley had put upon it. They had, one and all, consciously set themselves to make the college a place where young men's minds should be rendered fit for affairs, for the public ministry of the bench and senate, as well as of the pulpit. It was in Finley's day, but just now gone by, that the college had sent out such men as William Paterson, Luther Martin, and Oliver Ellsworth. Witherspoon but gave quickened life to the old spirit and method of the place where there had been drill from the first in public speech and public spirit.

And the Revolution, when it came, seemed but an object lesson in his scheme of life. It was not simply fighting that was done at Princeton. The little town became for a season the centre of politics, too; once and again the Legislature of the State sat in the college hall, and its revolutionary Council of Safety. Soldiers and public men whose names the war was making known to every man frequented the quiet little place, and racy talk ran high in the jolly tavern where hung the sign of Hudibras. Finally the Federal Congress itself sought the place and filled the college hall with a new scene, sitting a whole season there to do its business,—its president a trustee of the college. A commencement day came which saw both Washington and Witherspoon on the platform together,—the two men, it was said, who could not be matched for striking presence in all the country,— and the young salutatorian turned to the country's leader to say what it was in the hearts of all to utter. The sum of the town's excitement was made up when,

upon that notable last day of October, in the year
1783, news of peace came to that secluded hall, to
add a crowning touch of gladness to the gay and
brilliant company met to receive with formal welcome
the Minister Plenipotentiary but just come from the
Netherlands, Washington moving amongst them the
hero whom the news enthroned.

It was no single stamp that the college gave its
pupils. James Madison, Philip Freneau, Aaron Burr,
and Harry Lee had come from it almost at a single
birth, between 1771 and 1773—James Madison, the
philosophical statesman, subtly compounded of learning and practical sagacity; Philip Freneau, the careless poet and reckless pamphleteer of a party; Aaron
Burr, with genius enough to have made him immortal
and unschooled passion enough to have made him
infamous; "Lighthorse Harry" Lee, a Rupert in
battle, a boy in counsel, highstrung, audacious, wil-
ful, lovable, a figure for romance. These men were
types of the spirit of which the college was full; the
spirit of free individual development which found its
perfect expression in the president himself.

It has been said that Mr. Madison's style in writing is like Dr. Witherspoon's, albeit not so apt a
weapon for the quick thrust and instant parry; and
it is recalled that Madison returned to Princeton after
his graduation and lingered yet another year in
study with his master. But in fact his style is no
more like Witherspoon's than Harry Lee's way of
fighting was. No doubt there was the same firmness
of touch, the same philosophical breadth, the same
range of topic and finished force of argument in Dr.

Witherspoon's essays upon public questions that are
to be found in Madison's papers in the "Federalist";
but Dr. Witherspoon fought, too, with the same over-
coming dash that made men know Harry Lee in the
field, albeit with different weapons and upon another
arena.

Whatever we may say of these matters, however,
one thing is certain: Princeton sent upon the public
stage an extraordinary number of men of notable
quality in those days; became herself for a time in
some visible sort the academic centre of the Revolution, fitted, among the rest, the man in whom the
country was one day to recognize the chief author
of the Federal Constitution. Princetonians are never
tired of telling how many public men graduated from
Princeton in Witherspoon's time,—twenty Senators,
twenty-three Representatives, thirteen Governors,
three Judges of the Supreme Court of the Union;
one Vice-President, and a President; all within a
space of twenty years, and from a college which seldom had more than a hundred students. Nine Princeton men sat in the Constitutional Convention of 1787;
and, though but six of them were Witherspoon's
pupils, there was no other college that had there so
many as six, and the redoubtable Doctor might have
claimed all nine as his in spirit and capacity. Madison guided the convention through the critical stages
of its anxious work, with a tact, a gentle quietness, an
art of leading without insisting, ruling without commanding,—an authority, not of tone or emphasis,
but of apt suggestion,—such as Dr. Witherspoon
could never have exercised. Princeton men fathered

both the Virginia plan, which was adopted, and the
New Jersey plan, which was rejected; and Princeton
men advocated the compromises without which no
plan could have won acceptance. The strenuous
Scotsman's earnest desire and prayer to God to see
a government set over the nation that should last was
realized as even he might not have been bold enough
to hope. No man had ever better right to rejoice
in his pupils.

It would be absurd to pretend that we can distinguish Princeton's touch and method in the Revolution or her distinctive handiwork in the Constitution
of the Union. We can show nothing more of historical fact than that her own president took a great
place of leadership in that time of change, and became one of the first figures of the age; that the college which he led and to which he gave his spirit contributed more than her share of public men to the
making of the nation, outranked her elder rivals in
the roll-call of the Constitutional Convention, and
seemed for a little a seminary of statesmen rather
than a quiet seat of academic learning. What takes
our admiration and engages our fancy in looking
back to that time is the generous union then established in the college between the life of philosophy
and the life of the state.

It moves her sons very deeply to find Princeton
to have been from the first what they know her to
have been in their own day,—a school of duty. The
revolutionary days are gone, and you shall not find
upon her rolls another group of names given to public life that can equal her muster in the days of the

Revolution and the formation of the government. But her rolls read since the old days, if you know but a little of the quiet life of scattered neighborhoods, like a roster of trustees, a list of the silent men who carry the honorable burdens of business and of social obligations,—of such names as keep credit and confidence in heart. They suggest a soil full of the old seed, and ready, should the air of the time move shrewdly upon it as in the old days, to spring once more into the old harvest. The various, boisterous strength of the young men of affairs who went out with Witherspoon's touch upon them, is obviously not of the average breed of any place, but the special fruitage of an exceptional time. Later generations inevitably reverted to the elder type of Paterson and Ellsworth, the type of sound learning and stout character, without bold impulse added or any uneasy hope to change the world. It has been Princeton's work, in all ordinary seasons, not to change but to strengthen society, to give, not yeast, but bread for the raising.

It is in this wise Princeton has come into our own hands; and to-day we stand as those who would count their force for the future. The men who made Princeton are dead; those who shall keep it and better it still live: they are even ourselves. Shall we not ask ere we go forward, what gave the place its spirit and its air of duty? "We are now men, and must accept in the highest spirit the same transcendent destiny, and not pinched in a corner, not cowards fleeing before a revolution, but redeemers and benefactors, pious aspirants to be noble clay plastic under the Almighty effort, let us advance and advance on chaos and the dark!''

No one who looks into the life of the Institution shall find it easy to say what gave it its spirit and kept it in its character the generations through; but some things lie obvious to the view in Princeton's case. She had always been a school of religion, and no one of her sons, who has really lived her life, has escaped that steadying touch which has made her a school of duty. Religion, conceive it but liberally enough, is the true salt wherewith to keep both duty and learning sweet against the taint of time and change; and it is a noble thing to have conceived it thus liberally, as Princeton's founders did.

Churches among us, as all the world knows, are free and voluntary societies separated to be nurseries of belief, not suffered to become instruments of rule; and those who serve them can be free citizens, as well as faithful churchmen. The men who founded Princeton were pastors, not ecclesiastics. Their ideal was the service of congregations and communities, not the service of a church. Duty with them was a practical thing, concerned with righteousness in this world, as well as with salvation in the next. There is nothing that gives such pith to public service as religion. A God of truth is no mean prompter to the enlightened service of mankind; and character formed as if in His eye has always a fibre and sanction such as you shall not obtain for the ordinary man from the mild promptings of philosophy.

This, I cannot doubt, is the reason why Princeton has formed practical men, whom the world could

trust to do its daily work like men of honor. There
were men in Dr. Witherspoon's day who doubted him
the right preceptor for those who sought the ministry
of the church, seeing him "as high a son of liberty
as any man in America," and turned agitator rather
than preacher; and he drew about him, as troubles
thickened, young politicians rather than candidates
for the pulpit. But it is noteworthy that observing
men in far Virginia sent their sons to be with Dr.
Witherspoon because they saw intrigue and the taint
of infidelity coming upon their own college of William and Mary, Mr. Madison among the rest; and
that young Madison went home to read theology with
earnest system ere he went out to the tasks of his
life. He had no thought of becoming a minister, but
his master at Princeton had taken possession of his
mind and had enabled him to see what knowledge
was profitable.

The world has long thought that it detected in the
academic life some lack of sympathy with itself, some
disdain of the homely tasks which make the gross
globe inhabitable,—not a little proud aloofness and
lofty superiority, as if education always softened the
hands and alienated the heart. It must be admitted
that books are a great relief from the haggling of
the market, libraries a very welcome refuge from the
strife of commerce. We feel no anxiety about ages
that are past; old books draw us pleasantly off from
responsibility, remind us nowhere of what there is
to do. We can easily hold the services of mankind
at arm's length while we read and make scholars of
ourselves. But we shall be very uneasy, the while,

if the high mandates of religion are let in upon us
and made part of our thought. The quiet scholar has
his proper breeding, and truth must be searched out
and held aloft for men to see for its own sake, by
such as will not leave off their sacred task until death
takes them away. But not many pupils of a college
are to be investigators; they are to be citizens and
the world's servants in every field of practical endeavor, and in their instruction the college must use
learning as a vehicle of spirit, interpreting literature
as the voice of humanity,—must enlighten, guide,
and hearten its sons, that it may make men of them.
If it give them no vision of the true God, it has
given them no certain motive to practice the wise
lessons they have learned.

It is noteworthy how often God-fearing men have
been forward in those revolutions which have vindicated rights, and how seldom in those which have
wrought a work of destruction. There was a spirit
of practical piety in the revolutionary doctrines
which Dr. Witherspoon taught. No man, particularly
no young man, who heard him could doubt his cause
a righteous cause, or deem religion aught but a
prompter in it. Revolution was not to be distinguished from duty in Princeton. Duty becomes the
more noble when thus conceived the "stern daughter
of the voice of God"; and that voice must ever seem
near and in the midst of life if it be made to sound
dominant from the first in all thought of men and
the world. It has not been by accident, therefore,
that Princeton men have been inclined to public life.
A strong sense of duty is a fretful thing in confine-

ment, and will not easily consent to be kept at home
cooped up within a narrow round. The university
in our day is no longer inclined to stand aloof from
the practical world, and, surely, it ought never to have
had the disposition to do so. It is the business of a
university to impart to the rank and file of the men
whom it trains the right thought of the world, the
thought which it has tested and established, the principles which have stood through the seasons and become at length a part of the immemorial wisdom of
the race. The object of education is not merely to
draw out the powers of the individual mind; it is
rather its object to draw all minds to a proper adjustment to the physical and social world in which
they are to have their life and their development: to
enlighten, strengthen, and make fit. The business
of the world is not individual success, but its own
betterment, strengthening, and growth in spiritual
insight. "So teach us to number our days that we
may apply our hearts unto wisdom" is its right
prayer and aspiration.

It was not a work of destruction which Princeton
helped forward even in that day of storm which
came at the Revolution, but a work of preservation.
The American Revolution wrought, indeed, a radical
work of change in the world; it created a new nation and a new polity; but it was a work of conservation after all, as fundamentally conservative as the
revolution of 1688 or the extortion of Magna Charta.
A change of allegiance and the erection of a new
nation in the West were its inevitable results, but not
its objects. Its object was the preservation of a body

of liberties, to keep the natural course of English development in America clear of impediment. It was meant, not in rebellion, but in self-defence. If it brought change, it was the change of maturity, the fulfilment of destiny, the appropriate fruitage of wholesome and steady growth. It was part of English liberty that America should be free. The thought of our Revolution was as quick and vital in the minds of Chatham and of Burke as in the minds of Otis and Henry and Washington. There is nothing so conservative of life as growth; when that stops, decay sets in and the end comes on apace. Progress is life, for the body politic as for the body natural. To stand still is to court death.

Here, then, if you will but look, you have the law of conservatism disclosed: it is a law of progress. But not all change is progress, not all growth is the manifestation of life. Let one part of the body be in haste to outgrow the rest and you have malignant disease, the threat of death. The growth that is a manifestation of life is equable, draws its springs gently out of the old fountains of strength, builds upon old tissue, covets the old airs that have blown upon it time out of mind in the past. Colleges ought surely to be the best nurseries of such life, the best schools of the progress which conserves. Unschooled men have only their habits to remind them of the past, only their desires and their instinctive judgments of what is right to guide them into the future: the college should serve the State as its organ of recollection, its seat of vital memory. It should give the country men who know the probabilities of failure and success, who can separate the tendencies which are permanent from the tendencies which are of the moment merely, who can distinguish promises from threats, knowing the life men have lived, the hopes they have tested, and the principles they have proved.

This college gave the country at least a handful of such men, in its infancy, and its president for leader. The blood of John Knox ran in Witherspoon's veins. The great drift and movement of English liberty, from Magna Charta down, was in all his teachings; his pupils knew as well as Burke did that to argue the Americans out of their liberties would be to falsify their pedigree. "In order to prove that the Americans have no right to their liberties," Burke cried, "we are every day endeavoring to subvert the maxims which preserve the whole spirit of our own"; the very antiquarians of the law stood ready with their proof that the colonies could not be taxed by Parliament. This Revolution, at any rate, was a keeping of faith with the past. To stand for it was to be like Hampden, a champion of law though he withstood the king. It was to emulate the example of the very men who had founded the government then for a little while grown so tyrannous and forgetful of its great traditions. This was the compulsion of life, not of passion, and college halls were a better school of revolution than colonial assemblies.

Provided, of course, they were guided by such a spirit as Witherspoon's. Nothing is easier than to falsify the past; lifeless instruction will do it. If you rob it of vitality, stiffen it with pedantry, sophisticate it with argument, chill it with unsympathetic comment, you render it as dead as any academic exercise. The safest way in all ordinary seasons is to let it speak for itself; resort to its records, listen to its poets and to its masters in the humbler art of prose. Your real and proper object, after all, is not to expound, but to realize it, consort with it, and make your spirit kin with it, so that you may never shake the sense of obligation off. In short, I believe that the catholic study of the world's literature as a record of spirit is the right preparation for leadership in the world's affairs, if you undertake it like a man and not like a pedant.

Age is marked in the case of every people, just as it is marked in the case of every work of art, into which enters the example of the masters, the taste of long generations of men, the thought that has matured, the achievement that has come with assurance. The child's crude drawing shares the primitive youth of the first hieroglyphics; but a little reading, a few lessons from some modern master, a little time in the Old World's galleries set the lad forward a thousand years and more, make his drawings as old as art itself. The art of thinking is as old, and it is the university's function to impart it in all its length: the stiff and difficult stuffs of fact and experience, of prejudice and affection, in which the hard art is to work its will, and the long and tedious combinations of cause and effect out of which it is to build up its results. How else would you avoid a ceaseless round of error? The world's memory must be kept alive, or we shall never see an end of its old mistakes.

We are in danger of losing our identity and becoming infantile in every generation. That is the real menace under which we cower everywhere in this age of change. The Old World trembles to see its proletariat in the saddle; we stand dismayed to find ourselves growing no older, always as young as the information of our most numerous voters. The danger does not lie in the fact that the masses whom we have enfranchised seek to work any iniquity upon us, for their aim, take it in the large, is to make a righteous polity. The peril lies in this, that the past is discredited among them, because they played no choosing part in it. It was their enemy, they say, and they will not learn of it. They wish to break with it forever; its lessons are tainted to their taste.

In America, especially, we run perpetually this risk of newness. Righteously enough, it is in part a consequence of boasting. To enhance our credit for originality, we boasted for long that our institutions were one and all our own inventions, and the pleasing error was so got into the common air by persistent discharges of oratory that every man's atmosphere became surcharged with it, and it seems now quite too late to dislodge it. Three thousand miles of sea, moreover, roll between us and the elder past of the world. We are isolated here. We cannot see other nations in detail, and looked at in the large they do not seem like ourselves. Our problems, we say, are our own, and we will take our own way of solving them. Nothing seems audacious among us, for our case seems to us to stand singular and without parallel. We run in a free field, without recollection of failure, without heed of example.

This danger is nearer to us now than it was in the days of armed revolution. The men whom Madison led in the making of the Constitution were men who regarded the past. They had flung off from the mother country, not to get a new liberty but to preserve an old, not to break a Constitution but to keep it. It was the glory of the Convention of 1787 that it made choice in the framing of the government of principles which Englishmen everywhere had tested, and of an organization of which in every part Americans themselves had somewhere made trial. In every essential part they built out of old stuffs whose grain and fibre they knew.

" 'Tis not in battles that from youth we train
    The Governor who must be wise and good,
    And temper with the sternness of the brain
    Thoughts motherly, and meek as womanhood.
    Wisdom doth live with children round her knees:
    Books, leisure, perfect freedom, and the talk
    Man holds with week-day man in the hourly walk
    Of the mind's business: these are the degrees
    By which true sway doth mount; this is the stalk
    True power doth grow on; and her rights are these."

The men who framed the government were not radicals. They trimmed old growths, and were not forgetful of the old principles of husbandry.

It is plain that it is the duty of an institution of learning set in the midst of a free population and amidst signs of social change, not merely to implant a sense of duty, but to illuminate duty by every lesson that can be drawn out of the past. It is not a dogmatic process. I know of no book in which the lessons of the past are set down. I do not know of any man whom the world could trust to write such a book. But it somehow comes about that the man who has travelled in the realms of thought brings lessons home with him which make him grave and wise beyond his fellows, and thoughtful with the thoughtfulness of a true man of the world.

He is not a true man of the world who knows only the present fashions of it. In good breeding there is always the fine savor of generations of gentlemen, a tradition of courtesy, the perfect knowledge of long practice. The world of affairs is so old no man can know it who knows only that little last segment of it which we call the present. We have a special name for the man who observes only the present fashions of the world, and it is a less honorable name than that which we use to designate the grave and thoughtful gentlemen who keep so steadily to the practices that have made the world wise and at ease these hundreds of years. We cannot pretend to have formed the world, and we are not destined to reform it. We cannot even mend it and set it forward by the reasonable measures of a single generation's work if we forget the old processes or lose our mastery over them. We should have scant capital to trade on were we to throw away the wisdom we have inherited and seek our fortunes with the slender stock we have ourselves accumulated. This, it seems to me, is the real, the prevalent argument for holding every man we can to the intimate study of the ancient classics. Latin and Greek, no doubt, have a grammatical and syntactical habit which challenges the mind that

would master it to a severer exercise of analytical
power than the easy-going synthesis of any modern
tongue demands; but substitutes in kind may be
found for that drill. What you cannot find a substitute for is the classics as literature; and there can
be no first-hand contact with that literature if you
will not master the grammar and the syntax which
convey its subtle power. Your enlightenment depends on the company you keep. You do not know
the world until you know the men who have possessed it and tried its ways before ever you were
given your brief run upon it. And there is no sanity
comparable with that which is schooled in the
thoughts that will keep. It is such a schooling that
we get from the world's literature. The books have
disappeared which were not genuine,—which spoke
things which, if they were worth saying at all, were
not worth hearing more than once, as well as the
books which spoke permanent things clumsily and
without the gift of interpretation. The kind air
which blows from age to age has disposed of them
like vagrant leaves. There was sap in them for a
little, but now they are gone, we do not know where.
All literature that has lasted has this claim upon
us: that it is not dead; but we cannot be quite so
sure of any as we are of the ancient literature that
still lives, because none has lived so long. It holds a
sort of primacy in the aristocracy of natural selection.

Read it, moreover, and you shall find another proof
of vitality in it, more significant still. You shall
recognize its thoughts, and even its fancies, as your
long-time familiars—shall recognize them as the

thoughts that have begotten a vast deal of your own literature. We read the classics and exclaim, in our vanity: "How modern! it might have been written yesterday." Would it not be more true, as well as more instructive, to exclaim concerning our own ideas: "How ancient! they have been true these thousand years"? It is the general air of the world a man gets when he reads the classics, the thinking which depends upon no time but only upon human nature, which seems full of the voices of the human spirit, quick with the power which moves ever upon the face of affairs. "What Plato has thought he may think; what a saint has felt he may feel; what at any time has befallen any man he can understand." There is the spirit of a race in the Greek literature, the spirit of quite another people in the books of Virgil and Horace and Tacitus; but in all a mirror of the world, the old passion of the soul, the old hope that keeps so new, the informing memory, the persistent forecast.

It has always seemed to me an odd thing, and a thing against nature that the literary man, the man whose citizenship and freedom are of the world of thought, should ever have been deemed an unsafe man in affairs; and yet I suppose there is not always injustice in the judgment. It is a perilously pleasant and beguiling comradeship, the company of authors. Not many men when once they are deep in it will leave its engaging thought of things gone by to find their practical duties in the present. But you are not making an undergraduate a man of letters when you keep him four short years at odd, or even at

stated, hours in the company of authors. You shall
have done much if you make him feel free among
them.

This argument for enlightenment holds scarcely
less good, of course, in behalf of the study of modern literature, and especially the literature of your
own race and country. You should not belittle culture by esteeming it a thing of ornament, an accomplishment rather than a power. A cultured mind is
a mind quit of its awkwardness, eased of all impediment and illusion, made quick and athletic in the
acceptable exercise of power. It is a mind at once
informed and just,—a mind habituated to choose its
course with knowledge, and filled with full assurance,
like one who knows the world and can live in it
without either unreasonable hope or unwarranted
fear. It cannot complain, it cannot trifle, it cannot
despair. Leave pessimism to the uncultured, who do
not know reasonable hope; leave fantastic hopes to
the uncultured, who do not know the reasonableness
of failure. Show that your mind has lived in the
world ere now; has taken counsel with the elder dead
who still live, as well as with the ephemeral living
who cannot pass their graves. Help men, but do not
delude them.

I believe, of course, that there is another way of
preparing young men to be wise. I need hardly say
that I believe in full, explicit instruction in history
and in politics, in the experiences of peoples and the
fortunes of governments, in the whole story of what
men have attempted and what they have accomplished through all the changes both of form and

of purpose in their organization of their common life.
Many minds will receive and heed this systematic instruction which have no ears for the voice that is in
the printed page of literature. But, just as it is
one thing to sit here in republican America and hear
a credible professor tell of the soil of allegiance in
which the British monarchy grows, and quite another
to live where Victoria is queen and hear common men
bless her with full confession of loyalty, so it is one
thing to hear of systems of government in histories
and treatises and quite another to feel them in the
pulses of the poets and prose writers who have lived
under them.

It used to be taken for granted—did it not?—that
colleges would be found always on the conservative
side in politics (except on the question of free trade) ;
but in this latter day a great deal has taken place
which goes far toward discrediting the presumption.
The college in our day lies very near indeed to the
affairs of the world. It is a place of the latest experiments; its laboratories are brisk with the spirit
of discovery; its lecture rooms resound with the discussion of new theories of life and novel programmes
of reform. There is no radical like your learned radical, bred in the schools; and thoughts of revolution
have in our time been harbored in universities as
naturally as they were once nourished among the
Encyclopedists. It is the scientific spirit of the age
which has wrought the change. I stand with my
hat off at very mention of the great men who have
made our age an age of knowledge. No man more
heartily admires, more gladly welcomes, more ap-

provingly reckons the gain and the enlightenment
that have come to the world through the extraordinary advances in physical science which this great
age has witnessed. He would be a barbarian and a
lover of darkness who should grudge that great study
any part of its triumph. But I am a student of society and should deem myself unworthy of the comradeship of great men of science should I not speak
the plain truth with regard to what I see happening
under my own eyes. I have no laboratory but the
world of books and men in which I live; but I am
much mistaken if the scientific spirit of the age is
not doing us a great disservice, working in us a certain great degeneracy. Science has bred in us a
spirit of experiment and a contempt for the past.
It made us credulous of quick improvement, hopeful of discovering panaceas, confident of success in
every new thing.

I wish to be as explicit as carefully chosen words
will enable me to be upon a matter so critical, so
radical as this. I have no indictment against what
science has done: I have only a warning to utter
against the atmosphere which has stolen from laboratories into lecture rooms and into the general air of
the world at large. Science—our science—is new. It
is a child of the nineteenth century. It has transformed the world and owes little debt of obligation
to any past age. It has driven mystery out of the
Universe; it has made malleable stuff of the hard
world, and laid it out in its elements upon the table
of every class-room. Its own masters have known
its limitations: they have stopped short at the con-

fines of the physical universe; they have declined to
reckon with spirit or with the stuffs of the mind,
have eschewed sense and confined themselves to sen-
sation. But their work has been so stupendous that
all other men of all other studies have been set star-
ing at their methods, imitating their ways of thought,
ogling their results. We look in our study of the
classics nowadays more at the phenomena of language
than at the movement of spirit; we suppose the world
which is invisible to be unreal; we doubt the efficacy
of feeling and exaggerate the efficacy of knowledge;
we speak of society as an organism and believe that
we can contrive for it a new environment which will
change the very nature of its constituent parts; worst
of all, we believe in the present and in the future
more than in the past, and deem the newest theory
of society the likeliest. This is the disservice scientific study has done us: it has given us agnosticism
in the realm of philosophy, scientific anarchism in
the field of politics. It has made the legislator confident that he can create, and the philosopher sure
that God cannot. Past experience is discredited and
the laws of matter are supposed to apply to spirit
and the make-up of society.

Let me say once more, this is not the fault of the
scientist; he has done his work with an intelligence
and success which canot be too much admired. It
is the work of the noxious, intoxicating gas which
has somehow got into the lungs of the rest of us
from out the crevices of his workshop—a gas, it
would seem, which forms only in the outer air, and
where men do not know the right use of their lungs. I

should tremble to see social reform led by men who had breathed it; I should fear nothing better than utter destruction from a revolution conceived and led in the scientific spirit. Science has not changed the laws of social growth or betterment. Science has not changed the nature of society, has not made history a whit easier to understand, human nature a whit easier to reform. It has won for us a great liberty in the physical world, a liberty from superstitious fear and from disease, a freedom to use nature as a familiar servant; but it has not freed us from ourselves. It has not purged us of passion or disposed us to virtue. It has not made us less covetous or less ambitious or less self-indulgent. On the contrary, it may be suspected of having enhanced our passions, by making wealth so quick to come, so fickle to stay. It has wrought such instant, incredible improvement in all the physical setting of our life, that we have grown the more impatient of the unreformed condition of the part it has not touched or bettered, and we want to get at our spirits and reconstruct them in like radical fashion by like processes of experiment.

We have broken with the past and have come into a new world.

Can any one wonder, then, that I ask for the old drill, the old memory of times gone by, the old schooling in precedent and tradition, the old keeping of faith with the past, as a preparation for leadership in days of social change? We have not given science too big a place in our education; but we have made a perilous mistake in giving it too great a preponderance in method in every other branch of study. We must make the humanities human again; must recall what manner of men we are; must turn back once more to the region of practicable ideals.

Of course, when all is said, it is not learning but the spirit of service that will give a college place in the public annals of the nation. It is indispensable, it seems to me, if it is to do its right service, that the air of affairs should be admitted to all its class-rooms. I do not mean the air of party politics, but the air of the world's transactions, the consciousness of the solidarity of the race, the sense of the duty of man toward man, of the presence of men in every problem, of the significance of truth for guidance as well as for knowledge, of the potency of ideas, of the promise and the hope that shine in the face of all knowledge. There is laid upon us the compulsion of the national life. We dare not keep aloof and closet ourselves while a nation comes to its maturity. The days of glad expansion are gone, our life grows tense and difficult; our resource for the future lies in careful thought, providence, and a wise economy; and the school must be of the nation.

I have had sight of the perfect place of learning in my thought: a free place, and a various, where no man could be and not know with how great a destiny knowledge had come into the world—itself a little world; but not perplexed, living with a singleness of aim not known without; the home of sagacious men, hard-headed and with a will to know, debaters of the world's questions every day and used to the rough ways of democracy; and yet a place removed

—calm Science seated there, recluse, ascetic, like a nun; not knowing that the world passes, not caring, if the truth but come in answer to her prayer; and Literature, walking within her open doors, in quiet chambers, with men of olden time, storied walls about her, and calm voices infinitely sweet; here "magic casements, opening on the foam of perilous seas, in fairy lands forlorn," to which you may withdraw and use your youth for pleasure; there windows open straight upon the street, where many stand and talk, intent upon the world of men and business. A place where ideals are kept in heart in an air they can breathe; but no fool's paradise. A place where to hear the truth about the past and hold debate about the affairs of the present, with knowledge and without passion; like the world in having all men's life at heart, a place for men and all that concerns them; but unlike the world in its self-possession, its thorough way of talk; its care to know more than the moment brings to light; slow to take excitement, its air pure and wholesome with a breath of faith; every eye within it bright in the clear day and quick to look toward heaven for the confirmation of its hope. Who shall show us the way to this place?

MR. CLEVELAND AS PRESIDENT

FROM THE "ATLANTIC MONTHLY," MARCH, 1897, VOL. LXXIX, PP. 289-300. WALTER H. PAGE WAS THEN EDITOR OF THE "ATLANTIC MONTHLY."

IT is much too early to attempt to assign to Mr. Cleveland his place in the history of our government and policy. That he has played a very great and individual part in our affairs no one can doubt. But we are still too near him to see his work in its just perspective; we cannot yet see or estimate him as an historical figure.

It is plain, however, that Mr. Cleveland has rendered the country great services, and that his singular independence and force of purpose have made the real character of the government of the United States more evident than it ever was before. He has been the sort of President the makers of the Constitution had vaguely in mind: more man than partisan; with an independent executive will of his own; hardly a colleague of the Houses so much as an individual servant of the country; exercising his powers like a chief magistrate rather than like a party leader. Washington showed a like individual force and separateness; but he had been the country's leader through all its Revolution, and was always a kind of hero, whom parties could not absorb. Jackson worked his own will as President, and seemed to change the very nature of the government while he reigned; but it was a new social force that spoke in him, and he re-created a great party. Lincoln made the presidency the government while the war lasted, and gave the nation a great ruler; but his purposes were those of a disciplined and determined party, and his time was a time of fearful crisis, when men studied power, not law. No one of these men seems the normal President, or affords example of the usual courses of administration. Mr. Cleveland has been President in ordinary times, but after an extraordinary fashion; not because he wished to form or revolutionize or save the government, but because he came fresh to his tasks without the common party training, a direct, fearless, somewhat unsophisticated man of action. In him we got a President, as it were, by immediate choice from out the body of the people, as the Constitution has all along appeared to expect, and he has refreshed our notion of an American chief magistrate.

It is plain that Mr. Cleveland, like every other man, has drawn his character and force in large part from his origin and breeding. It would be easy to describe him as a man of the people, and he would, I suppose, be as proud as any other man of that peculiar American title to nobility. But, after all, no man comes from the people in general. We are each of us derived from some small group of persons in particular; and unless we were too poor to have any family life at all, it is the life and associations of the family that have chiefly shaped us in our youth. Mr. Cleveland had a very definite home training: wholesome, kindly, Christian. He was bred in a home where character was disciplined and the thoughts were formed, where books were read and the right rules of life obeyed. He was early thrown, indeed, into the ordinary and common school of life, had its rough work thrust upon him, and learned, by his own part in it, the life of the people. But he never got those first lessons, conned in plain village manses, out of his blood. "If mother were alive I should feel so much safer," he wrote to his brother upon the night he was elected governor of New York. Grover Cleveland certainly got good usury in his steadfast youth out of the capital stock of energy and principle he brought away, as his only portion, from his mother and father.

The qualities which have given him his place in his profession and in the history of the country seem commonplace enough in their customary manifestation: industry, thoroughness, uprightness, candor, courage. But it is worth while to remember that the same force and adjustment that will run a toy machine, made for a child's use, will also bring to bear the full might of a Corliss engine, with strength enough to drive a city's industries. It is the size and majesty of moral and intellectual qualities that make them great; and the point the people have noted about Mr. Cleveland is that his powers, though of a kind they know and have often had experience of, are made upon a great scale, and have lifted him to the view of the world as a national force, a maker and unmaker of policies. Men have said that Mr. Cleveland was without genius or bril-

liancy, because the processes of his mind were calculable and certain, like a law of nature; that his utterances were not above the common, because they
told only in the mass, and not sentence by sentence,
were cast rather than tempered; that he was stubborn because he did not change, and self-opinionated
because he did not falter. He has made no overtures
to fortune; has obtained and holds a great place in
our affairs by a sort of inevitable mastery, by a law
which no politician has ever quite understood or at
all relished, by virtue of a preference which the people themselves have expressed without analyzing.
We have seen how there is genius in mere excellence
of gift, and prevailing power merely in traits of
chastened will.

When a city or a nation looks for a man to better
its administration, it seeks character rather than
gifts of origination, a clear purpose that can be depended upon to work its will without fear or favor.
Mr. Cleveland never struck so straight towards the
confidence of practical men as when he spoke of the
tariff question as "a condition, not a theory." His
mind works in the concrete; lies close always to the
practical life of the world, which he understands by
virtue of lifelong contact with it. He was no prophet
of novelties, but a man of affairs; had no theories,
but strove always to have knowledge of fact. There
is as great a field for mind in thinking a situation
through and through as in threading the intricacies
of an abstract problem and it has heartened men
from the first to find that Mr. Cleveland could do
thinking of that sort with a sure, unhurried, stead-

fast power, such as no less practical man could even
have simulated. He was an experiment when he was
chosen mayor of Buffalo, did not know his own
powers, had given no one else their true measure; but
he was thereafter a known and calculable force, and
grew from station to station with an increase of
vigor, and withal a consistency of growth, which
showed his qualities such as waited only the invita-
tion of fortune and opportunity. It may be that
there are other men, of like parts and breeding, who
could rise in like fashion to a great rôle, but it is
certain that Mr. Cleveland has made a place of his
own among the Presidents of the United States.

The ordinary rules of politics have been broken
throughout his career. He came almost like a novice
into the field of national politics, despite his previous
experience as mayor and governor. He had always
identified himself, indeed, with the Democratic
party; but his neighbors in Buffalo had chosen him
to better rather than to serve his party, when they
elected him to local office. He had elevated the office
of sheriff, when they called him to it, by executing
it with conscientious energy and with an enlightened
sense of public duty; and he had made it his business, when they chose him mayor of their city, to see
municipal affairs put upon a footing of efficiency,
such as might become a great corporation whose object was the welfare of its citizens, and no partisan
interest whatever. It was inevitable that he should
shock and alienate all mere partisans, alike by his
temper and by his methods. He called himself a
party man, and had no weak stomach for the proc-

esses of party management; but he had not sought
office as a career, and he deemed his party better
served by manliness and integrity than by chicanery.
He was blunt, straightforward, plain-spoken, stalwart
by nature, used to choosing and pushing his own
way; and he had a sober audacity which made him no
caucus man. His courses of action were incalculable
to the mere politician, simply because they were not
based upon calculation.

It commonly turns out that the fearlessness of
such a man is safer than the caution of the professional party manager. A free and thoughtful
people loves a bold man, who faces the fight without
too much thought of himself or of his party's fortunes. Mr. Cleveland's success as mayor of Buffalo
attracted the attention of the whole State,—was
too pronounced and conspicuous to be overlooked.
Party managers saw in him a man to win with, little
as they understood the elements of his power. Even
they stared, nevertheless, to see him elected governor
of the State by the astounding majority of 192,854.
He evidently had not studied the art of pleasing; he
had been known as the "veto mayor" of Buffalo,
and his vetoes as the "plain speech" vetoes. He
had an odd way of treating questions of city government as if they were questions of individual official
judgment, and not at all questions of party advantage. He brought his exact habits as a lawyer to bear
upon his tasks as a public officer, and made a careful business of the affairs of city and State. There
was nothing puritanical about him. He had a robust
and practical spirit in all things. But he did not

seem to regard politics as in any way a distinct
science, set apart from the ordinary business of life.
He treated the legislature of the State, when he became governor, as he had treated the city council of
Buffalo, as if he were the president of a great industrial concern with incidental social functions, and
they were its board of directors, often unwise, sometimes unscrupulous, in their action; as if it were
his chief duty to stand between them and the stock-
holders, protecting the latter's interests at all
hazards. He used his veto as freely when governor
as he had used it when mayor. "Magnificent,"
cried the trained politicians about him, under their
breath,—"magnificent, but it is not politics!"

And yet they found him thrust inevitably upon
them as their candidate for President before his term
as governor had drawn to its close. Evidence was
accumulating that the country was ready to put an
end to the long succession of Republican administra-
tions which had held the federal executive departments for more than twenty years as a sort of party
property; but it was also plain enough that the old,
the real party leaders among the Democrats would
by no means be acceptable substitutes. The Democratic party, moreover, had been too long in opposition to be ready to assume, as it stood, the responsibilities of government. It had no real union; it was
little more than an assemblage of factions, a more or
less coherent association of the various groups and
interests opposed to the Republicans and bent upon
breaking their supremacy. It did not itself know
whether it was of one mind or not. For, though

popular majorities had been running its way for ten
years and more, and both Houses of Congress had
once come into its hands, it had never had leave to
undertake constructive legislation. The President's
veto had stood always in its way, and its legislation
had often been proposed for effect rather than with
a view to actual execution. It was necessary it
should go outside its own confused and disordered
ranks if it would choose a successful presidential
candidate, in order both to unite its own factions
and to win the country's confidence; and so it chose
Mr. Cleveland, and the country accepted him.

It was a novel experiment. The very considerations that made it wise to nominate Mr. Cleveland
as President were likely to render it difficult to live
under his presidency with an unbroken party discipline; and the circumstances of his election made it
all the more probable that he would choose to be
President of the country rather than leader of the
Democrats. The Democrats, in fact, did not recognize him as their leader, but only as their candidate
for the office of President. If he was leader at all in
the ordinary sense,—if he spoke and acted for the
views of any body of men,—he was the leader of
those independent Republicans who had broken with
their own party, and were looking for some one who
should open a new era in party politics and give
them efficient and public-spirited principles to believe in and vote for again. Men everywhere wished
to see parties reform themselves, and old-line Democrats had more reason to expect to see their party
fall apart into its contituent elements once more

than to hope that Mr. Cleveland would unite and
vivify it as an aggressive and triumphant organization. He had been made President, there was good
reason to believe, rather because thoughtful men
throughout the country wanted a pure and businesslike administration than because they wanted Democratic legislation or an upsetting of old policies;
he had been chosen as a man, not as a partisan,—
taken up by his own party as a likely winner rather
than as an acceptable master.

Apparently there was no reason, however, to fear
that Mr. Cleveland would arrogate to himself the
prerogatives of political leadership, or assume the
rôle of guide and mentor in matters of policy. At
first he regarded the great office to which he had
been chosen as essentially executive, except of course
in the giving or withholding of his assent to bills
passed by Congress. His veto he used with extraordinary freedom, particularly in the disapproval
of private pension bills, vetoing no less than one
hundred and forty-six measures during the sessions
of the first Congress of his administration; and he
filled his messages with very definite recommenda-
tions; but he thought it no part of his proper function to press his preferences in any other way upon
the acceptance of Congress. In the public interest,
he had addressed a letter to Mr. A. J. Warner, a
member of Congress, and others, only eight days before his inauguration as President, in which he had
declared in urgent terms his strong conviction that
the purchase and coinage of silver should be stopped
at once, to prevent radical and perhaps disastrous

disturbances in the currency; and he joined with
Mr. Manning, his Secretary of the Treasury, in speaking very plainly to the same effect when Congress
met. But he deemed his duty done when he had
thus used the only initiative given him by the Constitution, and expressly declined to use any other
means of pressing his views upon his party. He
meant to keep aloof, and be President with a certain
separateness, as the Constitution seemed to suggest.

It cost him at least one sharp fight with the
Senate to carry his purpose of executive independence into effect. Mr. Cleveland saw fit to remove
certain federal officers from office before the expira-
tion of their terms, and to appoint Democrats in
their places, and the Senate demanded the papers
which would explain the causes of the removals.
The President declined to send them, holding that
the Senate had no right to judge of anything but
the fitness of the men named as successors to the
officers removed. It was not certain that the moral
advantage lay with the President. He had been put
into the presidency chiefly because independent
voters all over the country, and particularly in his
own State, regarded him a tried champion of civil
service reform; but his choice and method in appointments had by no means satisfied the reformers.
They had stared to see him make Mr. Daniel Manning Secretary of the Treasury, not because Mr.
Manning lacked ability, but because he was notori-
ously a politician of the very "practical" sort, and
seemed to those who did not know him the very kind
of manager Mr. Cleveland ought to have turned his

back upon; and they did not like any more than the
Senate did to see men deprived of their offices to
make room for Democrats without good reason given,
reason that had no taint of partisanship upon it.
The truth was that the public service had been too
long in the hands of the Republicans to be susceptible of being considered an unpartisan service as it
stood.   Mr. Cleveland said simply, to those who
spoke to him in private about the matter, that he
had not made any removal which he did not, after
careful inquiry, believe to be for the good of the
public service.   This could not satisfy his critics.   It
meant that he must be permitted to use his judgment not only as a man, but also as a Democrat, in
reconstructing a civil service which had been for a
generation in the hands of the opposite political
party.   The laws could not be made mandatory upon
him in this matter, under the Constitution, and he
took leave to exercise his discretion here and there,
as his judgment as a practical and strong-willed man
suggested.   That the operation of the laws passed
for the reform of the civil service was strengthened
in the main, and their administration thoroughly
organized and very much bettered under him, no candid man could deny; and with that he asked the
country to be content.

The whole question afforded an excellent opportunity for studying Mr. Cleveland's character.   The
key quality of that character is, perhaps, a sort of
robust sagacity.   He had never for a moment called
himself anything but a party man.   He had not
sought personal detachment, and had all along

known the weakness that would come with isolation and the absolute rejection of the regular means of party management; and he had dared to make his own choices in cases which seemed too subtle or exceptional for the law. It was unsafe ground often; blunders were made which appeared to defeat the purposes he had in view in making removals and appointments; it looked in the end as if it would have been wiser to make no exceptions at all to the ordinary rules of appointment: but the mistakes were those of a strong nature,—too strong to strip itself absolutely of such choice as might serve what was to him legitimate party strength. Who shall judge the acts in question who does not know the grounds upon which the President proceeded? Not all of government can be crowded into the rules of the law.

At any rate, criticism did not disturb Mr. Cleveland's serenity; and it pleased the fancy of men of all sorts to see the President bear himself so steadfastly and do his work so calmly in the midst of all the talk. Outsiders could not know whether the criticism cut or not; they only knew that the President did not falter or suffer his mind to be shaken. He had an enormous capacity for work, shirked no detail of his busy function, carried the government steadily upon his shoulders. There is no antidote for worry to be compared with hard labor at important tasks which keep the mind stretched to large views; and the President looked upon himself as the responsible executive of the nation, not as the arbiter of policies. There is something in such a character that men of quick and ardent thought cannot like

or understand. They want all capable men to be
thinking, like themselves, along lines of active advance; they are impatient of performance which is
simply thorough without also being regenerative, and
Mr. Cleveland has not commended himself to them.
They themselves would probably not make good
Presidents. A certain tough and stubborn fibre is
necessary, which does not easily change, which is
unelastically strong.

The attention of the country, however, was presently drawn off from Mr. Cleveland's pension vetoes
and individual methods of appointment, from his
attitude and temper as a power standing aloof from
Congress, to note him a leader and master after all,
as if in spite of himself. He was too good a Democrat and too strenuous a man of business to stand by
and see the policy of the country hopelessly adrift
without putting his own influence to the test to direct it. He could not keep to his rôle of simple
executive. He saw his party cut into opposing factions upon the question of the tariff, upon the reform
to which it had been pledged time out of mind. Mr.
Carlisle, who wished to see the tariff brought to a
revenue basis, was Speaker of the Democratic House,
and Mr. Morrison was chairman of the Committee of
Ways and Means; but Mr. Randall checkmated them
at every turn, and nothing was done to redeem the
party's promises. No man of strong convictions
could stand there, where all the country watched
him, waiting for him to speak, the only representative of the nation as a whole in all the government, and let a great opportunity and a great duty

go by default. He had intended to make his a strictly business administration, to cleanse the public service and play his assigned part in legislation with a clear judgment to do right. But the President stands at the centre of legislation as well as of administration in executing his great office, and Mr. Cleveland grew to the measure of his place as its magnitude and responsibilities cleared to his view. The breath of affairs was at last in his lungs, and he gave his party a leader, of a sudden, in the plain-spoken, earnest, mandatory tariff message of December, 1887. It was such a stroke as no mere politician would have hazarded, and it sadly disconcerted the men who had supposed themselves the leaders of the Democrats. Mr. Cleveland had not consulted them about his manifesto. He had made the issue of the next presidential campaign for them before they were aware of it, and that campaign was immediately at hand. The Congress to which he sent his messages showed already a sad cutting off in the ranks of the Democrats. In the first Congress of his administration his party had had a majority of close upon forty in the House, though the Senate was still against them. In the Congress of which he demanded tariff reform the Democratic majority in the House had dwindled to eleven, though the Senate was almost equally divided. It seemed as if he would commit his party to a dangerous and aggressive policy at the very moment when its power was on the decline, and risk everything with regard to the next choice of President. Some resented his action as a sudden usurpation; others doubted what they should think; a few took the changed aspect of politics with zest and relish. It was bravely done. The situation produced was even dramatic; and yet the calmest man anywhere touched by the business was Mr. Cleveland himself. It was no trick or impulse. It was the steadily delivered blow of a stalwart and thoughtful man, thoroughly sick of seeing a great party drift and dally while the nation's finances suffered waste and demoralization.

He had certainly settled the way the next campaign should go: that the country's reception of his message showed; and the politicians adjusted themselves as best they might to his policy of plain speech and no circumspection. The House passed a tariff measure, drafted by Mr. Mills, which was thrown aside in the Senate, but not rejected by the party. Mr. Cleveland was renominated for the presidency by acclamation, not because the politicians wanted him, but because their constituents did. The two parties went to the country, and Mr. Cleveland lost by the vote of his own State.

The odd thing about it was that defeat did not seem to lessen Mr. Cleveland's importance. Some persons did not like to see their ex-President return to the ordinary duties of legal practice, as he did in New York, apparently expecting a healthy, practical man to accept a merely ornamental part in society after once having been their chief magistrate. There was no denying the fact that he had wrought his own defeat and his party's by forcing a hot fight when matters were going peacefully enough. He himself kept as much as might be from unnecessary publicity. But

the country could not cease to be interested in him,
and he was the only man it would take seriously,
even now, as the leader of the Democrats. Practical men could not for the life of them think of any
more suitable candidate for the next campaign.
Whether he had united or pleased his party or not,
he had, in any case, given it a programme and made
himself its chief representative. Through all the
four years of Mr. Harrison's administration Mr.
Cleveland was the most conspicuous man in the
country out of office, and a sort of popular expectation followed him in all his movements.

The Republicans, moreover, delivered themselves
into his hands. They took his defeat as a mandate
from the people to make a tariff as little like that
which Mr. Cleveland had desired as it might be possible to construct. The committee of Ways and
Means, of which Major McKinley was chairman,
framed a measure unmistakably fit to meet the demand; and the congressional elections of 1890 went
overwhelmingly against the Republicans. Apparently, the country had come at last to Mr. Cleveland's mind in respect of the tariff, and he became
once more the logical as well as the popular candidate of the Democrats for the presidency. Once
more he became President, and essayed the difficult
rôle of leader of a composite party. He had created
an additional difficulty, meanwhile, obeying an imperative conviction without regard to policy or opportune occasion. He had ventured a frank public
letter in opposition to the free coinage of silver,
notwithstanding the fact that he knew free coinage

to be much more distinctively a Democratic than a Republican measure. The habit of independent initiative in respect of questions of legislative policy was growing upon him, as he felt his personal power grow and his familiarity with public questions; and he knew that he was striking straight home, this time, to the confidence, at any rate, of every enlightened man of business in the country. Such men he had known from his youth up, and could assess: his courage and self-confidence in such a case was stuff of his whole training and character, and he felt that he could afford to lose the presidency upon that issue.

Mr. Cleveland's second term has shown the full strength and the full risk of the qualities which, during his first administration, the country had seen displayed only in the disturbing tariff message of 1887, in his energetic treatment of the fisheries question, which the Senate did not like, and in certain appointments which the whole country had criticised. He gave warning at the outset of the individual rôle he meant to play in the selection of his Cabinet. He bestowed the secretaryship of state upon a man come but the other day out of the Republican ranks to support him; the secretaryship of war upon a man who had formerly been his private secretary; the post-office upon his one-time law partner; the department of the interior upon a Georgian whose name the country smiled to hear for the first time; the attorney-generalship upon a lawyer who was no politician; and the secretaryship of agriculture upon a quiet gentleman of his own picking out.

Only the navy and the headship of the treasury
went to men whom his party knew and followed in the
House. His first Cabinet had contained men whom
everybody knew as accredited leaders among the
Democrats,—Mr. Bayard, Mr. Whitney, Mr. Lamar,
Mr. Vilas; only the minority of his counsellors had
then been selected as if to please himself, rather
than to draw a party following about him by recog-
nizing the men who exercised authority among the
Democrats. But his second Cabinet seemed chosen
as if of deliberate and set purpose to make a personal
and private choice, without regard to party support.

And yet there was less difference between the two
Cabinets than appeared upon the surface. Though
there had been some representative Democrats in the
first Cabinet, they had not been men who controlled
their party. Mr. Carlisle, of the second Cabinet,
was undoubtedly more influential than any of them,
and Mr. Herbert more truly a working, capital
member of the party's force in the House. The
truth was that Mr. Cleveland had, throughout his first
administration, been all the while held at arm's
length by his party,—an ally, perhaps, but not a
partner in its undertakings,—had been compelled to
keep the place of separateness and independence
which had at first seemed to be his choice. In his
second administration he apparently made no effort
to force his way into its counsels, but accepted his
place as the independent voters' President,—content
if only he could have a personal following, carry out
the real pledges of his party, and make his purpose
felt as the nation's spokesman. Not that he broke with

his party either in thought or in purpose; but he saw
that it would not take counsel with him, and that, if
he would fulfill his trust, he must force partisan
leaders, for their own good, to feel his power from
without. It might be they would draw about him more
readily through mastery than through persuasion.

It was singular how politics began at once to centre in the President, waiting for his initiative, and
how the air at Washington filled with murmurs
against the domineering and usurping temper and
practice of the Executive. Power had somehow gone
the length of the avenue, and seemed lodged in one
man. No one who knew Mr. Cleveland, or who
judged him fairly, for a moment deemed him too
covetous of authority, or in any degree disregardful
of the restraints the Constitution has put upon the
President. But the Democrats in the House were
made conscious that the eye of the country had been
withdrawn from them in matters of policy, and
Washington seemed full of Mr. Cleveland, his Secretary of the Treasury and his Secretary of State. A
position of personal isolation had been thrust upon
him, but he used the power which had come to him
to effect the purposes to which, as a Democrat, he
felt himself pledged. If the party would not act
with him, he must act for it. There was no touch
of cant in him when he declared his allegiance to
the Democratic party; there was only a danger that
if the leaders of the party in Congress continued to
follow him merely when they were obliged, he would
himself presently be all the Democratic party that
was left in the country.

On June 30, 1893, four months after his second
inauguration, he took steps to force action upon the
silver question. He called Congress to meet in extra
session upon the 7th of August following, to deal
with the finances of the country and prevent a panic;
telling them plainly that the law which compelled
the purchase and coinage of silver by the government ought to be repealed, and that this question
must be settled even if the tariff had to wait. There
was already serious disturbance in business circles,
arising in large part from the condition of the currency, when, on the 26th of June, the British authorities in India closed the mints of that country to
the free coinage of silver, and sent the price of the
unstable metal down with a disastrous tumble in all
the world's markets. It looked then as if there would
certainly be a fatal panic, and Mr. Cleveland saw
that Congress must meet and face the situation at
once.

It was evident, even before Congress came together, that the battle was to be, not between Democrats and Republicans, but between the advocates
and the opponents of the free coinage of silver, without regard to party. Conventions called by the
silver men met in Denver and in Chicago before
Congress assembled, and denounced the proposal to
repeal the silver purchase law as a scheme devised by
American and English bankers, with the assistance
of Mr. Cleveland, to drive silver out of use as money;
and when Congress took the matter up, old party
lines seemed, for the moment at any rate, to have disappeared. It was the "friends" of silver against

its "enemies." The advocates of Mr. Cleveland's policy of repeal won a decisive victory in the House of Representatives, and won it at once, before August was out; but in the Senate the fight dragged with doubtful and wavering fortunes, until the very end of October,—would have ended in some weak compromise had not the President stood resolute,—and kept the country waiting so long for the issue that business suffered almost as much as if repeal had been defeated.

It was the President's victory that the law was at last repealed, and every one knew it. He had forced the consideration of the question; he had told Senators plainly, almost passionately, when they approached him, that he would accept no compromise, —that he would veto anything less than absolute repeal, and let them face the country as best they might afterwards. Until he came on the stage both parties had dallied and coquetted with the advocates of silver. Now he had brought both to a parting of the ways. The silver men were forced to separate themselves and look their situation in the face, choose which party they should plan to bring under their will and policy, if they could, and no longer camp in the tents of both. Such a stroke settled what the course of congressional politics should be throughout the four years of Mr. Cleveland's term, and made it certain that at the end of that term he should either have won his party to himself or lost it altogether. It was evident that any party that rejected the gold standard for the currency must look upon him as its opponent.

He showed his fixed purpose in the matter once
again by his veto of the so-called Seigniorage Bill in
March, 1894. The silver men had already so far rallied as to induce substantial majorities in both Houses
to agree to the practically immediate coinage of all
the silver bullion owned by the treasury as a result
of the purchases of silver made under the law which
had but just now been repealed in the special session. It would not be wise to put forth so great a
body of silver, at such a time, to the fresh disturbance of the currency, said the President, and the bill
was negatived. The issue of more silver was defeated, and the silver men quietly set about forming
their party lines anew.

Meanwhile, issue was joined once more upon the
question of the tariff, not only as between Democrats
and Republicans, but also as between Democrat and
Democrat, and new lines of divergence were run
through Mr. Cleveland's party. The Committee of
Ways and Means, of which Mr. W. L. Wilson was
chairman, had formulated a tariff bill during the
special session, and when Congress came together for
its regular sittings they added to their tariff scheme
a bill providing for an income tax, to meet the probable deficiency in the revenue likely to result from
the reduction of import duties which they had proposed. The two measures were made one. There
was keen opposition in the East to the adoption of the
income tax, and though the composite bill went
through the House by a majority of sixty-four, many
Democrats voted against it, and party lines were
again broken. In the Senate, the tariff bill was

changed beyond recognition by more than six hundred amendments. Many of the *ad valorem* duties proposed by Mr. Wilson's committee were made specific; the Senate would not consent to put iron and lead ores or coal upon the free list with wool; above all, it insisted upon an increase rather than a reduction of the duty on sugar. In the Committee of Conference, irreconcilable differences of opinion emerged between the two Houses; a letter from Mr. Cleveland to Mr. Wilson, supporting the plans of the House and severely criticising those of the Senate, only stiffened a little more the temper of the Senate conferees; and the House at last yielded, rather than have no change at all in the tariff.

Mr. Cleveland did not sign the bill, but suffered it to become law without his signature. It was not such a law as he wanted, he said, nor such a law as fulfilled the pledges of the party; but the party had accepted it, and he would not cast himself loose from it in this critical matter by the use of his veto. No one believed that the Senators who had insisted upon the chief matter of contention, the change in the sugar duties, had acted as Democrats. It was the universal opinion that they had acted as the representatives of a particular vested interest. But in the nice balance of parties which existed in the Senate they were in a position to dictate. The party leaders in the House thought it better to pass some measure of tariff reform than to suffer a total miscarriage; and Mr. Cleveland tacitly consented to their judgment.

The Supreme Court completed the discomfiture of

the party by declaring the income tax law unconstitutional. Without that tax there was not revenue
enough to meet the expenditures of the government,
as presently became evident. Deficiency of revenue,
coupled with the obligation of the government to redeem its notes in gold on demand, cut into the gold
reserve, and the money question grew acute again.
To maintain the gold reserve the administration was
obliged again and again to resort to the issue of
bonds. The President was in league, the silver men
said, with the bankers and the men who controlled
the gold of the world everywhere. Mr. Carlisle earn-
estly urged a radical reform of the currency system:
the repeal of the law compelling a constant reissue of
the government's legal tender notes, and such legislation as would make provision for a sufficiently elastic
currency by means of liberal changes in the banking
laws. But his plans were not acted upon; the revenue did not increase; the government was obliged to
pay out gold, upon demand, from its reserve; and
there was nothing for it but to obtain gold of the
bankers, and of those who had hoarded it, by issu-
ing new bonds and increasing the interest charges of
the government. The silver men grew every day
more hostile to the administration.

The administration bulked very large the while,
not only in the business world, but also in the field
of foreign affairs. A treaty providing for the an-
nexation of Hawaii was pending in the Senate when
Mr. Cleveland came into office in March, 1893; but
Mr. Cleveland promptly withdrew it, and, in characteristic fashion, set about finding out for himself

the real situation of affairs in the islands. The outcome showed his transparent honesty and rare courage very plainly, if not his skill in a delicate affair. He found that it was the countenance and apparent assistance of the agent of the United States in Hawaii that had facilitated the dethronement of the Queen and the setting up of a revolutionary government, and he took steps to undo so far as possible the mischievous work of interference. The apologies of the United States were made to the Queen, and the provisional government was informed that the government of the United States would expect it to withdraw and make way for the reëstablishment of the legitimate government of the islands. But the provisional government refused to withdraw, and the President was obliged to submit the whole matter to Congress, without whose sanction he did not feel justified in employing force or in taking any further step in the unhappy affair. It seemed a lame ending, and the papers found it easy to scoff, though hard to say what other honorable course could have been taken; and every man who was not a Jingo perceived that the President had not in fact lost credit. He had simply followed his conscience without regard to applause or failure, and given one more proof of his unsophisticated character.

At any rate, everybody forgot Hawaii upon the emergence of Venezuela. Diplomatic relations had been suspended between Great Britain and Venezuela because of a dispute regarding the boundary line between Venezuela and British Guiana, and Mr. Cleveland's administration had intervened, and had

insisted that the whole question be submitted to arbitration. The position it took was based explicitly
upon the Monroe Doctrine, and the course it proposed was virtually a demand that the United States
be accorded the right of intervention in all questions arising between South American states and
European powers. Lord Salisbury declined to make
any such concession to the United States, or to submit any more of the question between Great Britain
and Venezuela to arbitration than he had already
expressed his willingness to submit to adjudication in
his correspondence with the Venezuelan government;
and Mr. Cleveland sent to Congress his startling message of December 17, 1895.

Here again he showed himself a strong man, but
no diplomatist. It was like a blunt, candid, fearless
man to say that it was the duty of the United
States to ascertain for herself the just rights of Venezuela, and resist any encroachment upon her southern
neighbor by every means in her power, and to add
that he fully realized the consequences that might
follow such a declaration of purpose. But only our
kinsmen oversea would have yielded anything or
sought peace by concession, after such words had been
spoken. England presently showed that she would
not have taken such a defiance from William of
Germany; but good feeling, good temper, good
sense, soon brought the two governments to a better
understanding. Our commission of inquiry acted
with the utmost sobriety and tact; Mr. Olney pursued his correspondence with Lord Salisbury with a
strength of good manners, good reasoning, and dis-

interested purpose that carried its own assurance of victory; we had in Mr. Bayard a representative in London of an old and excellent school of behavior; and the end was a diplomatic triumph for the United States which attracted the attention of the world. The successful settlement of the particular question in controversy was even followed by a treaty of general arbitration between England and the United States, such as multitudes of peace-loving men had prayed for, but few had dared to hope to see. What had at first seemed to threaten to mar Mr. Cleveland's fame once and for all turned out in the end its greatest title to honorable dignity. We are at last enabled to read the famous message aright. There spoke a man as desirous and capable of peace and moderation as any in the nation, but accustomed, when he spoke at all, to speak his whole mind without reserve, and willing to speak to Europe, if she must hear, as freely as he would speak to his own people. It was the perilous indiscretion of a frank nature incapable of disguises.

The Cuban question had shown us the same man. He has satisfied neither the Democrats nor the Republicans, because neither cared to observe the restraints of international law or set themselves any bounds of prudence; but he has made Spain feel the pressure of our opinion and of our material interest in the Cuban struggle none the less, and by his very self-restraint has brought the sad business sensibly nearer to its end.

In this, as in other things, he has been a man without a party. His friends have been the silent men

who watch public affairs without caring too much
about the fortunes of parties. He has carried civil
service reform to its completion at last; but that did
not give him a party. To extend the rules of the
classified merit service to all branches of the public
business was a work of non-partisanship, and no man
need expect a party following because of that. Mr.
Cleveland did not do this work hurriedly. At the
close of his first administration the friends of reform stood disappointed and not a little disheartened.
But he has done the work in his own way and thoroughly, and no man need doubt his record now. He
can look back with deep satisfaction upon the fact
that while he directed the affairs of the government
vast tracts of the public lands were reclaimed for
the use of the people; that he was enabled to put system and a little economy into the management of the
Pension Bureau; that more than one of the executive departments has received a complete reorganization at his hands; that he gave the country the businesslike administration he promised. None of these
things, however, secures any man the support of a
party. Mr. Cleveland never seemed so utterly without a party as in the extraordinary campaign which
has made Mr. McKinley his successor. But it is the
country's debt to him now that he thus stood alone.
He forced the fight which drove the silver men to
their final struggle for a party. They chose the
Democratic party, because it was strong in the West
where the silver ore was mined, and in the South
and in all the agricultural areas of the continent
where those business interests are weak which most

sensitively feel the movements of the money market. They drove thousands of men out of the Democratic party when they took it,—Mr. Cleveland, their chief enemy, with the rest. And the Republicans routed them upon the issue which Mr. Cleveland had made definite and final.

We need not pretend to know what history shall say of Mr. Cleveland; we need not pretend that we can draw any common judgment of the man from the confused cries that now ring everywhere from friend and foe. We know only that he has played a great part; that his greatness is authenticated by the passion of love and of hatred he has stirred up; that no such great personality has appeared in our politics since Lincoln; and that, whether greater or less, his personality is his own, unique in all the varied history of our government. He has made policies and altered parties after the fashion of an earlier age in our history, and the men who assess his fame in the future will be no partisans, but men who love candor, courage, honesty, strength, unshaken capacity, and high purpose such as his.

THE PURITAN

SPEECH BEFORE THE NEW ENGLAND SOCIETY OF NEW
    YORK CITY, DECEMBER 22, 1900. PROCEEDINGS
    PRINTED BY WILLIAM GREEN, NEW YORK, 1900, PP.
    39-49.

MR. DODGE, Ladies and Gentlemen: I cannot
but regard it as a whimsical fortune that a
Scotch-Irishman should be brought here to pay
tribute to the New England Society. The Scotch-
Irishman is not fond of paying anything except his
just debts, and there is always a certain risk in
letting him speak his real mind. Mr. Dodge himself
has given you some intimation of the risk he knows
he is incurring by intimating to you—he was thinking of the Irish in me, I hope, rather than of the
Scotch—that if I spoke long enough it would be a
desecration of the Sabbath.

And yet I believe, gentlemen, that nothing gives
one strong race so much satisfaction as to pay its
respects to another strong race. We came later to
this continent than you did, but we had the better
opportunity for observing your characters and the
cut of your jibs. We saw how important was the
task which you had half completed. We saw how
necessary it was that certain other elements should be
added which you had not contributed, and so we are
here, gentlemen, and we don't mind talking about

it. We, like you, are beginning to form societies to
annex the universe; we, like you, are beginning to
elect memorialists who shall record how every line of
strength in the history of the world is a line colored
by Scotch-Irish blood. There is a great deal in that.
[Laughter and applause.] I believe that it is
necessary that races of different characters should
exchange their ideas as well as their compliments,
and that we should understand just what our relative parts are to be in the great game that we are
to play upon this continent. The Puritan was—
as Dr. Hadley has said—intensely human; but you
will remember that he apologized to God as many as
three times a day for the fact [laughter], and that
it was an imperative part of his creed that he should
root out diligently, in season and out of season, the
pestiferous elements of the flesh that were in him.
[Laughter.] Now, I have no objection to the hatred
that Dr. Hadley referred to. I believe in a certain
degree of intolerance. It is an eminently comfortable indulgence. I believe that intolerance can express itself, if not exactly as a dear old President of
Princeton expressed it, at any rate, in more parliamentary form. I refer to that occasion when
he brought all the strong flavor of his Scotch-
Presbyterianism to a meeting of the Evangelical
Alliance—one of the early gatherings of that interesting association—when Dr. Huntington arose
and proposed that they adopt the Apostles' Creed as
a platform upon which all could stand. "Tut! tut!"
said Dr. McCosh in an undertone, to a neighbor, "I'll
not descend into hell with the Episcopalians."

[Laughter.] There is in this, gentlemen, the flavor and the definiteness which go with the Scotch character.

I believe that if you will look into it you will find that you are worshipping your ancestors at a safe distance. Dr. Hadley said that we had met this evening to celebrate your *descent* from those Fathers [laughter], and the old phrase came into my mind: *Facilis descensus.* It is not very much to your credit that you have descended; it will be to your credit if you ascend to the standards which they established. I sometimes recall when I think of the shock and the change which the Puritan principles underwent when they came to the City of New York [laughter], the story, half-pathetic and half-amusing, which is told of an old lady who, unaccustomed to travel, boarded a train somewhere in the neighborhood of New Haven, coming in this direction, and nervously asked the brakeman if that train stopped at Forty-second Street. "Well, ma'am, if it don't, you'll get the dumbdest bumping you ever got!" Now, I have sometimes thought that the New England principles, when they stopped at Forty-second Street, got the "dumbdest bumping" they ever got. [Laughter and applause.]

And yet, seriously, gentlemen, there is a great deal which you have preserved besides your handsome persons. You have preserved what I may be allowed to call, in rhetorical phrase, a great deal of the old structural iron, though you have changed a good deal about the exterior of the building and you have employed new and French architects. I ask you to consider with me just what contribution it was that the Puritans seem to have made to the civilization of this country. Of course I can tell you. [Laughter.] That contribution is worth considering, because, having been obliged to read many of the historians of this country, and having found that most of them were also celebrating their descent from the Pilgrim Fathers, I have read in their pages, and for a long time believed, that the history of this country was the expansion of New England. If it was the expansion of New England, it was spread thin. [Laughter.] And having been born, as I was born, in the valley of Virginia, where they do not accept that view, except as heretical, I was led in my maturer years to question its validity. I did not see reason to believe that all the elements of this country came out of what was, after all, the not very productive soil of New England, because when I looked at the character of those Puritan men they seemed to me to stand for one single principle—a very splendid principle, I allow you, but, nevertheless, the single principle of discipline, of order, of polity. It was for the discipline that pulls in harness; it was for subjection to authority; it was for crucifixion of the things which did not comport with a fixed and rigid creed that they strove [for]. These men stood for the discipline of life. They did not stand for the quick pulses which have operated in some of the most momentous things that have taken place on this continent, but they stood for those lessons of duty which they read out of a Bible, interpreted in the light of a Calvinistic creed, cut in a definite pattern, not allowing elasticity of interpretation; which forced men to settle in different parts of New England, because, if they differed with each other, they had to go and live somewhere else [laughter]; they could not continue to live with each other. The churches of Massachusetts did indeed pay their tribute of respect, and very generously, to Mr. Thomas Hooker, but Mr. Hooker found it more convenient to live at Hartford, and he lived at Hartford, because he did not like the doctrine of Mr. Cotton; because he did not like the doctrine of Mr. Wilson—a very respectable name; because he did not feel that there was just the sort of room for his doctrine in Newtown that there might be in the new places on the Connecticut. There is a sense in which the development of America is represented by the movement of people out of Massachusetts into that wild Cave of Adullam in Rhode Island whither all who were heretical, all who were discontented, all who were ungovernable, betook themselves, and where they combined to form that fine, effervescent mixture which is more like the rest of the country than the plain, unmixed material of the places of older settlements. Those men who struggled south through the Narragansett country, through the cold, forbidding woods, and made their new homes on the delightful prospects along the Bay of Narragansett—who made those places destined to have the distinction of containing the most fashionable summer resort in the United States— they represented that expulsive power of New England which certainly has been one of the causes of the growth of this country. [Applause.] There is

an application here for an old theme of Dr. Chalmers,
who preached one of the greatest of his sermons on
the subject: "The Expulsive Power of a New Affec-
tions." These men got an affection for new things,
and they found that only old things would not be
permitted in the places where they were living, and
so they had to seek homes elsewhere.

So when the race to which I belong landed on this
continent and made its way in its principal migra-
tions through the State of Pennsylvania and down
through the Cumberland Valley and the valley of
the Shenandoah and into the country of the South-
west; and then crossed the mountains and was
amongst the first to face the French on the Ohio,
and, going with the vanguard of the whole movement, deployed at last upon the plains that led to the
Great Valley of the Mississippi, it saw the thing
which it remained for another principle than that of
discipline to do—the principle of aspiration, the
principle of daring, the principle of unrest, the principle of mere adventure, which made the level lines
of the prairie seem finer and more inviting than the
uplifted lines of the mountain; that made it seem as
if the world were bigger on the plains, and as if the
feet of young men were the feet of leaders. And
this was a place where all those new things should
be tried and all those ungoverned adventures should
be made which filled this continent with an abounding life. For there is something, gentlemen, of this
balance in our lives between the discipline of restraint, the discipline of the old reminders of moral
principle, and that uplifting power of an unregulated

ambition. I believe that there is a sense, if you will
permit me to say so in all soberness, in which there
is a contrast between the New England spirit and the
national spirit. You contributed something without
which the national spirit would have simply set the
world on fire, without being able to confine its power
in piston rods, to drive the heart of machines, to make
furnaces hold the abounding heat. You contributed
the restraint—that mechanical combination, that
poise, that power of union, which is the spirit of
discipline. But there was besides a national spirit
which, if it had not received this restraint, would
have broken all bonds. The spirit of progression is
this spirit of aspiration which has led us into new
conditions and to face a new destiny. [Applause.]

I pray that sober principle may ever be whispered
at our ear, that we may be ever critical of our motives, that we may ever be self-examining men with
regard to our lives and conduct; but I also pray
that that fine discipline of the heart may but precede the expansion of power; that that fine elevation
and expansion of nature which ventures everything
may go with us to the ends of the earth, so be it
we go to the ends of the earth carrying conscience and
the principles that make for good conduct. I believe that it is necessary that when we get reformers
upon our platforms we should see that their function
is properly spelled. [Applause.] Most of our reformers are retro-reformers. They want to hale us
back to an old chrysalis which we have broken; they
want us to resume a shape which we have outgrown;
they want us to take back the outward form of prin-

ciples which they think cannot live in a new habiliment, or prosper under new forms and conditions. It is not the forms of our lives; it is the principles of our lives that count. I can quote Scripture for this [laughter], though not Scripture which, I am afraid, would be regarded as exactly orthodox in Princeton. There was an old darky preacher who said, "The Lord said unto Moses, Come fo'th; and he came fifth, and lost the race." [Great laughter.] Now, I think we ought to come forth, and not to come fifth and lose the race; and if we sufficiently obey this fine, expansive impulse in us we shall not make it necessary that we should forget the fine old discipline of ancient doctrine; we should not forget to have some sense of duty, something of a faith, some reverence for the laws ourselves have made.

I believe that the principal menace of a democracy is that the disciplinary power of the common thought should overwhelm the individual instinct of man's originative power, and that that individuality should be a little rubbed off and lost. I should wish to hear every man dare speak his thoughts. I should wish to have every man use a boldness, which I should also wish to see in the nation. I pray that the time may never come when we are not ready to do new things, when we are not ready to acknowledge that the age has changed. I suppose you have all heard Mr. Joseph Jefferson tell the story about the little boy who was to be taken by his mother to hear the play of "Rip Van Winkle." His mother fell ill and could not take him, but rather than disappoint him she turned the ticket over to his aunt and asked

her to take the lad. "But," she said, "you must remember that he never has been to the theatre before,
and you must explain things to him, as he cannot
understand it." But the aunt, being less solicitous
than the mother, forgot all about the boy until the
curtain went down on the young "Rip Van Winkle"
and was about to rise on the old "Rip Van Winkle,"
when it occurred to the aunt to say to the boy, "You
know, Johnny, twenty years have gone by since the
curtain went down." He said, "Where's my
mamma?" [Laughter.] Now, that is the attitude
of a great many people whom I very sincerely
respect. You say to them, "Twenty years have gone
by since we fought Spain," and they say, "Where
are our papas?" [Laughter.] They go to consult
a generation that did not know anything about it.
They even take liberties with the Father of his Country. Now Washington was a Virginian, and, perhaps, since I am a Virginian, I may be allowed to
interpret Washington. [Laughter.] We all know
each other down there. [Applause.] When you
reflect that Washington wrote his Farewell Address
to something over three million people, to whom he
was, if his letters are to be believed, very willing to
say good-bye [laughter], and if you will understand
that Address to have meant, as it would seem to have
meant: "I want you to discipline yourselves and
stay still and be good boys until you grow up, until
you are big enough to stand the competition of foreign countries, until you are big enough to go abroad
in the world," I think you will have put the proper
interpretation on it. "Wait," he said, "until you

need not be afraid of foreign influence, and then you shall be ready to take your part in the field of the world.'' I do not accept the interpretation of Washington's Farewell Address that those people who have but seen the curtain go down accept. [Laughter and applause.]

Now, gentlemen, will you follow the Scotch-Irish across the continent and into the farther seas of the Pacific? Will you follow the Star of Empire with those men who will follow anything which they think will drop profit or amusement? [Laughter.] Are you ready, are we ready, to go shoulder to shoulder, forgetting our differences of origin, forgetting our fatal descent, forgetting all the things which might restrain us, not going with faces averted over shoulder, but going with faces to the front, faces that will scorn to face a shame but will dare to face a glory? [Applause.]

DEMOCRACY AND EFFICIENCY

FROM THE "ATLANTIC MONTHLY," MARCH, 1901, VOL.
LXXXVII. PP. 289-299.

IT is no longer possible to mistake the reaction against democracy. The nineteenth century was above all others a century of democracy; and yet the world is no more convinced of the benefits of democracy as a form of government at its end than it was at its beginning. The history of closeted Switzerland has not been accepted as proving the stability of democratic institutions; the history of the United States has not been accepted as establishing their tendency to make governments just and liberal and pure. Their eccentric influence in France, their disastrous and revolutionary operation in South America, their power to intoxicate and their powerlessness to reform,—except where the states which use them have had in their training and environment what Switzerland or the colonies and commonwealths sprung from England have had, to strengthen and steady them,—have generally been deemed to offset every triumph or success they can boast. When we praise democracy, we are still put to our proofs; when we excuse its errors, we are understood to have admitted its failure.

There need be in this, however, no serious discouragement for us, whose democratic institutions have in all large things succeeded. It means nothing more than that the world is at last ready to accept the moral long ago drawn for it by de Tocqueville. He predicted the stability of the government of the United States, not because of its intrinsic excellence, but because of its suitability to the particular social, economic, and political conditions of the people and the country for whose use and administration it had been framed; because of the deliberation and sober sagacity with which it had been devised and set up; because it could reckon upon a sufficient "variety of information and excellence of discretion" on the part of the people who were to live under it to insure its intelligent operation; because he observed a certain uniformity of civilization to obtain throughout the country, and saw its affairs steadied by their fortunate separation from European politics; because he found a sober, religious habit of thought among our people, and a clear sense of right. Democracy was with us, he perceived, already a thing of principle and custom and nature, and our institutions admirably expressed our training and experience. No other people could expect to succeed by the same means, unless those means equally suited their character and stage of development. Democracy, like every other form of government, depended for its success upon qualities and conditions which it did not itself create, but only obeyed.

Many excellent suggestions, valid and applicable everywhere, we have given the world, with regard to the spirit in which government should be conducted. No doubt class privilege has been forever discredited

because of our example. We have taught the world
the principle of the general welfare as the object and
end of government, rather than the prosperity of any
class or section of the nation, or the preferment of
any private or petty interest. We have made the law
appear to all men an instrument wherewith to secure
equality of rights and a protection which shall be
without respect of persons. There can be no misgivings about the currency or the permanency of the
principles of right which we have exalted. But we
have not equally commended the forms or the organizations of the government under which we live.

A federal union of diverse commonwealths we have
indeed made to seem both practicable and efficient
as a means of organizing government on a great
scale, while preserving at the same time the utmost
possible latitude and independence in local self-
government. Germany, Canada, Australia, Switzerland herself, have built and strengthened their constitutions in large part upon our model. It would
be hard to exaggerate the shock which has been
given to old theories, or the impetus which has been
given to hopeful experiment, in the field of political
action, by our conspicuous successes as constitution-
makers and reformers. But those successes have not
been unlimited. We have not escaped the laws of
error that government is heir to. It is said that
riots and disorders are more frequent amongst us
than in any other country of the same degree of
civilization; justice is not always done in our courts;
our institutions do not prevent, they do not seem
even to moderate, contests between capital and labor;

our laws of property are no more equitable, our laws of marriage no more moralizing, than those of undemocratic nations, our contemporaries; our cities are perhaps worse governed than any in Europe outside the Turkish Empire and Spain; crime defies or evades the law amongst us as amongst other peoples, less favored in matters of freedom and privilege; we have no monopoly either of happiness or of enlightened social order. As we grow older, we grow also perplexed and awkward in the doing of justice and in the perfecting and safeguarding of liberty. It is character and good principle, after all, which are to save us, if we are to escape disaster.

That moral is the justification of what we have attempted. It is for this that we love democracy: for the emphasis it puts on character; for its tendency to exalt the purposes of the average man to some high level of endeavor; for its just principle of common assent in matters in which all are concerned; for its ideals of duty and its sense of brotherhood. Its forms and institutions are meant to be subservient to these things. Democracy is merely the most radical form of "constitutional" government. A "constitutional" government is one in which there is a definite understanding as to the sphere and powers of government; one in which individual liberty is defined and guaranteed by specific safeguards, in which the authority and the functions of those who rule are limited and determined by unmistakable custom or explicit fundamental law. It is a government in which these understandings are kept up, alike in the making and in the execution of laws, by

frequent conferences between those who govern and
those who are governed. This is the purpose of representation: stated conference and a cordial agreement between those who govern and those who are
governed. The process of the understanding is discussion,—public and continuous, and conducted by
those who stand in the midst of affairs, at the official
centre and seat of management, where affairs can
be looked into and disposed with full knowledge and
authority; those intrusted with government being
present in person, the people by deputy.

Representative government has had its long life
and excellent development, not in order that common
opinion, the opinion of the street, might prevail,
but in order that the best opinion, the opinion gen-
erated by the best possible methods of general
counsel, might rule in affairs; in order that some
sober and best opinion might be created, by thoughtful and responsible discussion conducted by men
intimately informed concerning the public weal, and
officially commissioned to look to its safeguarding
and advancement,—by discussion in parliaments, discussion face to face between authoritative critics and
responsible ministers of state.

This is the central object to which we have devoted
our acknowledged genius for practical politics.
During the first half century of our national life we
seemed to have succeeded in an extraordinary degree
in approaching our ideal, in organizing a nation for
counsel and coöperation, and in moving forward
with cordial unison and with confident and buoyant
step toward the accomplishment of tasks and duties

upon which all were agreed. Our later life has disclosed serious flaws, has even seemed ominous of pitiful failure, in some of the things we most prided ourselves upon having managed well: notably, in pure and efficient local government, in the successful organization of great cities, and in well-considered schemes of administration. The boss—a man elected by no votes, preferred by no open process of choice, occupying no office of responsibility—makes himself a veritable tyrant amongst us, and seems to cheat us of self-government; parties appear to hamper the movements of opinion rather than to give them form and means of expression; multitudinous voices of agitation, an infinite play of forces at cross-purpose, confuse us; and there seems to be no common counsel or definite union for action, after all.

We keep heart the while because still sure of our principles and of our ideals: the common weal, a common and cordial understanding in matters of government, secure private rights and yet concerted public action, a strong government and yet liberty also. We know what we have to do; what we have missed and mean to find; what we have lost and mean to recover; what we still strive after and mean to achieve. Democracy is a principle with us, not a mere form of government. What we have blundered at is its new applications and details, its successful combination with efficiency and purity in governmental action. We tell ourselves that our partial failure in these things has been due to our absorption in the tasks of material growth, that our practical genius has spent itself upon wealth and the

organization of industry. But it is to be suspected
that there are other elements in the singular fact.
We have supposed that there could be one way of
efficiency for democratic governments and another
for monarchial. We have declined to provide ourselves with a professional civil service, because we
deemed it undemocratic; we have made shift to do
without a trained diplomatic and consular service,
because we thought the training given by other governments to their foreign agents unnecessary in the
case of affairs so simple and unsophisticated as the
foreign relations of a democracy in politics and
trade,—transactions so frank, so open, so straightforward, interests so free from all touch of chicane
or indirection; we have hesitated to put our presidents or governors or mayors into direct and responsible relations of leadership with our legislatures and
councils in the making of laws and ordinances, because such a connection between lawmakers and
executive officers seemed inconsistent with the theory
of checks and balances whose realization in practice
we understood Montesquieu to have proved essential
to the maintenance of a free government. Our
theory, in short, has paid as little heed to efficiency
as our practice. It has been a theory of non-
professionalism in public affairs; and in many great
matters of public action non-professionalism is non-
efficiency.

"If only we had our old leisure for domestic affairs, we should devise a way of our own to be efficient, consonant with our principles, characteristic
of our genius for organization," we have heard men

say. "How fatal it may prove to us that our attention has been called off from a task but half done to the tasks of the world, for which we have neither inclination nor proper training nor suitable organization,—from which, until now, we were so happily free! We shall now be forever barred from perfection, our own perfection, at home!" But may it not be that the future will put another face upon the matter, and show us our advantage where least we thought it to lie? May it not be that the way to perfection lies along these new paths of struggle, of discipline, and of achievement? What will the reaction of new duty be? What self-revelations will it afford; what lessons of unified will, of simplified method, of clarified purpose; what disclosures of the fundamental principles of right action, the efficient means of just achievement, if we but keep our ideals and our character?

At any rate, it is clear that we could not have held off. The affairs of the world stand in such a case, the principles for which we have battled the long decades through are now put in such jeopardy amidst the contests of nations, the future of mankind faces so great a peril of reactionary revolution, that our own private business must take its chances along with the greater business of the world at large. We dare not stand neutral. All mankind deem us the representatives of the moderate and sensible discipline which makes free men good citizens, of enlightened systems of law and a temperate justice, of the best experience in the reasonable methods and principles of self-government, of public force made consistent with individual liberty; and we shall not realize these ideals at home, if we suffer them to be hopelessly discredited amongst the peoples who have yet to see liberty and the peaceable days of order and comfortable progress. We should lose heart ourselves, did we suffer the world to lose faith in us as the champions of these things.

There is no masking or concealing the new order of the world. It is not the world of the eighteenth century, nor yet of the nineteenth. A new era has come upon us like a sudden vision of things unprophesied, and for which no polity has been prepared. Here is straightway a new frontage for the nations,—this frontage toward the Orient. Our almost accidental possession of the Philippines has put us in the very presence of the forces which must make the politics of the twentieth century radically unlike the politics of the nineteenth; but we must have taken cognizance of them and dealt with them in any event. They concern us as nearly as they concern any other nation in the world. They concern all nations, for they shall determine the future of the race. Fortunately, they have not disclosed themselves before we were ready. I do not mean that our thought was prepared for them; I do not mean that our domestic affairs were in such shape as to seem fairly well ordered, so that we might in good conscience turn from them as from things finished and complete, and divert our energies to tasks beyond our borders. I mean that this change in the order of the world came, so far as we are concerned, at the natural point in our national development. The matter is worth looking into.

There has been a certain singular unity in our national task, hitherto; and these new duties now thrust upon us will not break that unity. They will perpetuate it, rather, and make it complete, if we keep but our integrity and our old-time purpose true. Until 1890 the United States had always a frontier; looked always to a region beyond, unoccupied, unappropriated, an outlet for its energy, a new place of settlement and of achievement for its people. For nearly three hundred years their growth had followed a single law,—the law of expansion into new territory. Themselves through all their history a frontier, the English colonies in America grew into a nation whose life poured still with strong tide along the old channel. Over the mountains on to the long slopes that descended to the Mississippi, across the great river into the plains, up the plains to the crowning heights of the Rockies, beyond the Rockies to the Pacific, slowly moved the frontier nation. England sought colonies at the ends of the earth to set her energy free and give vent to her enterprise; we, a like people in every impulse of mastery and achievement, had our own vast continent and were satisfied. There was always space and adventure enough and to spare, to satisfy the feet of our young men.

The great process put us to the making of states; kept the wholesome blood of sober and strenuous and systematic work warm within us; perpetuated in us the spirit of initiative and of practical expediency which had made of the colonies vigorous and heady states; created in us that national feeling which

finally put sectionalism from the field and altered
the very character of the government; gave us the
question of the extension of slavery, brought on the
civil war, and decided it by the weight of the West.
From coast to coast across the great continent our
institutions have spread, until the western sea has
witnessed the application upon a great scale of what
was begun upon a small scale on the shores of the
Atlantic, and the drama has been played almost to its
last act,—the drama of institutional construction on
the vast scale of a continent. The whole European
world, which gave us our materials, has been moralized and liberalized by the striking and stupendous
spectacle.

No other modern nation has been schooled as we
have been in big undertakings and the mastery of
novel difficulties. We have become confirmed in energy, in resourcefulness, in practical proficiency, in
self-confidence. We have become confirmed, also, so
far as our character is concerned, in the habit of
acting under an odd mixture of selfish and altruistic
motives. Having ourselves a population fit to be
free, making good its freedom in every sort of un-
hampered enterprise, determining its own destiny
unguided and unbidden, moving as it pleased within
wide boundaries, using institutions, not dominated
by them, we have sympathized with freedom everywhere; have deemed it niggardly to deny an equal
degree of freedom to any race or community that
desired it; have pressed handsome principles of
equity in international dealings; have rejoiced to
believe that our principles might some day make

every government a servant, not a master, of its people. Ease and prosperity have made us wish the whole world to be as happy and well to do as ourselves; and we have supposed that institutions and principles like our own were the simple prescription for making them so. And yet, when issues of our own interest arose, we have not been unselfish. We have shown ourselves kin to all the world, when it came to pushing an advantage. Our action against Spain in the Floridas, and against Mexico on the coasts of the Pacific; our attitude toward first the Spaniards, and then the French, with regard to the control of the Mississippi; the unpitying force with which we thrust the Indians to the wall wherever they stood in our way, have suited our professions of peacefulness and justice and liberality no better than the aggressions of other nations that were strong and not to be gainsaid. Even Mr. Jefferson, philanthropist and champion of peaceable and modest government though he was, exemplified this double temper of the people he ruled. "Peace is our passion," he had declared; but the passion abated when he saw the mouth of the Mississippi about to pass into the hands of France. Though he had loved France and hated England, he did not hesitate then what language to hold. "There is on the globe," he wrote to Mr. Livingston at Paris, "one single spot the possessor of which is our natural and habitual enemy. The day that France takes possession of New Orleans seals the union of two nations, who, in conjunction, can maintain exclusive possession of the sea. From that moment we must marry ourselves to the British fleet and nation.'' Our interests must march forward, altruists though we are: other nations must see to it that they stand off, and do not seek to stay us.

It is only just now, however, that we have awakened to our real relationship to the rest of mankind. Absorbed in our own development, we had fallen into a singular ignorance of the rest of the world. The isolation in which we lived was quite without parallel in modern history. Our only near neighbor of any consequence was like ourselves in every essential particular. The life of Canada has been unlike ours only in matters which have turned out in the long run to be matters of detail; only because she has had direct political connection with the mother country, and because she has had to work out the problem of forming a real union of life and sentiment between alien strains of French and English blood in her population. The contrast grows less and less between the two sides of the friendly border. And so we have looked upon nothing but our own ways of living, and have been formed in isolation. This has made us—not provincial, exactly; upon so big and various a continent there could not be the single pattern of thought and manners and purpose to be found cloistered in a secluded province. But if *provincial* be not the proper word, it suggests the actual fact. We have, like provincials, too habitually confined our view to the range of our own experiences. We have acquired a false self-confidence, a false self-sufficiency, because we have heeded no successes or failures but our own.

There could be no better illustration of this than the constant reargument, *de novo*, of the money question among us, and the easy currency to be obtained, at every juncture of financial crisis, for the most childish errors with regard to the well-known laws of value and exchange. No nation not isolated like ourselves in thought and experience could possibly think itself able to establish a value of its own for gold and silver, by legislation which paid no regard either to the commercial operations or to the laws of coinage and exchange which obtained outside its own borders. That a great political party should be able to win men of undoubted cultivation and practical sense to the support of a platform which embodied palpable and thrice-proven errors in such matters, and that, too, at a great election following close upon protracted, earnest, frank, and universal discussion, and should poll but little less than half the votes of the nation, is startling proof enough that we have learned to think, for the most part, only in terms of our own separate life and independent action, and have come to think ourselves a divided portion of mankind, masters and makers of our own laws of trade.

We have been equally deceived in matters in which we might more reasonably have deemed ourselves accredited experts. Misled by our own splendid initial advantage in the matter of self-government, we have suffered ourselves to misunderstand self-government itself, when the question was whether it could be put into practice amidst conditions totally unlike those with which, and with which alone, we

have been familiar. The people of the United States
have never known anything but self-government
since the colonies were founded. They have forgotten the discipline which preceded the founding of
the colonies, the long drill in order and in obedience
to law, the long subjection to kings and to parliaments which were not in fact of the people's choosing. They have forgotten how many generations
were once in tutelage in order that the generations
which discovered and settled the coasts of America
might be mature and free. No thoughtful student
of history or observer of affairs needs to be told the
necessary conditions precedent to self-government:
the slow growth of the sense of law; the equally slow
growth of the sense of community and of fellowship
in every general interest; the habit of organization,
the habit of discipline and obedience to those intrusted with authority, the self-restraint of give and
take; the allegiance to ideals, the consciousness of
mutual obligation; the patience and intelligence
which are content with a slow and universal growth.
These things have all been present in abundant measure in our own national life; but we have not deemed
them singular, and have assumed that they were
within reach of all others as well, and at as little
cost of conscious effort.

Our own form of self-government is, in fact, by
no means the one necessary and inevitable form.
England is the oldest home of self-government in the
modern world; our own principles and practices of
self-government were derived from her; she has
served as the model and inspiring example of self-

government for every country in Europe throughout
a century of democratic reform. And yet Eng-
gland did not have what we should call local self-
government until 1888, outside her boroughs. Until
1888, influential country gentlemen, appointed justices of the peace by the crown upon the nomination
of the Lord Chancellor, were the governing officers of
her counties. Practically every important matter
of local administration was in their hands, and yet
the people of the counties had absolutely no voice in
their selection. Things had stood so for more than
four hundred years. Professor Rudolph Gneist, the
great German student of English institutions, in ex-
pounding English ideas of self-government as he
found them exemplified in the actual organization of
local administration, declared that the word *government* was quite as emphatic in the compound as the
word *self*. The people of the counties were not self-
directed in affairs: they were governed by crown
officials. The policy of the crown was indeed moderated and guided in all things by the influence of a
representative parliament; the justices received no
salaries; were men resident in the counties for which
they were commissioned, identified with them in life
and interest, landlords and neighbors among the men
whose public affairs they administered. They had
nothing to gain by oppression, much to gain by the
real advancement of prosperity and good feeling
within their jurisdictions: they were in a very excellent and substantial sense representative men. But
they were not elected representatives; their rule was
not democratic either in form or in principle. Such

was the local self-government of England during
some of the most notable and honorable periods of
her history.

Our own, meanwhile, though conceived in the same
atmosphere and spirit, had been set up upon a very
different pattern, suitable to a different order of
society. The appointment of officials was discredited
amongst us; election everywhere took its place. We
made no hierarchy of officials. We made laws,—laws
for the selectmen, laws for the sheriff, laws for the
county commissioners, laws for the district attorney,
laws for each official from bailiff to governor,—and
bade the courts see to their enforcement; but we did
not subordinate one officer to another. No man was
commanded from the capital, as if he were a servant
of officials rather than of the people. Authority
was put into commission and distributed piecemeal;
nowhere gathered or organized into a single commanding force. Oversight and concentration were
omitted from the system. Federal administration,
it is true, we constituted upon a different principle,—
the principle of appointment and of responsibility
to the President; but we did not, when that new
departure was made, expect the patronage of the
President to be large, or look to see the body of federal officials play any very important or intimate
part in our life as a people. The rule was to be,
as before, the dispersion of authority. We printed
the *SELF* large and the *government* small in almost
every administrative arrangement we made; and that
is still our attitude and preference.

We have found that even among ourselves such

arrangements are not universally convenient or serviceable. They give us untrained officials, and an expert civil service is almost unknown amongst us. They give us petty officials, petty men of no ambition, without hope or fitness for advancement. They give us so many elective offices that even the most conscientious voters have neither the time nor the opportunity to inform themselves with regard to every candidate on their ballots, and must vote for a great many men of whom they know nothing. They give us, consequently, the local machine and the local boss; and where population crowds, interests compete, work moves strenuously and at haste, life is many-sided and without unity, and voters of every blood and environment and social derivation mix and stare at one another at the same voting places, government miscarries, is confused, irresponsible, unintelligent, wasteful. Methods of electoral choice and administrative organization, which served us admirably well while the nation was homogeneous and rural, serve us ofttimes ill enough now that the nation is heterogeneous and crowded into cities.

It is of the utmost importance that we should see the unmistakable truth of this matter and act upon it with all candor. It is not a question of the excellence of self-government: it is a question of the method of self-government, and of choosing which word of the compound we shall emphasize in any given case. It is a matter of separating the essentials from the non-essentials, the principle of self-government from its accidental forms. Democracy is unquestionably the most wholesome and livable

kind of government the world has yet tried. It supplies as no other system could the frank and universal criticism, the free play of individual thought,
the open conduct of public affairs, the spirit and
pride of community and of coöperation, which make
governments just and public-spirited. But the question of efficiency is the same for it as for any other
kind of polity; and if only it have the principle of
representation at the centre of its arrangements,
where counsel is held and policy determined and law
made, it can afford to put into its administrative
organization any kind of businesslike power or official
authority and any kind of discipline as if of a profession that it may think most likely to serve it.
This we shall see, and this we shall do.

It is the more imperative that we should see and
do it promptly, because it is our present and immediate task to extend self-government to Porto
Rico and the Philippines, if they be fit to receive
it,—so soon as they can be made fit. If there is to
be preparation, we must know of what kind it should
be, and how it ought to be conducted. Although
we have forgotten our own preparatory discipline in
that kind, these new tasks will undoubtedly teach us
that some discipline—it may be prolonged and
tedious—must precede self-government and prepare
the way for it; that one kind of self-government is
suitable for one sort of community, one stage of development, another for another; that there is no universal form or method either of preparation or of
practice in the matter; that character and the moralizing effect of law are conditions precedent, obscure,

and difficult, but absolutely indispensable. An examination of our own affairs will teach us these things; an examination of the affairs of the peoples we have undertaken to govern will confirm us in the understanding of them.

We shall see now more clearly than ever before that we lack in our domestic arrangements, above all things else, concentration, both in political leadership and in administrative organization; for the lack will be painfully emphasized, and will embarrass us sadly in the career we have now set out upon. Authority has been as much dispersed and distributed in the making of law and the choice of policy, under the forms we have used hitherto, as it has been in administrative action. We have been governed in all things by mass meetings. Committees of Congress, as various in their make-up as the body itself, sometimes guided by the real leaders of party, oftener guided by men whom the country at large neither knew nor looked to for leadership, have determined our national policy, piece by piece, and the pieces have seldom been woven together into any single or consistent pattern of statesmanship. There has been no leadership except the private leadership of party managers, no integration of the public business except such as was effected by the compromises and votes of party caucuses. Such methods will serve very awkwardly, if at all, for action in international affairs or in the government of distant dependencies. In such matters leadership must be single, open, responsible, and of the whole. Leadership and expert organization have become impera-

tive, and our practical sense, never daunted hitherto,
must be applied to the task of developing them at
once and with a will.

We did not of deliberate choice undertake these
new tasks which shall transform us. All the world
knows the surprising circumstances which thrust
them upon us. Sooner or later, nevertheless, they
would have become inevitable. If they had not come
upon us in this way, they would have come in another. They came upon us, as it was, though unexpected, with a strange opportuneness, as if part
of a great preconceived plan for changing the world.
Every man now knows that the world is to be
changed,—changed according to an ordering of Providence hardly so much as foreshadowed until it came;
except, it may be, to a few Europeans who were
burrowing and plotting and dreaming in the mysterious East. The whole world had already become
a single vicinage; each part had become neighbor to
all the rest. No nation could live any longer to itself, the tasks and the duties of neighborhood being
what they were. Whether we had had a material
foothold there or not, it would have been the duty
of the United States to play a part, and a leading
part at that, in the opening and transformation of
the East. We might not have seen our duty, had
the Philippines not fallen to us by the willful fortune of war; but it would have been our duty, nevertheless, to play the part we now see ourselves obliged
to play. The East is to be opened and transformed,
whether we will or no; the standards of the West
are to be imposed upon it; nations and peoples which

have stood still the centuries through are to be quickened, and make part of the universal world of commerce and of ideas which has so steadily been
a-making by the advance of European power from
age to age. It is our peculiar duty, as it is also England's, to moderate the process in the interests of
liberty : to impart to the peoples thus driven out upon
the road of change, so far as we have opportunity
or can make it, our own principles of self-help; teach
them order and self-control in the midst of change;
impart to them, if it be possible by contact and sympathy and example, the drill and habit of law and
obedience which we long ago got out of the strenuous
processes of English history; secure for them, when
we may, the free intercourse and the natural development which shall make them at least equal members of the family of nations. In China, of course,
our part will be indirect, but in the Philippines it
will be direct; and there in particular must the moral
of our polity be set up and vindicated.

This we shall do, not by giving them out of hand
our codes of political morality or our methods of
political action, the generous gifts of complete individual liberty or the full-fangled institutions of
American self-government,—a purple garment for
their nakedness,—for these things are not blessings,
but a curse, to undeveloped peoples, still in the childhood of their political growth; but by giving them,
in the spirit of service, a government and rule which
shall moralize them by being itself moral, elevate
and steady them by being itself pure and steadfast,
inducting them into the rudiments of justice and

freedom. In other words, it is the aid of our character they need, and not the premature aid of our institutions. Our institutions must come after the ground of character and habit has been made ready for them; as effect, not cause, in the order of political growth. It is thus that we shall ourselves recognize the fact, at last patent to all the world, that the service of democracy has been the development of ideals rather than the origination of practical methods of administration of universal validity, or any absolute qualification of the ultimate conceptions of sovereignty and the indispensable disciplinary operation of law. We must aid their character and elevate their ideals, and then see what these will bring forth, generating after their kind. As the panacea for oppressive taxation lies in honesty and economy rather than in this, that, or the other method of collection, in reasonable assessment rather than in a particular machinery of administration, so the remedy for oppressive government in general is, not a constitution, but justice and enlightenment. One set of guarantees will be effective under one set of circumstances, another under another.

The best guarantee of good government we can give the Filipinos is, that we shall be sensitive to the opinion of the world; that we shall be sensitive in what we do to our own standards, so often boasted of and proclaimed, and shall wish above all things else to live up to the character we have established, the standards we have professed. When they accept the compulsions of that character and accept those standards, they will be entitled to partnership with us, and shall have it. They shall, meanwhile, teach us, as we shall teach them. We shall teach them order as a condition precedent to liberty, self-control as a condition precedent to self-government; they shall teach us the true assessment of institutions,— that their only invaluable content is motive and character. We shall no doubt learn that democracy and efficiency go together by no novel rule. Democracy is not so much a form of government as a set of principles. Other forms of government may be equally efficient; many forms of government are more efficient,—know better ways of integrating and purifying administration than we have yet learned, more successful methods of imparting drill and order to restless and undeveloped peoples than we are likely to hit upon of ourselves, a more telling way of getting and a more effectual way of keeping leadership in a world of competitive policies, doubtful concerts, and international rivalries. We must learn what we can, and yet scrupulously square everything that we do with the high principles we brought into the world: that justice may be done to the lowly no less than to the great; that government may serve its people, not make itself their master,—may in its service heed both the wishes and the needs of those who obey it; that authority may be for leadership, not for aggrandizement; that the people may be the state.

The reactions which such experiments in the universal validity of principle and method are likely to bring about in respect of our own domestic institutions cannot be calculated or forecast. Old principles

applied in a new field may show old applications to
have been clumsy and ill considered. We may ourselves get responsible leadership instead of government by mass meeting; a trained and thoroughly
organized administrative service instead of administration by men privately nominated and blindly
elected; a new notion of terms of office and of standards of policy. If we but keep our ideals clear, our
principles steadfast, we need not fear the change.

THE IDEALS OF AMERICA [1]

FROM THE "ATLANTIC MONTHLY," DECEMBER, 1902, VOL.
XC, PP. 721-734. THIS ARTICLE APPEARED THE FIRST
YEAR MR. WILSON WAS PRESIDENT OF PRINCETON
UNIVERSITY.

WE do not think or speak of the War for
Independence as if we were aged men who,
amidst alien scenes of change, comfort themselves
with talk of great things done in days long gone by,
the like of which they may never hope to see again.
The spirit of the old days is not dead. If it were,
who amongst us would care for its memory and distant, ghostly voice? It is the distinguishing mark,
nay the very principle of life in a nation alive and
quick in every fibre, as ours is, that all its days are
great days,—are to its thought single and of a piece.
Its past it feels to have been but the prelude and
earnest of its present. It is from its memories of
days old and new that it gets its sense of identity,
takes its spirit of action, assures itself of its power
and its capacity, and knows its place in the world.
Old colony days, and those sudden days of revolution
when debate turned to action and heady winds as
if of destiny blew with mighty breath the long continent through, were our own days, the days of our
childhood and our headstrong youth. We have not

[1] An address delivered on the one hundred and twenty-fifth anniversary of the battle of Trenton, December 26, 1901.

forgotten.   Our memories make no effort to recall
the time.   The battle of Trenton is as real to us as
the battle of San Juan hill.

We remember the chill, and the ardor, too, of that
gray morning when we came upon the startled outposts of the town, the driving sleet beating at our
backs; the cries and hurrying of men in the street,
the confused muster at our front, the sweeping fire
of our guns and the rush of our men, Sullivan coming up by the road from the river.   Washington at
the north, where the road to Princeton is; the showy
Hessian colonel shot from his horse amidst his bewildered men; the surrender; the unceasing storm.
And then the anxious days that followed: the re-
crossing of the icy river before even we had rested;
the troop of surly prisoners to be cared for and sent
forward to Philadelphia; the enemy all the while to
be thought of, and the way to use our advantage.

How much it meant a third time to cross the river,
and wait here in the town for the regiments Sir
William Howe should send against us!   How sharp
and clear the night was when we gave Cornwallis the
slip and took the silent, frosty road to Allentown
and Princeton!   Those eighteen miles between bed-
time and morning are not easily forgot, nor that
sharp brush with the redcoats at Princeton: the
moving fight upon the sloping hillside, the cannon
planted in the streets, the gray old building where
the last rally was made,—and then the road to Bruns-
wick, Cornwallis at our heels!

How the face of things was changed in those brief
days!   There had been despair till them.   It was but

a few short weeks since the men of the Jersey towns
and farms had seen us driven south across the river
like fugitives; now we came back an army again,
the Hessians who had but the other day harried and
despoiled that countryside beaten and scattered before us, and they knew not whether to believe their
eyes or not. As we pushed forward to the heights
at Morristown we drew in the British lines behind
us, and New Jersey was free of the redcoats again.
The Revolution had had its turning point. It was
easy then to believe that General Washington could
hold his own against any adversary in that terrible
game of war. A new heart was in everything!

And yet what differences of opinion there were,
and how hot and emphatic every turn of the war
made them among men who really spoke their minds
and dissembled nothing! It was but six months since
the Congress had ventured its Declaration of Independence, and the brave words of that defiance
halted on many lips that read them. There were
men enough and to spare who would not speak them
at all; who deemed the whole thing madness and
deep folly, and even black treason. Men whose
names all the colonies knew held off and would take
no part in armed resistance to the ancient crown
whose immemorial sovereignty kept a great empire
together. Men of substance at the ports of trade
were almost all against the Revolution; and where
men of means and principle led, base men who played
for their own interest were sure to follow. Every
movement of the patriotic leaders was spied upon
and betrayed; everywhere the army moved there

were men of the very countryside it occupied to be
kept close watch against.

Those were indeed "times that tried men's souls"!
It was no light matter to put the feeling as of a
nation into those scattered settlements: to bring the
high-spirited planters of the Carolinas, who thought
for themselves, or their humble neighbors on the
upland farms, who ordered their lives as they pleased,
to the same principles and point of view that the
leaders of Virginia and Massachusetts professed and
occupied,—the point of view from which everything
wore so obvious an aspect of hopeful revolt, where
men planned the war at the north. There were great
families at Philadelphia and in Boston itself who
were as hard to win, and plain men without number
in New York and the Jerseys who would not come
for the beckoning. Opinion was always making and
to be made, and the campaign of mind was as hard
as that of arms.

To think of those days of doubt and stress, of
the swaying of opinion this way and that, of counsels
distracted and plans to be made anew at every turn
of the arduous business, takes one's thoughts forward to those other days, as full of doubt, when the
war had at last been fought out and a government
was to be made. No doubt that crisis was the
greatest of all. Opinion will form for a war, in the
face of manifest provocation and of precious rights
called in question. But the making of a government
is another matter. And the government to be made
then was to take the place of the government cast
off: there was the rub. It was difficult to want any

common government at all after fighting to be quit
of restraint and overlordship altogether; and it went
infinitely hard to be obliged to make it strong, with
a right to command and a power to rule. Then it
was that we knew that even the long war, with its
bitter training of the thoughts and its hard discipline
of union, had not made a nation, but only freed a
group of colonies. The debt is the more incalculable
which we owe to the little band of sagacious men
who labored the summer through, in that far year
1787, to give us a Constitution that those heady little
commonwealths could be persuaded to accept, and
which should yet be a framework within which the
real powers of a nation might grow in the fullness
of time, and gather head with the growth of a mighty
people.

They gave us but the outline, the formula, the
broad and general programme of our life, and left
us to fill it in with such rich store of achievement
and sober experience as we should be able to gather
in the days to come. Not battles or any stirring scene
of days of action, but the slow processes by which
we grew and made our thought and formed our purpose in quiet days of peace, are what we find it
hard to make real to our minds again, now that we
are mature and have fared far upon the road. Our
life is so broad and various now, and was so simple
then; the thoughts of those first days seem crude to
us now and unreal. We smile upon the simple
dreams of our youth a bit incredulously, and seem
cut off from them by a great space. And yet it
was by those dreams we were formed. The lineage

of our thoughts is unbroken.   The nation that was
making then was the nation which yesterday intervened in the affairs of Cuba, and to-day troubles the
trade and the diplomacy of the world.

It was clear to us even then, in those first days
when we were at the outset of our life, with what
spirit and mission we had come into the world.
Clear-sighted men oversea saw it too, whose eyes were
not holden by passion or dimmed by looking steadfastly only upon things near at hand.   We shall
not forget those deathless passages of great speech,
compact of music and high sense, in which Edmund
Burke justified us and gave us out of his riches our
philosophy of right action in affairs of state.
Chatham rejoiced that we had resisted.   Fox clapped
his hands when he heard that Cornwallis had been
trapped and taken at Yorktown.   Dull men without
vision, small men who stood upon no place of elevation in their thoughts, once cried treason against
these men,—though no man dared speak such a taunt
to the passionate Chatham's face; but now all men
speak as Fox spoke, and our Washington is become
one of the heroes of the English race.   What did
it mean that the greatest Englishmen should thus
cheer us to revolt at the very moment of our rebellion?   What is it that has brought us at last the
verdict of the world?

It means that in our stroke for independence we
struck a blow for all the world.   Some men saw it
then; all men see it now.   The very generation of
Englishmen who stood against us in that day of our
struggling birth lived to see the liberating light of

that day shine about their own path before they
made an end and were gone. They had deep reason
before their own day was out to know what it was
that Burke had meant when he said, "We cannot
falsify the pedigree of this fierce people, and per-
suade them that they are not sprung from a nation
in whose veins the blood of freedom circulates. The
language in which they would hear you tell them
this tale would detect the imposition, your speech
would betray you. An Englishman is the unfittest
person on earth to argue another Englishman into
slavery." . . . "For, in order to prove that the
Americans have no right to their liberties, we are
every day endeavoring to subvert the maxims which
preserve the whole spirit of our own. To prove that
the Americans ought not to be free, we are obliged
to depreciate the value of freedom itself; and we
never seem to gain a paltry advantage over them in
debate, without attacking some of those principles, or
deriding some of those feelings, for which our ancestors have shed their blood."

It turned out that the long struggle in America
had been the first act in the drama whose end and
culmination should be the final establishment of constitutional government for England and for English
communities everywhere. It is easy now, at this
quiet distance, for the closeted student to be puzzled
how to set up the legal case of the colonists against
the authority of Parliament. It is possible now to
respect the scruples of the better loyalists, and even
to give all honor to the sober ardor of self-sacrifice
with which they stood four-square against the Revo-

lution. We no longer challenge their right. Neither
do we search out the motives of the mass of common
men who acted upon the one side or the other. Like
men in all ages and at every crisis of affairs, they
acted each according to his sentiment, his fear, his
interest, or his lust. We ask, rather, why did the
noble gentlemen to whom it fell to lead America
seek great action and embark all their honor in such
a cause? What was it they fought for?

A lawyer is puzzled to frame the answer; but no
statesman need be. "If I were sure," said Burke,
"that the colonists had, at their leaving this country,
sealed a regular compact of servitude, that they had
solemnly abjured all the rights of citizens, that they
had made a vow to renounce all ideas of liberty for
them and their posterity to all generations, yet I
should hold myself obliged to conform to the temper
I found universally prevalent in my own day, and
to govern two millions of men, impatient of servitude, on the principles of freedom. I am not determining a point of law; . . . the general character
and situation of a people must determine what sort
of government is fit for them." It was no abstract
point of governmental theory the leaders of the colonies took the field to expound. Washington, Henry,
Adams, Hancock, Franklin, Morris, Boudinot, Livingston, Rutledge, Pinckney,—these were men of affairs, who thought less of books than of principles of
action. They fought for the plain right of self-
government, which any man could understand. The
government oversea had broken faith with them,—
not the faith of law, but the faith that is in precedents

and ancient understandings, though they be tacit and nowhere spoken in any charter. Hitherto the colonies had been let live their own lives according to their own genius, and vote their own supplies to the crown as if their assemblies were so many parliaments. Now, of a sudden, the Parliament in England was to thrust their assemblies aside and itself lay their taxes. Here was too new a thing. Government without precedent was government without license or limit. It was government by innovation, not government by agreement. Old ways were the only ways acceptable to English feet. The revolutionists stood for no revolution at all, but for the maintenance of accepted practices, for the inviolable understandings of precedent,—in brief, for *constitutional government*.

That sinister change which filled the air of America with storm darkened the skies of England too. Not in America only did George, the king, and his counsellors make light of and willfully set aside the ancient understandings which were the very stuff of liberty in English eyes. That unrepresentative Parliament, full of placemen, which had taxed America, contained majorities which the king could bestow at his will upon this minister or that; and the men who set America by the ears came or went from their places at his bidding. It was he, not the Parliament, that made and unmade ministries. Behind the nominal ministers of the crown stood men whom Parliament did not deal with, and the nation did not see who were the king's favorites, and therefore the actual rulers of England. There was here the real revolution. America, with her sensitive make-up, her assemblies that were the real representatives of her people, had but felt sooner than the mass of Englishmen at home the unhappy change of air which seemed about to corrupt the constitution itself. Burke felt it in England, and Fox, and every man whose thoughts looked soberly forth upon the signs of the times. And presently, when the American war was over, the nation itself began to see what light the notable thing done in America shed upon its own affairs. The king was to be grappled with at home, the Parliament was to be freed from his power, and the ministers who ruled England were to be made the real servants of the people. Constitutional government was to be made a reality again. We had begun the work of freeing England when we completed the work of freeing ourselves.

The great contest which followed oversea, and which was nothing less than the capital and last process of making and confirming the constitution of England, kept covert beneath the surface of affairs while the wars of the French Revolution swept the world. Not until 1832 was representation in Parliament at last reformed, and the Commons made a veritable instrument of the nation's will. Days of revolution, when ancient kingdoms seemed tottering to their fall, were no days in which to be tinkering the constitution of old England. Her statesmen grew slow and circumspect and moved in all things with infinite prudence, and even with a novel timidity. But when the times fell quiet again, opinion gathering head for a generation, moved forward at

last to its object; and government was once more by
consent in England. The Parliament spoke the real
mind of the nation, and the leaders whom the Commons approved were of necessity also the ministers
of the crown. Men could then look back and see that
America· had given England the shock, and the
crown the opportune defeat, which had awakened
her to save her constitution from corruption.

Meanwhile, what of America herself? How had
she used the independence she had demanded and
won? For a little while she had found it a grievous
thing to be free, with no common power set over her
to hold her to a settled course of life which should
give her energy and bring her peace and honor and
increase of wealth. Even when the convention at
Philadelphia had given her the admirable framework
of a definite constitution, she found it infinitely hard
to hit upon a common way of progress under a mere
printed law which had no sanction of custom or affection, which no ease of old habit sustained, and no
familiar light of old tradition made plain to follow.
This new law had yet to be filled with its meanings,
had yet to be given its texture of life. Our whole
history, from that day of our youth to this day of
our glad maturity, has been filled with the process.

It took the War of 1812 to give us spirit and full
consciousness and pride of station as a nation. That
was the real war of independence for our political
parties. It was then we cut our parties and our
passions loose from politics oversea, and set ourselves
to make a career which should be indeed our own.
That accomplished, and our weak youth turned to

callow manhood, we stretched our hand forth again to the west, set forth with a new zest and energy upon the western rivers and the rough trails that led across the mountains and down to the waters of the Mississippi. There lay a continent to be possessed. In the very day of first union Virginia and her sister states had ceded to the common government all the great stretches of western land that lay between the mountains and that mighty river into which all the western waters gathered head. While we were yet weak and struggling for our place among the nations, Mr. Jefferson had added the vast bulk of Louisiana, beyond the river, whose boundaries no man certainly knew. All the great spaces of the continent from Canada round and about by the great Rockies to the warm waters of the southern Gulf lay open to the feet of our young men. The forest rang with their noisy march. What seemed a new race deployed into those broad valleys and out upon those long, unending plains which were the common domain, where no man knew any government but the government of the whole people. That was to be the real making of the nation.

There sprang up the lusty states which now, in these days of our full stature, outnumber almost threefold the thirteen commonwealths which formed the Union. Their growth set the pace of our life; forced the slavery question to a final issue; gave us the civil war with its stupendous upheaval and its resettlement of the very foundations of the government; spread our strength from sea to sea; created us a free and mighty people, whose destinies daunt

the imagination of the Old World looking on. That
increase, that endless accretion, that rolling, resist-
less tide, incalculable in its strength, infinite in its
variety, has made us what we are; has put the resources of a huge continent at our disposal; has
provoked us to invention and given us mighty captains of industry. This great pressure of a people
moving always to new frontiers, in search of new
lands, new power, the full freedom of a virgin world,
has ruled our course and formed our policies like a
Fate. It gave us, not Louisiana alone, but Florida
also. It forced war with Mexico upon us, and gave
us the coasts of the Pacific. It swept Texas into the
Union. It made far Alaska a territory of the United
States. Who shall say where it will end?

The census takers of 1890 informed us, when their
task was done, that they could no longer find any
frontier upon this continent; that they must draw
their maps as if the mighty process of settlement
that had gone on, ceaseless, dramatic, the century
through, were now ended and complete, the nation
made from sea to sea. We had not pondered their
report a single decade before we made new frontiers
for ourselves beyond the seas, accounting the seven
thousand miles of ocean that lie between us and the
Philippine Islands no more than the three thousand
which once lay between us and the coasts of the
Pacific. No doubt there is here a great revolution in
our lives. No war ever transformed us quite as the
war with Spain transformed us. No previous years
ever ran with so swift a change as the years since
1898. We have witnessed a new revolution. We

have seen the transformation of America completed.
That little group of states, which one hundred and
twenty-five years ago cast the sovereignty of Britain
off, is now grown into a mighty power. That little
confederation has now massed and organized its energies. A confederacy is transformed into a nation.
The battle of Trenton was not more significant than
the battle of Manila. The nation that was one hundred and twenty-five years in the making has now
stepped forth into the open arena of the world.

I ask you to stand with me at this new turning-
point of our life, that we may look before and after,
and judge ourselves alike in the light of that old
battle fought here in these streets, and in the light
of all the mighty processes of our history that have
followed. We cannot too often give ourselves such
challenge of self-examination. It will hearten, it
will steady, it will moralize us to reassess our hopes,
restate our ideals, and make manifest to ourselves
again the principles and the purposes upon which we
act. We are else without chart upon a novel voyage.

What are our thoughts now, as we look back from
this altered age to the Revolution which to-day we
celebrate? How do we think of its principles and of
its example? Do they seem remote and of a time not
our own, or do they still seem stuff of our thinking,
principles near and intimate, and woven into the very
texture of our institutions? What say we now of
liberty and of self-government, its embodiment?
What lessons have we read of it on our journey
hither to this high point of outlook at the beginning
of a new century? Do those old conceptions seem

to us now an ideal modified, of altered face, and of a mien not shown in the simple days when the government was formed?

Of course forms have changed. The form of the Union itself is altered, to the model that was in Hamilton's thought rather than to that which Jefferson once held before us, adorned, transfigured, in words that led the mind captive. Our ways of life are profoundly changed since that dawn. The balance of the states against the federal government, however it may strike us now as of capital convenience in the distribution of powers and the quick and various exercise of the energies of the people, no longer seems central to our conceptions of governmental structure, no longer seems of the essence of the people's liberty. We are no longer strenuous about the niceties of constitutional law; no longer dream that a written law shall save us, or that by ceremonial cleanliness we may lift our lives above corruption. But has the substance of things changed with us, also? Wherein now do we deem the life and very vital principle of self-government to lie? Where is that point of principle at which we should wish to make our stand and take again the final risk of revolution? What other crisis do we dream of that might bring in its train another battle of Trenton?

These are intensely practical questions. We fought but the other day to give Cuba self-government. It is a point of conscience with us that the Philippines shall have it, too, when our work there is done and they are ready. But when will our work there be

done, and how shall we know when they are ready?
How, when our hand is withdrawn from her capitals
and she plays her game of destiny apart and for herself, shall we be sure that Cuba has this blessing of
liberty and self-government, for which battles are
justly fought and revolutions righteously set afoot?
If we be apostles of liberty and of self-government,
surely we know what they are, in their essence and
without disguise of form, and shall not be deceived
in the principles of their application by mere differences between this race and that. We have given
pledges to the world and must redeem them as we
can.

Some nice tests of theory are before us,—are even
now at hand. There are those amongst us who have
spoken of the Filipinos as standing where we stood
when we were in the throes of that great war which
was turned from fear to hope again in that battle
here in the streets of Trenton which we are met to
speak of, and who have called Aguinaldo, the winning, subtle youth now a prisoner in our hands at
Manila, a second Washington. Have they, then, forgotten that tragic contrast upon which the world
gazed in the days when our Washington was President: on the one side of the sea, in America, peace,
an ordered government, a people busy with the tasks
of mart and home, a group of commonwealths bound
together by strong cords of their own weaving, institutions sealed and confirmed by debate and the suffrages of free men, but not by the pouring out of
blood in civil strife,—on the other, in France, a nation frenzied, distempered, seeking it knew not what,

—a nation which poured its best blood out in a vain sacrifice, which cried of liberty and self-government until the heavens rang and yet ran straight and swift to anarchy, to give itself at last, with an almost glad relief, to the masterful tyranny of a soldier? "I should suspend my congratulations on the new liberty of France," said Burke, the master who had known our liberty for what it was, and knew this set up in France to be spurious,—"I should suspend my congratulations on the new liberty of France until I was informed how it had been combined with government; with public force; with the discipline and obedience of armies; with the collection of an effective and well-distributed revenue; with morality and religion; with the solidity of property; with peace and order; with social and civil manners." Has it not taken France a century to effect the combination; and are all men sure that she has found it even now? And yet were not these things combined with liberty amongst us from the very first?

How interesting a light shines upon the matter of our thought out of that sentence of Burke's! How liberty had been combined with government! Is there here a difficulty, then? Are the two things not kindly disposed toward one another? Does it require any nice art and adjustment to unite and reconcile them? Is there here some cardinal test which those amiable persons have overlooked, who have dared to cheer the Filipino rebels on in their stubborn resistance to the very government they themselves live under and owe fealty to? Think of Washington's passion for order, for authority, for some righteous

public force which should teach individuals their
place under government, for the solidity of property,
for morality and sober counsel. It was plain that
he cared not a whit for liberty without these things
to sustain and give it dignity. "You talk, my good
sir," he exclaimed, writing to Henry Lee in Congress, "you talk of employing influence to appease
the present tumults in Massachusetts. I know not
where that influence is to be found, or, if attainable,
that it would be a proper remedy for the disorders.
Influence is no *government*. Let us have one by
which our lives, liberties, and properties will be
secured, or let us know the worst at once." In brief,
the fact is this, that liberty is the privilege of maturity, of self-control, of self-mastery and a thoughtful
care for righteous dealings,—that some peoples may
have it, therefore, and others may not.

We look back to the great men who made our government as to a generation, not of revolutionists, but
of statesmen. They fought, not to pull down, but to
preserve,—not for some fair and far-off thing they
wished for, but for a familiar thing they had and
meant to keep. Ask any candid student of the history of English liberty, and he will tell you that these
men were of the lineage of Pym and Hampden, of
Pitt and Fox; that they were men who consecrated
their lives to the preservation intact of what had been
wrought out in blood and sweat by the countless generations of sturdy freemen who had gone before them.

Look for a moment at what self-government really
meant in their time. Take English history for your
test. I know not where else you may find an answer

to the question. We speak, all the world speaks, of England as the mother of liberty and self-government; and the beginning of her liberty we place in the great year that saw Magna Charta signed, that immortal document whose phrases ring again in all our own Bills of Rights. Her liberty is in fact older than that signal year; but 1215 we set up as a shining mark to hold the eye. And yet we know, for all we boast the date so early, for how many a long generation after that the monarch ruled and the Commons cringed; haughty Plantagenets had their way, and indomitable Tudors played the master to all men's fear, till the fated Stuarts went their stupid way to exile and the scaffold. Kings were none the less kings because their subjects were free men.

Local self-government in England consisted until 1888 of government by almost omnipotent Justices of the Peace appointed by the Lord Chancellor. They were laymen, however. They were country gentlemen and served without pay. They were of the neighborhood and used their power for its benefit as their lights served them; but no man had a vote or choice as to which of the country gentlemen of his county should be set over him; and the power of the Justices sitting in Quarter Sessions covered almost every point of justice and administration not directly undertaken by the officers of the crown itself. "Long ago," laughs an English writer, "lawyers abandoned the hope of describing the duties of a Justice in any methodic fashion, and the alphabet has become the only possible connecting thread. A justice must have something to do with 'Railroads, Rape, Rates, Recognizances, Records, and Recreation Grounds'; with 'Perjury, Petroleum, Piracy, and Playhouses'; with 'Disorderly Houses, Dissenters, Dogs, and Drainage.'" And yet Englishmen themselves call their life under these lay masters self-government.

The English House of Commons was for many a generation, many a century even, no House of the Commons at all, but a house full of country gentlemen and rich burghers, the aristocracy of the English counties and the English towns; and yet it was from this House, and not from that reformed since 1832, that the world drew, through Montesquieu, its models of representative self-government in the days when our own Union was set up.

In America, and in America alone, did self-government mean an organization self-originated, and of the stuff of the people themselves. America has gone a step beyond her mother country. Her people were for the most part picked men: such men as have the energy and the initiative to leave old homes and old friends, and go to far frontiers to make a new life for themselves. They were men of a certain initiative, to take the world into their own hands. The king had given them their charters, but within the broad definitions of those charters they had built as they pleased, and common men were partners in the government of their little commonwealths. At home, in the old country, there was need, no doubt, that the hand of the king's government should keep men within its reach. The countrysides were full of yokels who would have been brutes to deal with else. The counties were in fact represented very well by

the country gentlemen who ruled them: for they
were full of broad estates where men were tenants,
not freehold farmers, and the interests of masters
were generally enough the interests of their men.
The towns had charters of their own. There was
here no democratic community, and no one said or
thought that the only self-government was democratic self-government. In America the whole constitution of society was democratic, inevitably and of
course. Men lay close to their simple governments,
and the new life brought to a new expression the immemorial English principle, that the intimate affairs
of local administration and the common interests that
were to be served in the making of laws should be
committed to laymen, who would look at the government critically and from without, and not to the
king's agents, who would look at it professionally
and from within. England had had self-government
time out of mind; but in America English self-
government had become *popular* self-government.

"Almost all the civilized states derive their national unity," says a great English writer of our generation, "from common subjection, past or present,
to royal power; the Americans of the United States,
for example, are a nation because they once obeyed
a king." That example in such a passage comes upon
us with a shock: it is very unexpected,—"The
Americans of the United States, for example, are a
nation because they once obeyed a king!" And yet,
upon reflection, can we deny the example? It is
plain enough that the reason why the English in
America got self-government and knew how to use it,

and the French in America did not, was, that the English had had a training under the kings of England
and the French under the kings of France. In the
one country men did all things at the bidding of officers of the crown; in the other, officers of the crown
listened, were constrained to listen, to the counsels of
laymen drawn out of the general body of the nation.
And yet the kings of England were no less kings than
the kings of France. Obedience is everywhere the
basis of government, and the English were not ready
either in their life or in their thought for a free
régime under which they should choose their kings
by ballot. For that régime they could be made ready
only by the long drill which should make them respect above all things the law and the authority of
governors. Discipline—discipline generations deep—
had first to give them an ineradicable love of order,
the poise of men self-commanded, the spirit of men
who obey and yet speak their minds and are free, before they could be Americans.

No doubt a king did hold us together until we
learned how to hold together of ourselves. No doubt
our unity as a nation does come from the fact that
we once obeyed a king. No one can look at the processes of English history and doubt that the throne
has been its centre of poise, though not in our days
its centre of force. Steadied by the throne, the effective part of the nation has, at every stage of its development, dealt with and controlled the government
in the name of the whole. The king and his subjects
have been partners in the great undertaking. At
last, in our country, in this best trained portion of

the nation, set off by itself, the whole became fit to
act for itself, by veritable popular representation,
without the make-weight of a throne. That is the history of our liberty. You have the spirit of English
history, and of English royalty, from King Harry's
mouth upon the field of Agincourt:—

> "We few, we happy few, we band of brothers;
> For he to-day that sheds his blood with me
> Shall be my brother; be he ne'er so vile,
> This day shall gentle his condition:
> And gentlemen in England now a-bed
> Shall think themselves accursed they were not here,
> And hold their manhoods cheap whiles any speaks
> That fought with us upon Saint Crispin's day."

It is thus the spirit of English life has made comrades of us all to be a nation.

This is what Burke meant by combining government with liberty,—the spirit of obedience with the
spirit of free action. Liberty is not itself government. In the wrong hands,—in hands unpracticed,
undisciplined,—it is incompatible with government.
Discipline must precede it,—if necessary, the discipline of being under masters. Then will self-control
make it a thing of life and not a thing of tumult, a
tonic, not an insurgent madness in the blood. Shall
we doubt, then, what the conditions precedent to liberty and self-government are, and what their invariable support and accompaniment must be, in the
countries whose administration we have taken over in
trust, and particularly in those far Philippine Islands
whose government is our chief anxiety? We cannot

give them any quittance of the debt ourselves have paid. They can have liberty no cheaper than we got it. They must first take the discipline of law, must first love order and instinctively yield to it. It is the heathen, not the free citizen of a self-governed country, who "in his blindness bows down to wood and stone, and don't obey no orders unless they is his own." We are old in this learning and must be their tutors.

But we may set them upon the way with an advantage we did not have until our hard journey was more than half made. We can see to it that the law which teaches them obedience is just law and even-handed. We can see to it that justice be free and unpurchasable among them. We can make order lovely by making it the friend of every man and not merely the shield of some. We can teach them by our fairness in administration that there may be a power in government which, though imperative and irresistible by those who would cross or thwart it, does not act for its own aggrandizement, but is the guarantee that all shall fare alike. That will infinitely shorten their painful tutelage. Our pride, our conscience will not suffer us to give them less.

And, if we are indeed bent upon service and not mastery, we shall give them more. We shall take them into our confidence and suffer them to teach us, as our critics. No man can deem himself free from whom the government hides its action, or who is forbidden to speak his mind about affairs, as if government were a private thing which concerned the governors alone. Whatever the power of govern-

ment, if it is just, there may be publicity of governmental action and freedom of opinion; and public
opinion gathers head effectively only by concerted
public agitation. These are the things—knowledge
of what the government is doing and liberty to speak
of it—that have made Englishmen feel like free
men, whether they liked their governors or not: the
right to know and the right to speak out,—to speak
out in plain words and in open counsel. Privacy,
official reticence, governors hedged about and inac-
cessible,—these are the marks of arbitrary government, under which spirited men grow restive and
resentful. The mere right to criticise and to have
matters explained to them cools men's tempers and
gives them understanding in affairs. This is what we
seek among our new subjects: that they shall understand us, and after free conference shall trust us:
that they shall perceive that we are not afraid of
criticism, and that we are ready to explain and to
take suggestions from all who are ready, when the
conference is over, to obey.

There will be a wrong done, not if we govern and
govern as we will, govern with a strong hand that
will brook no resistance, and according to principles
of right gathered from our own experience, not from
theirs, which has never yet touched the vital matter we are concerned with; but only if we govern in
the spirit of autocrats and of those who serve themselves, not their subjects. The whole solution lies
less in our methods than in our temper. We must
govern as those who learn; and they must obey as
those who are in tutelage. They are children and

we are men in these deep matters of government and justice. If we have not learned the substance of these things no nation is ever likely to learn it, for it is taken from life, and not from books. But though children must be foolish, impulsive, headstrong, unreasonable, men may be arbitrary, self-opinionated, impervious, impossible, as the English were in their Oriental colonies until they learned. We should be inexcusable to repeat their blunders and wait as long as they waited to learn how to serve the peoples whom we govern. It is plain we shall have a great deal to learn; it is to be hoped we shall learn it fast.

There are, unhappily, some indications that we have ourselves yet to learn the things we would teach. You have but to think of the large number of persons of your own kith and acquaintance who have for the past two years been demanding, in print and out of it, with moderation and the air of reason and without it, that we give the Philippines independence and self-government now, at once, out of hand. It were easy enough to give them independence, if by independence you mean only disconnection with any government outside the islands, the independence of a rudderless boat adrift. But self-government? How is that "given"? *Can* it be given? Is it not gained, earned, graduated into from the hard school of life? We have reason to think so. I have just now been trying to give the reasons we have for thinking so.

There are many things, things slow and difficult to come at, which we have found to be conditions precedent to liberty,—to the liberty which can be combined with government; and we cannot, in our pres-

ent situation, too often remind ourselves of these
things, in order that we may look steadily and wisely
upon liberty, not in the uncertain light of theory, but
in the broad, sunlike, disillusioning light of experience. We know, for one thing, that it rests at bottom upon a clear experimental knowledge of what
are in fact the just rights of individuals, of what
is the equal and profitable balance to be maintained
between the right of the individual to serve himself
and the duty of government to serve society. I say,
not merely a *clear* knowledge of these, but a clear
experimental knowledge of them as well. We hold
it, for example, an indisputable principle of law in
a free state that there should be freedom of speech,
and yet we have a law of libel. No man, we say, may
speak that which wounds his neighbor's reputation
unless there be public need to speak it. Moreover we
will judge of that need in a rough and ready fashion.
Let twelve ordinary men, empanelled as a jury, say
whether the wound was justly given and of necessity. "The truth of the matter is very simple when
stripped of all ornaments of speech," says an eminent English judge. "It is neither more nor less
than this: that a man may publish anything which
twelve of his fellow countrymen think is not blam-
able." It is plain, therefore, that in this case at
least we do not inquire curiously concerning the
Rights of Man, which do not seem susceptible of being stated in terms of social obligation, but content
ourselves with asking, "What are the rights of men
living together, amongst whom there must be order
and fair give and take?" And our law of libel is

only one instance out of many. We treat all rights in like practical fashion. But a people must obviously have had experience to treat them so. You have here one image in the mirror of self-government.

Do not leave the mirror before you see another. You cannot call a miscellaneous people, unknit, scattered, diverse of race and speech and habit, a nation, a community. That, at least, we got by serving under kings: we got the feeling and the organic structure of a community. No people can form a community or be wisely subjected to common forms of government who are as diverse and as heterogeneous as the people of the Philippine Islands. They are in no wise knit together. They are of many races, of many stages of development, economically, socially, politically disintegrate, without community of feeling because without community of life, contrasted alike in experience and in habit, having nothing in common except that they have lived for hundreds of years together under a government which held them always where they were when it first arrested their development. You may imagine the problem of self-government and of growth for such a people,—if so be you have an imagination and are no doctrinaire. If there is difficulty in our own government here at home because the several sections of our own country are disparate and at different stages of development, what shall we expect, and what patience shall we not demand of ourselves, with regard to our belated wards beyond the Pacific? We have here among ourselves hardly sufficient equality of social and economic conditions to breed full community of feeling. We have learned of our own experience what the problem of self-government is in such a case.

That liberty and self-government are things of infinite difficulty and nice accommodation we above all other peoples ought to know who have had every adventure in their practice. Our very discontent with the means we have taken to keep our people clear-eyed and steady in the use of their institutions is evidence of our appreciation of what is required to sustain them. We have set up an elaborate system of popular education, and have made the maintenance of that system a function of government, upon the theory that only systematic training can give the quick intelligence, the "variety of information and excellence of discretion" needed by a self-governed people. We expect as much from school-teachers as from governors in the Philippines and in Porto Rico: we expect from them the *morale* that is to sustain our work there. And yet, when teachers have done their utmost and the school bills are paid, we doubt, and know that we have reason to doubt, the efficacy of what we have done. Books can but set the mind free, can but give it the freedom of the world of thought. The world of affairs has yet to be attempted, and the schooling of action must supplement the schooling of the written page. Men who have an actual hand in government, men who vote and sustain by their thoughts the whole movement of affairs, men who have the making or the confirming of policies, must have reasonable hopes, must act within the reasonable bounds set by hard experience.

By education, no doubt, you acquaint men, while they are yet young and quick to take impressions, with the character and spirit of the polity they live under; give them some sentiment of respect for it, put them in the air that has always lain about it, and prepare them to take the experience that awaits them. But it is from the polity itself and their own contact with it that they must get their actual usefulness in affairs, and only that contact, intelligently made use of, makes good citizens. We would not have them remain children always and act always on the preconceptions taken out of the books they have studied. Life is their real master and tutor in affairs.

And so the characters of the polity men live under has always had a deep significance in our thoughts. Our greater statesmen have been men steeped in a thoughtful philosophy of politics, men who pondered the effect of this institution and that upon morals and the life of society, and thought of character when they spoke of affairs. They have taught us that the best polity is that which most certainly produces the habit and the spirit of civic duty, and which calls with the most stirring and persuasive voice to the leading characters of the nation to come forth and give it direction. It must be a polity which shall stimulate, which shall breed emulation, which shall make men seek honor by seeking service. These are the ideals which have formed our institutions, and which shall mend them when they need reform. We need good leaders more than an excellent mechanism of action in charters and constitutions. We need men of devotion as much as we need good laws. The two cannot be divorced and self-government survive.

It is this thought that distresses us when we look upon our cities and our states and see them ruled by bosses. Our methods of party organization have produced bosses, and they are as natural and inevitable a product of our politics, no doubt, at any rate for the time being and until we can see our way to better things, as the walking delegate and the union president are of the contest between capital and federated labor. Both the masters of strikes and the masters of caucuses are able men, too, with whom we must needs deal with our best wits about us. But they are not, if they will pardon me for saying so, the leading characters I had in mind when I said that the excellence of a polity might be judged by the success with which it calls the leading characters of a nation forth to its posts of command. The polity which breeds bosses breeds managing talents rather than leading characters,—very excellent things in themselves, but not the highest flower of politics. The power to govern and direct primaries, combine primaries for the control of conventions, and use conventions for the nomination of candidates and the formulation of platforms agreed upon beforehand is an eminently useful thing in itself, and cannot be dispensed with, it may be, in democratic countries, where men must act, not helter skelter, but in parties, and with a certain party discipline, not easily thrown off; but it is not the first product of our politics we should wish to export to Porto Rico and the Philippines.

No doubt our study of these things which lie at
the front of our own lives, and which must be
handled in our own progress, will teach us how to be
better masters and tutors to those whom we govern.
We have come to full maturity with this new century
of our national existence and to full self-consciousness as a nation. And the day of our isolation is
past. We shall learn much ourselves now that we
stand closer to other nations and compare ourselves
first with one and again with another. Moreover, the
centre of gravity has shifted in the action of our federal government. It has shifted back to where it was
at the opening of the last century, in that early day
when we were passing from the gristle to the bone of
our growth. For the first twenty-six years that we
lived under our federal Constitution foreign affairs,
the sentiment and policy of nations oversea, dominated our politics, and our Presidents were our leaders. And now the same thing has come about again.
Once more it is our place among the nations that we
think of; once more our Presidents are our leaders.

The centre of our party management shifts accordingly. We no longer stop upon questions of
what this state wants or that, what this section will
demand or the other, what this boss or that may do
to attach his machine to the government. The scale
of our thought is national again. We are sensitive
to airs that come to us from off the seas. The President and his advisers stand upon our chief coign of
observation, and we mark their words as we did not
till this change came. And this centring of our
thoughts, this looking for guidance in things which

mere managing talents cannot handle, this union of
our hopes, will not leave us what we were when first
it came. Here is a new world for us. Here is a new
life to which to adjust our ideals.

It is by the widening of vision that nations, as men,
grow and are made great. We need not fear the ex-
panding scene. It was plain destiny that we should
come to this, and if we have kept our ideals clear, un-
marred, commanding through the great century and
the moving scenes that made us a nation, we may
keep them also through the century that shall see us
a great power in the world. Let us put our leading
characters at the front; let us pray that vision may
come with power; let us ponder our duties like men
of conscience and temper our ambitions like men who
seek to serve, not to subdue, the world; let us lift our
thoughts to the level of the great tasks that await us,
and bring a great age in with the coming of our day
of strength.

THE YOUNG PEOPLE AND THE CHURCH

AN ADDRESS DELIVERED BEFORE THE FORTIETH ANNUAL
CONVENTION OF THE PENNSYLVANIA STATE SABBATH
SCHOOL ASSOCIATION, AT PITTSBURGH, OCTOBER 13,
1904. COPYRIGHT, 1904, BY THE SUNDAY SCHOOL TIMES
COMPANY, PHILADELPHIA, PA.

WE bear a relationship to the rising generation whether we will or not. It is one of the principal tasks of each generation of mature persons in this world to hand on the work of the world to the next generation. We are engaged even more than we are aware in molding young people to be like ourselves. Those who have read that delightful book of Kenneth Grahame's entitled "The Golden Age," the age of childhood, will recall the indictment which he brings against the Olympians, as he calls them,—the grown-up people,—who do not understand the feelings of little folks not only, but do not seem to understand anything very clearly; who do not seem to live in the same world, who are constantly forcing upon the young ones standards and notions which they cannot understand, which they instinctively reject. They live in a world of delightful imagination; they pursue persons and objects that never existed; they make an Argosy laden with gold out of a floating butterfly,—and these stupid Olympians try to translate these things into uninteresting facts.

I suppose that nothing is more painful in the rec-

ollections of some of us than the efforts that were
made to make us like grown-up people. The delightful follies that we had to eschew, the delicious non-
sense that we had to disbelieve, the number of odious
prudences that we had to learn, the knowledge that
though the truth was less interesting than fiction, it
was more important than fiction,—the fact that
what people told you could not always be relied on,
and that it must be tested by the most uninteresting
tests.

When you think of it, we are engaged in the somewhat questionable practise of making all the world
uniform. We should be very sure that we are very
handsome characters to have a full heart in the undertaking of making youngsters exactly like ourselves. There is an amount of aggregate vanity in
the process which it is impossible to estimate. Moreover, you will notice that there are very whimsical
standards in this world. We speak of some persons
as being normal, and of others as being abnormal.
By normal we mean like ourselves; by abnormal we
mean unlike ourselves. The abnormal persons are in
the minority, and therefore most of them are in the
asylum. If they got to be in the majority, we would
go to the asylum. If we departed from that law of
the Medes and Persians which commands us to be
like other persons, we would be in danger of the bars.
The only thing that saves us is that abnormal people
are not all alike. If they were, they might be shrewd
enough to get the better of us, and put us where we
put them.

And we are engaged in rubbing off the differences.

We desire not to be supposed to be unlike other persons; we would prefer to abjure our individuality, and to say, as Dean Swift advised every man to say who desired to be considered wise, "My dear sir, I am exactly of your opinion." We try to avoid collisions of individuality, and go about to tell the younger people that they must do things as we have always done them, and as our parents made us do them, or else they will lose caste in the world.

There are two means by which we carry on this interesting work of making the next generation like the last. There is life itself, and that is the most drastic school there is. There is no school so hard in its lessons as the school of life. You are not excused from any one of its exercises. You are not excused for mistakes in any one of its lessons. We say a great many things that are harsh, and deservedly harsh, I will admit, about college hazing; but there is a more subtle hazing than that. The world hazes the persons that will not conform. It hazes after a manner that is worse than hazing their bodies,—it hazes their spirits, and teases them with the pointed finger and the curl of the lip, and says, "That man thinks he knows the whole thing." That, I say, is a very much more refined torture than making a man do a great many ridiculous things for the purpose of realizing that he is ridiculous, and so getting out of conceit with himself. I do not believe in hazing, but I do believe that there are some things worse than hazing. And I have suffered worse things from my fellow-men since I got out of college than I suffered while I was in college.

Life is a terrible master to those who cannot escape its more trying processes. The little urchin in the slums of the city knows more of the prudences of life when he is five than most of us knew at five and twenty. He knows just how hard a school he lives in, and just how astute he must be to win any of its prizes, to win even the tolerance of the powers that conduct it, even to live from day to day. He knows how many cars of Juggernaut must be dodged on the streets for the mere leave to live, and the keenness of his senses, his shrewdness in a bargain, is such as would predict him a man successful in commerce, would mean that some day he was going to overreach his fellow-man as now life seems to be overreaching him, and imposing upon him, and snatching every coveted thing from his grasp. The process of culture, the process of civilization, and the processes that can be bought by wealth, are largely processes of exemption from the harder classes of the school of life. Some young gentlemen brought up in the lap of luxury seem to have escaped all lessons, seem to know just as little about the world as it is possible for a person to live nineteen years and know. I have sometimes thought that if we could get a whole college of youngsters who had spent their boyhood in the slums, where they had to have wits in order to live, we would make extraordinary progress in scholarship; whereas, when in our discouraged moments,—I mean discouraged moments in our teaching,—we take some grim comfort in saying, as a Yale friend of mine said, that after teaching twenty years he had come to the conclusion that the human mind had infinite resources for resisting the introduction of knowledge. But you cannot resist the introduction of the knowledge that life brings. Life brings it and unloads it in your lap whether you want it or not.

The other means we have of indoctrinating the next generation and making the world uniform is organization. The individual process is not enough, we think, the process of working upon each other individually so that a miscellaneous set of influences prick each of us like so many currents of electricity. We think we must organize as a body to have a given, definite, predetermined effect upon others. So we take unfair advantage of a youngster in organizing a whole school so that he cannot escape having certain impressions made upon him. We tax the public in order to pay for the schools which will make it impossible for him to escape. And there are various instrumentalities which are organic. In the first place, there is the home; then there is the school; then there is the church; then there are all the political means, the means which we call social in their character, by which to mold and control the rising generation. All of these have their part in controlling the youth of the country and making them what we deem it necessary that they should be.

What do we wish that they should be? If forced to reason about it, we say they ought to be what we have found by experience it is prudent and wise to be; and they ought to be something more,—they ought to go one stage beyond the stage we have gone. But we cannot conduct them beyond the stage we

have reached. We can only point and say, "Here are
the boundaries which we have reached; beyond is an
undiscovered country; go out and discover it. We
can furnish you with a few probabilities; we can
supply you with a few tendencies; we can say to you
that we think that wisdom points in this direction;
but we cannot go with you; we cannot guide you;
we must part with you at the opening of the door,
and bid you Godspeed. But we want you to go on;
we do not want you to stop where we stopped."

What capital, after all, is it that we supply them
with? I take it that knowledge is a pretty poor com-
modity in itself and by itself. A ship does not sail
because of her cargo. There is no propulsion in that.
If the captain did not know his port, if he did not
know his rules of navigation, if he did not know
the management of his engines, or have somebody
aboard who did, if he did not know all the powers
that will carry the ship to the place where her cargo
will have additional value, the cargo would be nothing to him. What is his purpose? His purpose is
that the cargo should be used. Used for what? For
the convenience or the enlightenment, whatever it
may be, of the people to whom he is carrying it.

And so with knowledge. The knowledge you supply to the little fellow in the home is not merely con-
veyed to him in order that he may be full; the
knowledge that is supplied to him in school is not put
in him as if he were merely a little vessel to be filled
to the top. My father, who was a very plain-spoken
man, used to use a phrase which was rough, but it
expressed the meaning exactly. He said, "My son,

the mind is not a prolix gut to be stuffed.'' That is
not the object of it. It is not a vessel made to contain something; it is a vessel made to transmute
something. The process of digestion is of the essence,
and the only part of the food that is of any consequence is the part that is turned into blood and fruc-
tifies the whole frame. And so with knowledge. All
the wise saws and prudent maxims and pieces of information that we supply to the generation coming
on are of no consequence whatever in themselves unless they get into the blood and are transmuted.

And how are you going to get these things into the
blood? You know that nothing communicates fire
except fire. In order to start a fire you must originate a fire. You must have a little spark in order to
have a great blaze. I have often heard it said that a
speaker is dry, or that a subject is dry. Well, there
isn't any subject in the world that is dry. It is the
person that handles it and the person who receives it
that are dry. The subject is fertile enough. But the
trouble with most persons when they handle a subject is that they handle it as if it were a mere aggregate mass meant to stay where it is placed; whereas
it is something to be absorbed into the pores, to have
the life circulation communicated to it, and the moment you communicate that to it, it itself becomes a
vehicle of life. Every one who touches a live thing
knows he has touched living tissue, and not a dead
hand.

So that no knowledge is of any particular consequence in this world which is not incarnate. For example, we are taught the knowledge of the laws of

hygiene, but what earthly good are the laws of hygiene to us if we do not live in obedience to them? Presently disease springs upon us, and Nature says, "Thou fool. You knew these things. What profit is it to you to know them and not to regard them in your way of life? They were never yours. They were never part of you. You never possessed them." The moral of which is simply this, that the truths which are not translated into lives are dead truths, and not living truths. The only way to learn grammatical speech is to associate with those who speak grammatically.

And so of religion. Religion is communicable, I verily believe, aside from the sacred operations of the Holy Spirit, only by example. You have only to ask yourself what is the effect of a profession of religion on the part of a man who does not live a religious life. You know that the effect is not only not to communicate religion, but to delay indefinitely its influence. It is certainly true that we are not to judge religion by those who profess it but do not live it. But it is also true that if those who profess it are the only ones we live with, and they fail to live it, it cannot be communicated except by some mysterious grace of the Holy Spirit himself. So that no amount of didactic teaching in a home whose life is not Christian will ever get into the consciousness and life of the children. If you wish your children to be Christians, you must really take the trouble to be Christians yourselves. Those are the only terms upon which the home will work the gracious miracle.

And you cannot shift this thing by sending your

children to Sunday-school. You may remedy many
things, but you cannot shift this responsibility. If
the children do not get this into their blood atmospherically, they are not going to get it into their
blood at all until, it may be, they come to a period
of life where the influences of Christian lives outside
of the home may profoundly affect them and govern
their consciences. We must realize that the first and
most intimate and most important organization for
the indoctrinating of the next generation is the home,
is the family. This is the key to the whole situation.
That is the reason that you must get hold of the
whole family when you get hold of the children in
your Sunday-school work; that your work will not be
half done when you merely get the children there,
and it may be, their mothers. You must include
the fathers, and get your grip upon the home organization in such wise that the children will have
the atmospheric pressure of Christianity the week
through.

We are constantly debating and hearing it debated, How will the church get hold of the young
people? You cannot answer that question unless you
have a philosophy of the matter. And it seems to
me that the inevitable philosophy of the matter is
this: There are only a certain number of things that
impress young persons, only a certain number that
impress old ones, or, for that matter that impress
anybody. The things that impress the young person
and the old are convictions and earnestness in action
that looks like business, and a certain dignity and
simplicity that go along with being in earnest. You

will notice that when a man is going about his business he does not study his gestures, he does not consider his poses, he does not think how he looks when he is sitting at his desk in his chair. There is a directness and simplicity of approach in the thing which shows an utter lack of self-consciousness. He is not thinking about the machinery by which he is acting; he is after the thing.

When we say, therefore, that the way to get young people to the church is to make the church interesting, I am afraid we too often mean that the way to do is to make it entertaining. Did you ever know the theater to be a successful means of governing conduct? Did you ever know the most excellent concert, or series of concerts, to be the means of revolutionizing a life? Did you ever know any amount of entertainment to go further than hold for the hour that it lasted? If you mean to draw young people by entertainment, you have only one excuse for it, and that is to follow up the entertainment with something that is not entertaining, but which grips the heart like the touch of a hand. I dare say that there is some excuse for alluring persons to a place where good will be done them, but I think it would be a good deal franker not to allure them. I think it would be a great deal better simply to let them understand that that is the place where life is dispensed, and that if they want life they must come to that place.

If they believe that you believe what you say, they will come. If they have the least suspicion that you do not believe it, if they have the least suspicion that you are simply playing a game of social organization, if they have the notion that you are simply organizing a very useful instrumentality of society for moralizing the community, but that you don't after all believe that life itself lies in the doctrine and preaching of that place and nowhere else, you cannot keep hold of them very long. The only thing that governs any of us is authority. And the reason that it is harder to govern us when we are grown up than when we are young is that we question the authority, and you have to convince our minds of the reasonableness of the authority. But the young mind yields to the authority that believes in itself. That is the reason that consistency of conduct is indispensable to the maintenance of authority. You cannot make the young person do what you do not do yourself. You cannot make him believe what you do not believe yourself.

I have known some parents who had very deep doubt about some of the deeper mysteries of revelation, but who, nevertheless, tried to communicate those deep mysteries to their children, with an absolute lack of success that was to have been expected. They did not believe them themselves. Did you never have the uneasy experience of going into the presence of a child who did not care to speak to you? There are two beings who assess character instantly by looking into the eyes,—dogs and children. If a dog not naturally possessed of the devil will not come to you after he has looked you in the face, you ought to go home and examine your conscience; and if a little child, from any other reason than mere timidity,

looks you in the face, and then draws back and will
not come to your knee, go home and look deeper yet
into your conscience. There is no eye so searching
as the eye of simplicity. And you might as well give
up the attempt of trying to wear a mask before children, particularly the mask that you are so desirous
of wearing,—the mask of hypocrisy. It does not
work, and it is a very fortunate thing that it does
not work. If it did, we would make our children as
big hypocrites as we are. You must believe the
things you tell the children.

Have you not seen the flicker of the child's eye
when he first asked you if there was really any Santa
Claus, and you told him yes? He knows something
is the matter. He may not be shrewd enough or
thoughtful enough to know what is the matter, but
after that he has his doubts about Santa Claus,
simply because, by some electric communication that
you cannot stop, your doubts about Santa Claus have
been communicated to him. If you are a positivist,
he will be a positivist; if you believe, he will believe.

It is all in the atmosphere. Sometimes it seems to
me that nine-tenths of what we give other persons is
in our personality. The value of one man contrasted
with another is that some men have no electricity in
them. They might be in the room or out of the room;
it doesn't make any difference. Other men come
into the room, and the moment they come into it
something happens, either attraction or repulsion. I
cannot sit in a railroad station comfortably, because
men will come in whom I want to kick out, and persons will come in whom I want to go up and speak

to, and make friends with, and I am restrained because when I was small I was told that was not good form, and I would not for the world be unlike my fellow-men. So I sit still and try to think about something else, and my eye constantly wanders to some person whom it would, I am sure, be such fun to go and talk to, who I know has something I would like to have. And yet, as for nine-tenths of the persons in the room, they do nothing but vitiate the atmosphere, and you would rather have their breathing room than their presence.

And it is thus all through life. A man comes to you to press a piece of business upon you, and he goes away, and you say to yourself, "No, I won't go into that."

And some one else says, "Why not? Don't you believe in him?"

"No, I don't believe in him."

"Do you know anything wrong that he ever did?"

"No."

"Didn't he verify his statements?"

"Yes."

"Then why don't you go in with him?"

"Well, I don't know. I won't do it. I don't like his looks. There was something about him that made me think it was not all straight, and, at any rate, I will look into it, and hear about it from somebody else before going any further."

We are constantly having that feeling. And that is the feeling which illustrates my thought, though I have gone pretty far afield to illustrate it,—that it is conviction, authority, simplicity, the directness of one who is going about his business, and goes about it with genuineness, which governs young people. The moral of that is, that you are going the wrong way about accomplishing what you seek when you try to make that entertaining which, in the nature of things, though engrossing, is not entertaining in the ordinary sense of the word.

To tell a human being of the things that affect his eternal salvation I should say is decidedly under-described if you call it entertaining. It is not entertaining in any reasonable sense of the word to tell him of the things that most profoundly affect his welfare in this world and in the next. I know that there are ways of telling men the truth which repel them; I know that too many men are tried for by efforts which merely frighten. I believe that too much effort is made to get people to believe for fear of the consequences of unbelief. I don't believe any man was ever drawn into heaven for fear he would go to hell. Because, if I understand the Scriptures in the least, they speak a gospel of love. Except God draw you, you are not drawn. You are not brought in by whips, you are not drawn by a frowning face, you are not drawn by a threatening gesture. You are drawn by love, you are drawn by the knowledge that if you come you will be received as a son. Nothing but yearning draws you. Fear never drew you anywhere.

You must realize that it is all a question of personal relationship between man and his Maker, and a personal relationship founded upon love. For love is the only thing that I know that ever led to self-abnegation. Ambition does not lead to it; no use of power for power's sake leads to anything but self-aggrandizement. Can you name me any motive in the world that ever led a man to love another life more than his own except the motive of love? And yet what we are working for in the young people, as in the old, is to show them the perfect image of a Man who will draw all the best powers of their nature to Himself, and make them love him so that they will love him more than they love themselves, and loving him so, will love their fellow-men more than they love themselves. Everything heroic, everything that looks toward salvation, is due to this power of elevation. It is a noteworthy thing that we reserve the beautiful adjective "noble" for the men who think less of themselves than of some cause or of some person whom they serve. We elevate to the only nobility we have, the nobility of moral greatness, only those men who are governed by love.

You cannot create love by entertainment, but you can make love by the perfect exhibition of Christ-like qualities, and, with the assistance of the Holy Spirit, by the withdrawal of the veil which for most men hangs before the face of our Lord and Saviour. Our whole object, it seems to me, in church work is simply this: to enable all to see him, to realize him, and if we devote ourselves to that purpose with singleness of heart and without thought of ourselves, we shall suddenly find the seats filling, because where there is fire thither men will carry their lamps to be lighted. Where there is power, men will go to partake of it. Every human soul instinctively feels that

the only power he desires, the only power that can
relieve him from the tedium of the day's work, the
only thing which can put a glow upon the routine of
the day's task, the only thing that can take him back
to the golden age when everything had a touch of
magic about it, when everything was greater than
the fact, when everything had lurking behind it some
mysterious power, when there was in everything a
vision and a perfect image,—is this thing which he
sees enthroned upon the shining countenances of
those who really believe in the life and saving grace
of their Lord and Master.

THE BANKER AND THE NATION

ADDRESS DELIVERED AT THE ANNUAL CONVENTION OF THE AMERICAN BANKERS' ASSOCIATION AT DENVER, COLORADO, SEPTEMBER 30, 1908. FROM THE "CONGRESSIONAL RECORD," 62D CONGRESS, 2D SESSION, VOL. XLVIII, APPENDIX, PP. 502-503.

MR. PRESIDNET, ladies, and gentlemen: We have witnessed in recent years an extraordinary awakening of the public conscience with regard to the methods of modern business, and of the private conscience also, for scores of business men have become conscious, as they never were before, that the eager push and ambition and competition of modern business had hurried them, oftentimes unconsciously, into practices which they had not stopped, in the heat of the struggle, to question, but which they now see to have been immoral and against the public interest. Sometimes the process of their demoralization was very subtle, very gradual, very obscure and therefore hidden from their consciences. Sometimes it was crude and obvious enough, but they did not stop to be careful, thinking of their rivals and not of their morals. But now the moral and political aspects of the whole matter are laid bare to their own view as well as to the view of the world, and we have run out of quiet waters into a very cyclone of reform. No man is so poor as not to have his policies for everything. The whole structure of society is being critically looked over, and changes of the most radical character are being soberly discussed, which it would take generations to perfect, but which we are hopefully thinking of putting out to contract to be finished by a specified date well within the limits of our own time.

It is not my purpose on the present occasion to discuss particular policies and proposals. I wish, rather, to call your attention to some of the large aspects of the matter, which we should carefully consider before we make up our minds which way we should go and with what purpose we should act.

What strikes one most forcibly in the recent agitation of public opinion is the anatomy of our present economic structure which they seem to disclose. Sharp class contrasts and divisions have been laid bare—not class distinctions in the old world or the old-time sense, but sharp distinctions of power and opportunity quite as significant. For the first time in the history of America there is a general feeling that issue is now joined, or about to be joined, between the power of accumulated capital and the privileges and opportunities of the masses of the people. The power of accumulated capital is now, as at all other times and in all other circumstances, in the hands of a comparatively small number of persons, but there is a very widespread impression that those persons have been able in recent years as never before to control the national development in their own interest. The contest is sometimes said to be between capital and labor, but that is too narrow and too special a conception of it. It is, rather, between capital in all its larger accumulations and all other less concentrated, more dispersed, smaller, and more individual economic forces; and every new policy proposed has as its immediate or ultimate object the restraint of the power of accumulated capital for the protection and benefit of those who cannot command its use.

This anatomizing of our social structure, this pulling it to pieces and scrutinizing each part of it separately, as if it had an independent existence and interest and could live not only separately but in contrast and contest with its other parts, as if it had no organic union with them or dependence upon them, is a very dangerous and unwholesome thing at best; but there are periods of excitement and inquiry when it is inevitable, and we should make the best of it, if only to hasten the process of reintegration. This process of segregation and contrast is always a symptom of deep discontent. It is not set afoot accidentally. It generally comes about, as it has come about now, because the several parts of society have forgotten their organic connections, their vital interdependence, and have become individually selfish or hostile—because the attention of a physician is in fact necessary. It has given occasion to that extensive and radical programme of reform which we call socialism and with which so many hopeful minds are now in love. We shall be able to understand our present confused affairs thoroughly and handle them wisely only when we have made clear to ourselves how his situation arose, how this programme was provoked, and what we individually and collectively have to do with it.

The abstract principles of socialism it is not difficult to admire. They are, indeed, hardly distinguishable from the abstract principles of Democracy. The
object of the thoughtful Socialist is to effect such an
organization of society as will give the individual his
best protection and his best opportunity, and yet
serve the interest of all rather than the interest of
any one in particular; an organization of mutual
benefit based upon the principle of the solidarity of
all interests. But the programme of socialism is another matter. It is not unfair to say that the programmes of socialism so far put forth are either
utterly vague or entirely impracticable. That they
are now being taken very seriously and espoused very
ardently is evidence, not of their excellence or practicability, but only of the fact, to which no observant
man can any longer shut his eyes, that the contesting
forces in our modern society have broken its unity
and destroyed its organic harmony—not because that
was inevitable, but because men have used their
power thoughtlessly and selfishly, and legitimate
undertakings have been pushed to illegitimate
lengths. There has been an actual process of selfish
segregation, and society has so reacted from it that
almost any thorough-going programme of reintegration looks hopeful and attractive. Such programme
cannot be thrust aside or defeated by mere opposition and denial; it can be overcome only by wiser
and better programmes, and these it is our duty as
patriotic citizens to find.

The most striking fact about the actual organization of modern society is that the most conspicuous,

the most readily wielded, and the most formidable
power is not the power of government, but the power
of capital. Men of our day in England and America
have almost forgotten what it is to fear the Government, but have found out what it is to fear the power
of capital, to watch it with jealousy and suspicion,
and trace to it the source of every open or hidden
wrong. Our memories are not of history, but of what
our own lives and experiences and the lives and experiences of the men about us have disclosed. We
have had no experience in our day, or in the days of
which our fathers have told us, of the tyranny of
governments, of their minute control and arrogant
interference and arbitrary regulation of our business and of our daily life, though it may be that we
shall know something of it in the near future. We
have forgotten what the power of government means
and have found out what the power of capital means;
and so we do not fear government and are not jealous
of political power. We fear capital and are jealous
of its domination. There will be need of many cool
heads and much excellent judgment amongst us to
curb this new power without throwing ourselves back
into the gulf of the old from which we were the first
of the nations of the world to find a praticable way
of escape.

The only forces that can save us from the one ex-
treme or the other are those forces of social reunion
and social reintegration which every man of station
and character and influence in the country can in
some degree and within the scope of his own life set
afoot. We must open our minds wide to the new cir-

cumstances of our time, must bring about a new common understanding and effect a new coördination in the affairs which most concern us. Capital must give over its too great preoccupation with the business of making those who control it individually rich and must study to serve the interests of the people as a whole. It must draw near to the people and serve them in some intimate way of which they will be conscious. Voluntary coöperation must forestall the involuntary coöperation which legislators will otherwise seek to bring about by the coercion of law. Capital now looks to the people like a force and interest apart, with which they must deal as with a master and not as with a friend. Those who handle capital in the great industrial enterprises of the country know how mistaken this attitude is. They see how intimately the general welfare and the common interest are connected with every really sound process of business, and how all antagonisms and misunderstandings hamper and disorganize industry. But no one can now mistake the fact and no one knows better than the manipulators of capital how many circumstances there are to justify the impression. We can never excuse ourselves from the necessity of dealing with facts.

I am sure that many bankers must have become acutely and sensitively aware of the fact that the most isolated and the most criticized interest of all is banking. The banks are, in the general view and estimation, the special and exclusive instrumentalities of capital used on a large scale. They stand remote from the laborer and the body of the people, and put whatever comes into their coffers at the disposal of the captains of industry, the great masters of finance, the corporations which are in the way to crush all competitors.

I shall not now stop to ask how far this view of the banks is true. I need not tell you that in large part it is false. I know that the close connection of the banks with the larger operations of commerce and finance is natural and not illicit, and that the banks turn very cheerfully and very cordially to the smaller pieces of business. Time was when the banks never advertised, never condescended to solicit business; now they eagerly seek it in small pieces as well as big. The banks are in fact and in spirit at the service of every man to the limit of his known trustworthiness and credit, and they know very well that there is profit in multiplying small accounts and small loans. But, on the other hand, they are in fact singularly remote from the laborer and the body of the people. They are particularly remote from the farmer and the small trader of our extensive countrysides.

Let me illustrate what I mean. Roughly speaking, every town of any size and importance in the United States has its bank. But the large majority of our people live remote from banks, are unknown to the officers who manage them and dispense their credit. Moreover, our system of banking is such that local banks must for the most part be organized and maintained by local capital and have at their disposal only local resources. It is difficult for those of you who do not travel leisurely in the vast rural districts of this country to realize how few and far between the banks are, or how local and petty, and without extensive power to help the community most of them are when you find them. A friend of mine rode through seven counties of one of the oldest of our States before finding any place where he could change a $20 bill; and I myself was obliged one summer, in a thriving agricultural district, to get change for bills of any considerable denomination sent to me by express from banks 50 miles distant. The business of the country was done largely by barter. I do not wonder that the men thereabout thought that the money of the country was being hoarded somewhere, presumably in Wall Street. None of it was accessible to them, though they by no means lacked in this world's goods. They believed in the free coinage of silver, not realizing that the silver, too, would have to be handled by the banks and would be equally inaccessible. It would not have been shipped like ordinary merchandise.

"Where and whose is the money of the country?" is the question which the average voter wants his political representative to answer for him. Bankers can answer the question, but I have met very few of them who could answer it in a way the ordinary man could understand. Bankers, as a body of experts in a particular, very responsible business, hold, and hold very clearly, certain economic facts and industrial circumstances in mind, and possess a large and unusually interesting mass of specialized knowledge of which they are masters in an extraordinary degree. But I trust you will not think me impertinent if I say that they excuse themselves from knowing a great many things which it would manifestly be to their interest to know, and that they are oftentimes singularly ignorant, or at any rate singularly indifferent, about what I may call the social functions and the political functions of banking, particularly in a country governed by opinion. I am not here to advocate the establishment of branch banks or argue in favor of anything which you understand better than I do. But I have this to say, and to say with great confidence: That if a system of branch banks, very simply and inexpensively managed and not necessarily open every day in the week, could be organized, which would put the resources of the rich banks of the country at the disposal of whole countrysides to whose merchants and farmers only a restricted and local credit is now open, the attitude of plain men everywhere towards the banks and banking would be changed utterly within less than a generation. You know that you are looking out for investments; that even the colossal enterprises of our time do not supply you with safe investments enough for the money that comes in to you; and that banks here, there, and everywhere are tempted, as a consequence, to place money in speculative enterprises, and even themselves to promote questionable ventures in finance at a fearful and wholly unjustifiable risk in order to get the usury they wish from their resources. You sit only where these things are spoken of and big returns coveted. There would be plenty of investments if you carried your money to the people of the country at large and had agents in hundreds of villages who knew the men in their neighborhoods who could be trusted with loans and who would make profitable use of them. Your money, moreover, would quicken and fertilize the country, and that other result would follow which I think you will agree with me is not least important in my argument: The average voter would learn that the money of the country was not being hoarded; that it was at the disposal of any honest man who could use it; and that to strike at the banks was to strike at the general convenience and the general prosperity. I do not know what the arguments against branch banks are; but these I know from observation to be the arguments for them, and very weighty arguments they seem to me to be.

That, however, need not concern me. I am not so much interested in argument as in illustration. My theme is this: Bankers, like men of every other interest, have their lot and part in the Nation—their social function and their political duty. We have come upon a time of crisis when it is made to appear, and is in part true, that interest is arrayed against interest; and it is our duty to turn the war into peace. It is the duty of the banker, as it is the duty of men of every other class, to see to it that there be in his calling no class spirit, no feeling of antagonism to the people, to plain men whom the bankers, to their great loss and detriment, do not know. It is their duty to be intelligent, thoughtful, patriotic intermediaries between capital and the people at large; to understand and serve the general interest; to be public men serving the country as well as private men serving their depositors and the enterprises

whose securities and notes they hold. How capital is
to draw near to the people and serve them at once
obviously and safely is the question, the great and
now pressing question, which it is the particular duty
of the banker to answer. No one else can answer it
so intelligently; and if he does not answer it others
will, it may be to his detriment and to the general
embarrassment of the country. The occasion and the
responsibility are yours.

We live in a very interesting time of awakening, in
a period of reconstruction and readjustment, when
everything is being questioned and even old foundations are threatened with change. But it is not a
time of danger if we do not lose our heads and ignore
our consciences. It is, on the contrary, a time of
extraordinary privilege and opportunity when men
of every class have begun to think upon the themes
of the public welfare as they never thought before.
I feel that I have only to speak of your social duty
and political function to meet with a very instant
and effectual response out of your own thoughts and
purposes. I think that you will agree with me that
our responsibility in a democratic country is not only
for what we do and for the way and spirit in which
we do it, but also for the impression we make. We
are bound to make the right impression and to contribute by our action not only to the general prosperity and well-being of the country, but also to its
general instruction, so that men of different classes
can understand each other, can serve each other with
intelligence and energy. There is a sense in which a
democratic country statesmanship is forced upon

every man of initiative, every man capable of leading anybody; and this I believe to be the particular period when statesmanship is forced upon bankers and upon all those who have to do with the application and use of the vast accumulated wealth of this country. We should, for example, not only seek the best solution for our currency difficulties, not only the safest and most scientific system of elastic currency to meet the convenience of a country in which the amount of cash needed at different times fluctuates enormously and violently, but we should also seek to give the discussions of such matters such publicity and such general currency and such simplicity as will enable men of every kind and calling to understand what we are talking about and take an intelligent part in the discussion. We cannot shut ourselves in as experts to our own business. We must open our thoughts to the country at large and serve the general intelligence as well as the general welfare.

ROBERT E. LEE: AN INTERPRETATION

DELIVERED ON THE OCCASION OF THE HUNDREDTH AN-
NIVERSARY OF THE BIRTH OF ROBERT E. LEE, AT
THE UNIVERSITY OF NORTH CAROLINA, JANUARY 19,
1909, AND NOW REPRINTED FROM THE BOOK ENTITLED
"ROBERT E. LEE." BY WOODROW WILSON. PUBLISHED
IN 1924 BY THE UNIVERSITY OF NORTH CAROLINA
PRESS.

IN one sense, it is a superfluous thing to speak of General Lee,—he does not need the eulogy of any man. His fame is not enhanced, his memory is not lifted to any new place of distinction by any man's word of praise, for he is secure of his place. It is not necessary to recount his achievements; they are in the memory not only of every soldier, but of every lover of high and gifted men who likes to see achievements which proceed from character, to see those things done which are not done with the selfish purpose of self-aggrandizement, but in order to serve a country, and prove worthy of a cause. These are the things which make the name of this great man prominent not only, but in some regards unapproachable in the history of our country.

I happened the other day to open a book not printed in this part of the country, the *Century Cyclopædia of Names,* and to turn to the name of Lee, and I was very much interested, and I must say a little touched, by the simple characterization it gave of the man: "A celebrated American general

in the Confederate service.'' How perfectly that sums
the thing up,—a celebrated American general, a national character who won his chief celebrity in the
service of a section of the country, but who was not
sectionalized by the service, is recognized now as a
national hero; who was not rendered the less great
because he bent his energies towards a purpose which
many men conceived not to be national in its end.

I think this speaks something for the healing process of time. I think it says something for the age,
that it should have taken so short a time for the
whole nation to see the true measure of this man, and
it takes me back to my own feelings about one's necessary connection with the region in which he was
born.

There is an interesting and homely story of Daniel
Webster, how after one very tedious and laborious
session of the Senate he returned to his home in Boston quite worn out and told his servant that he was
going upstairs to lie down, and must not be disturbed
on any account. He had hardly reached his room
when some gentlemen from the little village in New
Hampshire which had been his original boyhood
home, called at the door and said they must see him,
—that a man's life was involved. They had come
down as the neighbours of a lad in his old home,
charged, as they believed falsely, with murder. They
believed in the lad but were confounded by circum-
stantial evidence; and they thought that there was
only one man in the United States who could unravel
the tangle of misleading indications; and they had
come to see Mr. Webster. The servant was afraid to

call him but yielded to their urgency, and he came down in no pleasant humour. To all their appeals he replied, "Gentlemen, it is impossible; I am worn out. I am not fit for the service, and cannot go." Seeing at last that it was probably hopeless, the spokesman of the little company at last rose and said, "Well, I don't know what the neighbours will say." "Oh! well," said Webster, "if it is the neighbours, I will go!" There came to his mind the vision of some little groups of old men in that village where he had lived as a boy whose comments he could surmise, and that was the particular condemnation he could not face. So all great patriots have had a deep local root-age. You can love a country if you begin by loving a community, but you cannot love a country if you do not have the true rootages of intimate affection which are the real sources of all that is strongest in human life. So this "celebrated American general" had his necessary local rootages, and the sap of his manhood united him with the soil on which he was bred. It was there he won his celebrity and made secure his fame. I think one of the most interesting things to remember about Lee is that he was an ideal combination of what a man inherits and what he may make of himself.

General Lee came of a distinguished family. His father, Light Horse Harry Lee, was of the finest breed of those gallant soldiers who made the country free; and the lad in his boyhood must have been bred to many memories of high deeds and to many fine conceptions of patriotic service at the hearth where his father sat.

I like to think, for my part, that Light Horse
Harry Lee was bred under the teaching of Doctor
John Witherspoon, the great Scotchman who at that
day presided over the college at Princeton, and that
there is some sort of Princetonian lineage in the man
whom we honor now.

But these soldierly traditions, this impulse from a
great father, were not what made Robert E. Lee.
After all, what makes and distinguishes a man is not
that he is derived from any family or from any training, but that he has discovered for himself the true
rôle of manhood in his own day. No man gains distinction who does not make some gift of his own individuality to the thing that he does,—to the generation which he serves.

This man was not great because he was born of a
soldier and bred in a school of soldiers, but because,
of whomsoever he may have been born, howsoever
he was bred, he was a man who saw his duty, who
conceived it in high terms, and who spent himself,
not upon his own ambitions, but in the duty that lay
before him. We like to remember all the splendid
family traditions of the Lees, but we like most of
all to remember that this man was greater than all
the traditions of his family; that there was a culmination here that could not have been reached by
the mere drift of what men remember, but must be
reached by what men originate and conceive.

I am not going to try to outline the career of Lee,
because I feel the compulsion of that last characteristic of General Lee. I do not want to live, and I do
not wish to ask you to live on the memory of what

General Lee did. I want to remind you of how General Lee turned immediately from war, when it was past, to the future which was to come, and said, "I will do my part in trying to make the young men of this country ready for the things which are yet to be done."

We are not at liberty to walk with our eyes over our shoulders, recalling the things which were done in the past; we are bound in conscience to march with our eyes forward, with the accents of such men in our ears saying, "We lived not as you must live. We lived for our generation; we tried to do its tasks. Turn your faces and your hands likewise to the tasks that you have to do." We would not be honouring General Lee if we did not think of him only enough to remind ourselves of what we have to do to be like him. The true eulogy of General Lee is a life which is meant to be patterned after his standards of duty and of achievement. And so I am not going to ask you to-night to look back at General Lee, but, rather to answer the question—"What does General Lee mean to us?"

It is a notable thing that we see when we look back to men of this sort. The Civil War is something which we cannot even yet uncover in memory without stirring embers which may spring into a blaze. There was deep colour and the ardour of blood in that contest. The field is lurid with the light of passion, and yet in the midst of that crimson field stands this gentle figure,—a man whom you remember, not as a man who loved war, but as a man moved by all the high impulses of gentle kindness, a man whom men did not fear, but loved; a man in whom everybody who approached him marked singular gentleness, singular sweetness, singular modesty,—none of the pomp of the soldier, but all the simplicity of the gentleman. This man is in the centre of that crimson field, is the central figure of a great tragedy. A singular tragedy it seems which centres in a gentleman who loved his fellow-men and sought to serve them by the power of love, and who yet, in serving them with the power of love, won the imperishable fame of a great soldier! A singular contradiction!

It is true that we do not think entirely correctly of Lee in supposing that he was compact entirely of gentleness. No man whom you deeply care for or look to for leadership is made up altogether of gentle qualities. When you come into the presence of a leader of men you know you have come into the presence of fire,—that it is best not incautiously to touch that man,—that there is something that makes it dangerous to cross him, that if you grapple his mind you will find that you have grappled with flame and fire. You do not want sweetness merely and light in men who lead you; and there was just as much fire in Lee as there was in Washington. In Washington it was more truly present. Every man who approached Washington had the singular impression that he was in the presence of a man of tremendous passions. He was always well in hand; but you knew that the man himself was aware that he was driving a mettlesome team, which he had to watch at every moment to avoid sudden runaway, when circumstances were exigent or exciting.

You did not get that impression when in the presence of Lee. I have only the delightful memory of standing, when a lad, for a moment by General Lee's side and looking up into his face, so that I have nothing but a child's memory of the man; but those who saw him when they were men and could judge say that you got no impression of constrained and governed passion such as men got from General Washington. But whenever General Lee was in the field no one dared cross him, no one dared neglect his orders, no one dared exercise a dangerous discretion in the carrying out of his commands. There would flare in the man a consuming fire of anger; those who were in his presence felt it was dangerous so much as to breathe naturally until it was past. There was something of the tiger in this man when his purpose was aroused and in action. It would immediately recede; quiet gentleness would come again, that perfect poise, that delightful sense of ease as he moved from one purpose to another; but you would not forget that moment of exposed fire,—you would know that you had been in the presence of consuming force.

But what strikes me as most interesting in the example of General Lee is that this was not in one sense of the word personal force at all. Touch General Lee about himself and you never saw the flash of fire, but touch him about things he regarded as his duty, and you saw it instantly. So the force that presided in him was no other than that moral force which may be said to be a principle in action. There is a sense, I sometimes think, in which every one of us in whose life principle forms a part is merely hold-

ing up a light which he himself did not kindle, not
his own principle, not something peculiar and individual to himself, but that light which must light
all mankind, the love of truth, the love of duty, the
love of those things which are not stated in the terms
of personal interest. That is the force and that the
fire that moulds men or else consumes them.

You need not be afraid of the fire that is in selfish
passion, you can crush that; but you cannot crush the
fire that is in unselfish passion. You know that there
you are in the presence of the greatest force in the
world, the only force that lifts men or nations to
greatness, or purifies communities; and that is the
consuming fire which we dare not touch. I apply
this thought sometimes to existing circumstances. I
grow tired often, as I tire of any futility, of hearing
certain abuses condemned and not having the condemnation followed by a list of the names of the
persons who are guilty of them; for there is not a
group of men in this country who could stand the
heat of the fire that would scorch those names. You
cannot scorch the abuse, but you can consume men
by merely exposing them to this moral fire, which
they know is the fire of their death; and that is the
sort of force that burned in General Lee. All his
life through you are aware of a conscious self-subor-
dination to principles which lay outside of his personal life.

I have sometimes noted with a great deal of interest how careless we are about most words in our
language, and yet how careful we are about some
others; for example, there is one word which we

do not use carelessly and that is the word "noble."
We use the word "great" indiscriminately. A
man is great because he has had great material
success and has piled up a fortune; a man is great
because he is a great writer, or a great orator; a
man is great because he is a great hero. We notice
in him some distinct quality that overtops like qualities in other men. But we reserve the word "noble"
carefully for those whose greatness is not spent in
their own interest. A man must have a margin of
energy which he does not spend upon himself in
order to win this title of nobility. He is noble in our
popular conception only when he goes outside the
narrow circle of self-interest, and begins to spend
himself for the interest of mankind. Then, however
humble his gifts, however undistinguished his intellectual force, we give him this title of nobility, and
admit him into the high peerage of men who will
not be forgotten.

Now that was the characteristic of General Lee's
life. It was not only moral force, but it was moral
force conscientiously guided by interests which were
not his own. You do not need to have me illustrate
that. It was manifestly not to General Lee's personal interest to take command of the armies of the
South. He could have taken command of the armies
of the North; and, in spite of the noble quality of the
Southern struggle, every man now sees that the
forces of the world were sure to crush the self-asser-
tion of the South; and General Lee knew enough of
the force of the world, has been schooled enough in
national armies to know upon which side the prob-

ability of material power lay and therefore the prob-
ability of success in arms.   He knew that the South
would be weak in that it could not count on the support of the world, and the North could.   A man seeking his own aggrandizement would not have chosen
as General Lee did.   But he did not choose with any,
even momentary regard for his personal fortune.   He
sacrificed himself for the things that were nearest,
the things I have illustrated in the homely anecdote
about Webster.   He thought of the neighbours; he
knew that a man's nearest attachments are his best
attachments, and his nearest duties his imperative
duties.   He had been born in Virginia, he was Virginia's.   Virginia could do with him as she pleased.
And wherever that spirit obtains, wherever men can
be found in the State of North Carolina, or in any
other State, who conscientiously live upon this principle, that they belong to North Carolina, that they
belong to their people and to their State and must
see to it that they yield themselves to the needs and
commands of their people and do the things that are
necessary to be done for their welfare, those are the
men who, if they do not look merely to their own
fame, will sometime be written upon the roll of
honour of the local and national history of this country.

So that there is brought to the surface in General
Lee, as it were, the consummate fire of a democratic
nation, the perfect product of a common conscience
and a common consciousness expressing itself in an
instrument excellently suitable because of its own
fine quality.   You may use a clumsy instrument for

the right purpose, but it is better to use a perfect instrument, and this man was like the finest steel adapting himself to the nicest strokes of precision and yet incapable of being snapped or broken by any impact. He was a perfect instrument for a thing which we too little think of.

I do not believe in a democratic form of government because I think it the best form of government. It is the clumsiest form of government in the world. If you wanted to make a merely effective government you would make it of fewer persons. If you wanted to invent a government that would act with speed and quick force, you would be doing a clumsy thing to make it democratic in structure. That is not purposed to be the best form, but to have the best sources.

Did you ever think how the world managed politically to get through the Middle Ages? It got through them without breakdown because it had the Roman Catholic Church to draw upon for native gifts, and by no other means that I can see. If you will look at the politics of the Middle Ages you will see that states depended for their guidance upon great ecclesiastics, and they depended upon them because the community itself was in strata, was in classes, and the Roman Catholic Church was a great democracy. Any peasant could become a priest, and any priest a chancellor. And this reservoir of democratic power and native ability was what brought the Middle Ages through their politics. If they had not had a democratic supply of capacity they could not have conducted a sterile aristocratic polity. An aristocratic polity goes to seed. The establishment of a democratic nation means that any man in it may, if he consecrate himself and use himself in the right way, come to be the recognized instrument of a whole nation. It is an incomparably resourceful arrangement, though it is not the best practical organization of government.

In a man like General Lee you see a common consciousness made manifest; and this singular thing revealed, that by a root which seems to be a root of failure a man may be lifted to be the model of a whole nation. For it is not an exaggeration to say that in all parts of this country the manhood and the self-forgetfulness and the achievements of General Lee are a conscious model to men who would be morally great. This man who chose the course which eventually led to practical failure is one of the models of the times. "A nation," Browning says, "is but the attempt of many to rise to the completer life of one; and those who live as the models for the mass are singly of more value than they all."

The moral force of a country like America lies in the fact that every man has it within his choice to express the nation in himself. I am interested in historical examples as a mere historian. I was found guilty myself of the indiscretion of writing a history, but I will tell you frankly, if you will not let it go further, that I wrote it, not to instruct anybody else, but to instruct myself. I wrote the history of the United States in order to learn it. That may be an expensive process for other persons who bought the book, but I lived in the United States and my interest in learning their history was, not to remember what happened, but to find which way we were going.

I remember a traveller telling me of being on a road in Scotland and asking a man breaking stone by the roadside if this was the road to so and so; the man said, "Where did you come from"; he answered, "I don't know whether it is any of your business where I came from." "Weel," said the man, "it's as muckle as whaur ye're ganging tae." There is a great deal of philosophy in that question asked by the roadside. If I am near a crossroad and ask if this is the road to so and so, it is a pertinent question to ask me where I came from.

We often speak of a man as having "lost himself," in a desert for example. Did you never reflect that that is the only thing he has not lost,—himself? He is there. The danger of the situation is that he has lost all the rest of the world. He doesn't know where the North is, or the South, or the East, or the West, —has lost every point of the compass. The only way by which he can start is to get some fixed and known point by which he can determine his direction. A nation that does not know its history and heed its history has lost itself. Unless you know where you came from you do not know where you are going to.

I am told by psychologists that if I did not remember who I was yesterday I would not know who I am to-day. Now the same is true of a nation. A nation which does not remember what it was yesterday does not know what it is to-day, or what it is trying to do. We are trying to do a futile thing if we do not know where we came from or what we have been about.

We have stumbled upon a confusing age; nothing is like it was fifteen years ago,—certainly in the field of economic endeavor, and we are casting about to discover a new world without any standards taken out of an older world by which we can make the comparison.

I was passing through the city of Omaha during the latter stages of the presidential campaign and I bought the morning paper, the *Omaha Bee,* and found in it an interesting article by my friend Mr. Rosewater in which he made capital fun of a quotation about the tariff from Mr. Bryan. I thought there was something odd about the quotation, and it turned out the next morning that Mr. Rosewater, himself a member of the Republican National Committee, had been making fun, not of a quotation from Bryan, but of a quotation from the Republican platform. Now the point is, that unless you had an experienced nose in that campaign, if you picked up either of the platforms you had to look at the label to see which it was. The reason is that in recent years we have been looking about for expedients and policies and have not been looking about for principles.

If you want me to bid against you for a popular policy I will probably resort to the expedient of matching your bid if I think it is a good one; but if I happen to be restrained by certain knowledge of what happened once before, I may choose differently and by a longer measurement. I may say there are certain things going to happen in this; they are going to happen upon well-known and ancient principles: having read history I would be a fool if I did not know it. I am going to hark back to those fundamental principles which hold good despite changes of policy. I am not going to hark back to old policies, but I shall try to find out whether there is not some new and suitable expression of those old principles in new policies. Although I may not assist my party to win at the next election by such a course, it is sure thereby to win at some election, at which it will give it such distinction that the country will thereafter for a whole generation recognize in it the only safe counsellor it has.

If you want to win at an election which occurs tomorrow probably you haven't time to remind your fellow-countrymen of the abiding principles upon which they should act; but if you form the habit of basing your advice upon definite principles you will presently gain a permanent following such as you could not possibly have gained upon any bidding for popularity by mere expedients.

I want to say that the lesson of General Lee's life to me is that it is not the immediate future that should be the basis of the statesman's calculation. If you had been in Lee's position, what would have been your calculation of expediency? Here was a great national power, material and spiritual, in the North. In the Northwest there had grown up by a slow process, as irresistible as the glacial movement, a great national feeling, a feeling in which was quite obliterated and lost the old idea of the separate sov-

ereignty of states. In the South there had been a
steadfast maintenance of the older conception of the
union. What in such a case would you have said to
your countrymen? "It will be most proper, as it
will certainly be most expedient, for you to give in to
the majority, and vote for the Northern conception?"
Not at all. If you had been of Lee's kind you would
have known that men's consciences, men's habits of
thought, lie deeper than that, and you would have
said: "No; this is not a time to talk about majorities; this is a time to express convictions; and if her
conviction is not expressed by the South in terms of
blood she will lose her character. These are her convictions, and if she yields them out of expediency
she will have proved herself of the soft fibre of those
who do not care to suffer for what they profess to
love." Even a man who saw the end from the beginning should, in my conception as a Southerner, have
voted for spending his people's blood and his own,
rather than pursue the weak course of expediency.
There is here no mere device, no regard to the immediate future. What has been the result?—ask yourself that. It has been that the South has retained
her best asset, her self-respect.

Let that great case serve as an example. Are you
going into political campaigns of a less fundamental
character on the ground of expediency, or are you
going in on the ground of your real opinions and
ultimate self-respect?

For my part, if I did not, after saturating myself
in the conceptions upon which this government was
formed, express my knowledge of those principles

and my belief in them by the way I voted, I would lose my self-respect; and I would not care to have anybody's company in the poor practice. What this country needs now in the field of politics is principle; not measures of expediency, but principle,— principles expressed in terms of the present circumstances, but principles nevertheless. And principles do not spring up in a night; principles are not new, principles are ancient.

There is one lesson that the peoples of the world have learned so often that they ought to esteem themselves contemptible if they have to learn it again, and that is that if you concentrate the management of a people's affairs in a single central government and carry that concentration beyond a certain point of oversight and regulation, you will certainly provoke again those revolutionary processes by which individual liberty was asserted. We have had so little excess of government in this country that we have forgotten that excess of government is the very antithesis of liberty. So it seems to me that the principle by which we should be guided above all others is this, that we do not want to harness men like Lee in the service of a managing government; we want to see to it that, though there is control, it is control of law and not the discretionary control of executive officials. We want to see to it that while there is the restraint of abuses, it is persons who are restrained, and not unnamed bodies of persons. There is only, historically speaking, one possible successful punishment of abuses of law, and that is, that when a wrong thing is done you find the man who did it and punish him. You can fine all the corporations there are, and fine them out of existence, and all you will have done will be to have embarrassed the commerce of the country. You will have left the men who did it free to repeat it in other combinations.

I am going to use an illustration which you can easily understand, but I am going to ask you not to misunderstand it. Suppose I could incorporate an association of burglars with the assurance that you would restrain their actions, not as individuals, but only as a corporation. Whenever a burglary occurred you would fine the corporation. They would be very much pleased with that arrangement, because it would leave them the services of their most accomplished burglars, who could fool you half the time and not be found out. Such a corporation would be willing to pay you a heavy fine for the privilege. Now I do not mean to draw a parallel between our great corporations and burglars,—that is where you are likely to misunderstand me, because I do not hold the general belief that the majority of the business men of this country are burglars; I believe, on the contrary, that the number of malicious men engaged in corporations in this country is very small. But that small number is singularly gifted, and until you have picked them out and distinguished them for punishment you have not touched the process by which they succeed in doing what they wish. You may say that this is a very difficult thing, that there is so much covert, so much undergrowth, the nation is so thickset with organizations that you cannot see them and run them to cover.

Perhaps you are right; but that does not make any difference to my argument; whether difficult, or not, it has got to be done. If you don't know enough to do it, it is none the less necessary to find the way.

What have we been doing in the last fifteen years? Trying to remedy things which we have not stopped long enough to understand.

I was talking the other day to a body of men which included a good many persons belonging to the profession to which I used to belong. I used to be a lawyer. I said to these men: "I am sure there are a great many corporation lawyers in this audience and I have something to say to them. You know exactly what is being done that ought not to be done. You complain that the legislators of this country are playing havoc with the industry of the country by trying to remedy things in the wrong way. Now, if you really want to save the corporations, you will tell the legislators you complain of what ought to be done and how. If you do not, they will continue their experiments and destroy your corporations, but having said that to you I must add that I don't expect you to have sense enough to do anything of the kind."

There is a hopeless sort of fidelity in men who are employed as advisers that prevents their seeing the coming of the deluge; and yet it is they who are to blame if it comes. If you and I had this difficult task in hand of regulating the corporations, whom would we call into counsel? The men who had handled the business. And yet they are the very men who will not yield us any service in the matter at all. They are the very men who are neglecting this great example we are recalling to-night. They are acting upon lines of self-interest, closing in the lines of self-interest as about themselves, and about those whom they represent, and forgetting those greater interests which, if they forget, they oppose, —the interests of the nation and of our common life. And so hostility has sprung up where there should be coöperation, and blunders are committed because men who know how the thing ought to be done will not give public counsel.

We must stop long enough to know what we are about and then go fearlessly forward and do it against the guilty individuals.

I think if I had an independent fortune, and could give up my present profession, I could find a delightful occupation. I would take up my residence in the city of Washington and would industriously find out from the central bureaus of inquiry what was going on in the larger business world of the United States. Then I would prepare one or two addresses upon the knowledge which I had gained and would make a careful list of the names of the gentle-who had been doing the things that ought not to be done. They could not do me any harm physically, and I woud enjoy the opinion they would have of me. If I could once get their names I would not need the assistance of the criminal law; I would only have to publish the names and prove the facts to put them out of business. Because the moral judgments of this country are as sound as they ever were, and if you direct them in the right channels they are irresistibly effective. At present we are directing them

into oratorical channels and not into legislative or
judicial channels.

The channels of legislation, the humdrum daily administration of courts of justice are the effective
channels of government, and I would rather have
government carried successfully on by such means
than hear all the fine speeches that have been uttered
by the most gifted speakers. I am not depreciating
speakers, because that is part of my own business,
and I would not ask you to look with contempt upon
the humble vocation which I attempt. But I would
look with contempt upon myself if I supposed speaking to be a kind of action.

Now, what does it mean that General Lee is accepted as a national hero? It means simply this delightful thing, that there are no sections in this
country any more; that we are a nation and are
proud of all the great heroes whom the great processes of our national life have elevated into conspicuous places of fame. I believe that the future lies
with all those men who devote themselves to national
thinking, who eschew those narrow calculations of
self-interest which affect only particular communities and try to conceive of communities as a part of a
great national life which must be purified in order
that it may be successful. For we may pile up wealth
until it exceeds all fables of riches in ancient fiction
and the nation which possesses it may yet use it to
malevolent ends. A poor nation such as the United
States was in 1812, for example, if it is in the right,
is more formidable to the world than the richest
nation in the wrong. For the rich nation in the

wrong destroys the fair work that God has permitted
and man has wrought; whereas, the poor nation, with
purified purpose, is the stronger. It looks into men's
hearts and sees the spirit there; finds some expression
of that spirit in life; bears the fine aspect of hope
and exhibits in all its purposes the irresistible quality
of rectitude. These are the things which make a
nation formidable. There is nothing so self-destruc-
tive as selfishness, and there is nothing so permanent
as the work of hands that are unselfish. You may
pile up fortunes and dissolve them, but pile up ideals
and they will never be dissolved. A quiet company
of gentlemen sitting through a dull summer in the
city of Philadelphia worked out for a poor and rural
nation an immortal constitution, which has made
statesmen all over the world feel confidence in the
political future of the race. They knew that human
liberty was a feasible basis of government.

There is always danger that certain men thinking
only of the material prospects of their section, wish-
ing to get the benefit of the tariff, it may be, or of
this thing, or of that, when it comes to the distribution of favors, will write only the history which has
been written again and again, whose reiteration has
been repeated since the world began; from which no
man will draw fresh inspiration; from which no ideal
can spring, from which no strength can be drawn.
Whereas the nation which denies itself material advantage and seeks those things which are of the spirit
works not only for each generation, but for all generations, and works in the permanent and durable
stuffs of humanity.

I spoke just now in disparagement of the vocation of the orator. I wish there were some great orator who could go about and make men drunk with this spirit of self-sacrifice. I wish there were some man whose tongue might every day carry abroad the golden accents of that creative age in which we were born a nation; accents which would ring like tones of reassurance around the whole circle of the globe, so that America might again have the distinction of showing men the way, the certain way, of achievement and of confident hope.

ABRAHAM LINCOLN: A MAN OF THE PEOPLE

ADDRESS ON THE OCCASION OF THE CELEBRATION OF
THE HUNDREDTH ANNIVERSARY OF THE BIRTH OF
ABRAHAM LINCOLN. CHICAGO, FEBRUARY 12, 1909.
TAKEN FROM "ABRAHAM LINCOLN, THE TRIBUTE OF
A CENTURY," PP. 14-30.

MY earliest recollection is of standing at my
father's gateway in Augusts, Georgia, when
I was four years old, and hearing some one pass and
say that Mr. Lincoln was elected and there was to be
war. Catching the intense tones of his excited voice,
I remember running in to ask my father what it
meant. What it meant, you need not be told. What
it meant, we shall not here to-day dwell upon. We
shall rather turn away from those scenes of struggle
and of unhappy fraternal strife, and recall what has
happened since to restore our balance, to remind us
of the permanent issues of history, to make us single-
hearted in our love of America, and united in our
purpose for her advancement. We are met here to-
day to recall the character and achievements of a
man who did not stand for strife, but for peace, and
whose glory it was to win the affection alike of those
whom he led and of those whom he opposed, as indeed
a man and a king among those who mean the right.

It is not necessary that I should rehearse for you
the life of Abraham Lincoln. It has been written in

every school book. It has been rehearsed in every family. It were to impeach your intelligence if I were to tell you the story of his life. I would rather attempt to expound for you the meaning of his life, the significance of his singular and unique career.

It is a very long century that separates us from the year of his birth. The nineteenth century was crowded with many significant events,—it seems to us in America as if it were more crowded with significant events for us than for any other nation in the world,—and that far year 1809 stands very near its opening, when men were only beginning to understand what was in store for them. It was a significant century, not only in the field of politics but in the field of thought. Do you realize that modern science is not older than the middle of the last century? Modern science came into the world to revolutionize our thinking and our material enterprises just about the time that Mr. Lincoln was uttering those remarkable debates with Mr. Douglas. The struggle which determined the life of the Union came just at the time when a new issue was joined in the field of thought, and men began to reconstruct their conceptions of the universe and of their relation to nature, and even of their relation to God. There is, I believe, no more significant century in the history of man than the nineteenth century, and its whole sweep is behind us.

That year 1809 produced, as you know, a whole group of men who were to give distinction to its annals in many fields of thought and of endeavor. To mention only some of the great men who were born in 1809: the poet Tennyson was born in that year, our own poet Edgar Allan Poe, the great Sherman, the great Mendelssohn, Chopin, Charles Darwin, William E. Gladstone, and Abraham Lincoln. Merely read that list and you are aware of the singular variety of gifts and purposes represented. Tennyson was, to my thinking, something more than a poet. We are apt to be so beguiled by the music of his verse as to suppose that its charm and power lie in its music; but there is something about the poet which makes him the best interpreter, not only of life, but of national purpose, and there is to be found in Tennyson a great body of interpretation which utters the very voice of Anglo-Saxon liberty. That fine line in which he speaks of how English liberty has "broadened down from precedent to precedent" embodies the noble slowness, the very process and the very certainty, of the forces which made men politically free in the great century in which he wrote. He was a master who saw into the heart of affairs, as well as a great musician who seemed to give them the symphony of sound.

And then there was our own Poe, that exquisite workman in the human language, that exquisite artisan in all the nice effects of speech, the man who dreamed all the odd dreams of the human imagination, and who quickened us with all the singular stories that the mind can invent, and did it all with the nicety and certainty of touch of the consummate artist.

And then there were Chopin and Mendelssohn, whose music constantly rings in our ears and lifts our spirits to new sources of delight. And there was Charles Darwin, with an insight into nature next to Newton's own; and Gladstone, who knew how to rule men by those subtle forces of oratory which shape the history of the world and determine the relations of nations to each other.

And then our Lincoln. When you read that name you are at once aware of something that distinguished it from all the rest. There was in each of those other men some special gift, but not in Lincoln. You cannot pick Lincoln out for any special characteristic. He did not have any one of those peculiar gifts that the other men on this list possessed. He does not seem to belong in a list at all; he seems to stand unique and singular and complete in himself. The name makes the same impression upon the ear that the name of Shakespeare makes, because it is as if he contained a world within himself. And that is the thing which marks the singular stature and nature of this great—and, we would fain believe, typical— American. Because when you try to describe the character of Lincoln you seem to be trying to describe a great process of nature. Lincoln seems to have been of general human use and not of particular and limited human use. There was no point at which life touched him that he did not speak back to it instantly its meaning. There was no affair that touched him to which he did not give back life, as if he had communicated a spark of fire to kindle it. The man seemed to have, slumbering in him, powers which he did not exert of his own choice, but which woke the moment they were challenged, and for

which no challenge was too great or comprehensive.
You know how slow, how almost sluggish the development of the man was. You know how those who
consorted with him in his youth noted the very thing
of which I speak. They would have told you that
Abraham Lincoln was good for nothing in particular;
and the singular fact is he *was* good for nothing in
particular—he was good for everything in general.
He did not narrow and concentrate his power, because it was meant to be diffused as the sun itself.
And so he went through his youth like a man who
has nothing to do, like a man whose mind is never
halted at any point where it becomes serious, to seize
upon the particular endeavor or occupation for which
it is intended. He went from one sort of partial
success to another sort of partial success, or, as his
contemporaries would have said, from failure to
failure, until—not until he found himself, but until,
so to say, affairs found him, and the crisis of a country seemed suddenly to match the universal gift of
his nature; until a great nature was summed up, not
in any particular business or activity, but in the affairs of a whole country. It was characteristic of
the man.

Have you ever looked at some of those singular
statues of the great French sculptor Rodin—those
pieces of marble in which only some part of a figure
is revealed and the rest is left in the hidden lines of
the marble itself; where there emerges the arm and
the bust and the eager face, it may be, of a man, but
his body disappears in the general bulk of the stone,
and the lines fall off vaguely? I have often been

made to think, in looking at those statues, of Abraham
Lincoln. There was a little disclosed in him, but not
all. You feel that he was so far from being exhausted
by the demands of his life that more remained unre-
vealed than was disclosed to our view. The lines run
off into infinity and lead the imagination into every
great conjecture. We wonder what the man might
have done, what he might have been, and we feel
that there was more promise in him when he died
than when he was born; that the force was so far
from being exhausted that it had only begun to display itself in its splendor and perfection. No man
can think of the life of Lincoln without feeling that
the man was cut off almost at his beginning.

And so it is with every genius of this kind, not
singular, but universal, because there were uses to
which it was not challenged. You feel that there is
no telling what it might have done in days to
come, when there would have been new demands
made upon its strength and upon its versatility. He
is like some great reservoir of living water which you
can freely quaff but can never exhaust. There is
something absolutely endless about the lines of such
a life.

And you will see that that very fact renders it
difficult indeed to point out the characteristics of a
man like Lincoln. How shall you describe general
human nature brought to its finest development?—
for such was this man. We say that he was honest:
men used to call him "Honest Abe." But honesty
is not a quality. Honesty is the manifestation of
character. Lincoln was honest because there was

nothing small or petty about him, and only smallness and pettiness in a nature can produce dishonesty. Such honesty is a quality of largeness. It is that openness of nature which will not condescend to subterfuge, which is too big to conceal itself. Little men run to cover and deceive you. Big men cannot and will not run to cover, and do not deceive you. Of course, Lincoln was honest. But that was not a peculiar characteristic of him; that is a general description of him. He was not small or mean, and his honesty was not produced by any calculation, but was the genial expression of the great nature that was behind it.

Then we also say of Lincoln that he saw things with his own eyes. And it is very interesting that we can pick out individual men to say that of them. The opposite of the proposition is, that most men see things with other men's eyes. And that is the pity of the whole business of the world. Most men do not see things with their own eyes. If they did they would not be so inconspicuous as they consent to be. What most persons do is to live up to formulas and opinions and believe them, and never give themselves the trouble to ask whether they are true or not; so that there is a great deal of truth in saying that the trouble is, that men believe so many things that are not so, because they have taken them at second hand; they have accepted them in the form they were given to them. They have not reëxamined them. They have not seen the world with their own eyes. But Lincoln saw it with his own eyes. And he not only saw the surface of it, but saw beneath the surface of it; for the characteristic of the seeing eye is that it is a discerning eye, seeing also that which is not caught by the surface; it penetrates to the heart of the subjects it looks upon. Not only did this man look upon life with a discerning eye. If you read of his youth and of his early manhood, it would seem that these were his only and sufficient pleasures. Lincoln seemed to covet nothing from his business except that it would give him leisure enough to do this very thing—to look at other people; to talk about them; to sit by the stove in the evening and discuss politics with them; to talk about all the things that were going on, to make shrewd, penetrating comments upon them, to speak his penetrating jests.

I had a friend once who said he seriously thought that the business of life was conversation. There is a good deal of Mr. Lincoln's early life which would indicate that he was of the same opinion. He believed that, at any rate, the most attractive business of life was conversation; and conversation, with Lincoln, was an important part of the business of life, because it was conversation which uncovered the meanings of things and illuminated the hidden places where nobody but Lincoln had ever thought of looking.

You remember the very interesting story told about Mr. Lincoln in his early practice as a lawyer. Some business firm at a distance wrote to him and asked him to look into the credit of a certain man who had asked to have credit extended to him by the firm. Mr. Lincoln went around to see the man at his place of business, and reported to this effect: that he had found the man in an office which contained one table and two chairs. "But," he added, "there is a hole in the corner that would bear looking into." That anecdote, slight as it is, is typical of Mr. Lincoln. He sometimes found the character of the man lurking in a hole; and when his speech touched that character it was illuminated; you could not frame otherwise a better characterization. That seemed to be the business of the man's life; to look at things and to comment upon them; and his comment upon them was just as fearless and just as direct as it was shrewd and penetrating.

I know some men can see anything they choose to see, but they won't say anything; who are dried up at the source by that enemy of mankind which we call Caution. God save a free country from cautious men,—men, I mean, cautious for themselves,—for cautious men are men who will not speak the truth if the speaking of it threatens to damage them. Caution is the confidential agent of selfishness.

This man had no caution. He was absolutely direct and fearless. You will say that he had very little worldly goods to lose. He did not allow himself to be encumbered by riches, therefore he could say what he pleased. You know that men who are encumbered by riches are apt to be more silent than others. They have given hostages to fortune, and for them it is very necessary to maintain the *status quo*. Now, Mr. Lincoln was not embarrassed in this way. A change of circumstances would suit him just as well as the permanency of existing circumstances.

But I am confident that if Mr. Lincoln had had the
gift of making money, he nevertheless would not have
restrained his gift for saying things; that he nevertheless would not have ignored the trammels and
despised caution and said what he thought. But one
interesting thing about Mr. Lincoln is that no matter
how shrewd or penetrating his comment, he never
seemed to allow a matter to grip him. He seemed so
directly in contact with it that he could define things
other men could not define; and yet he was detached.
He did not look upon it as if he were part of it. And
he was constantly salting all the delightful things
that he said, with the salt of wit and humour.

I would not trust a saturnine man, but I would
trust a wit; because a wit is a man who can detach
himself, and not get so buried in the matter he is
dealing with as to lose that sure and free movement
which a man can have only when he is detached. If
a man can comment upon his own misfortunes with
a touch of humour, you know that his misfortunes
are not going to subdue or kill him. You should try
to instill into every distressed friend the inclination
to hold himself off at arm's length, and should assure
him that, after all, there have been worse cases on
record. Mr. Lincoln was not under the impression
that his own misfortunes were unique, and he was
not under the impression that the misfortunes of his
fellow-men were unique or unalterable. Therefore he
was detached; therefore he was a wit; therefore he
told you a story to show that he was not so intense
upon a matter that he could not recognize the funny
side of it.

Not only that, but Lincoln was a singularly studious man—not studious in the ordinary conventional sense. To be studious in the ordinary, conventional sense, if I may judge by my observation at a university, is to do the things you have to do and not understand them particularly. But to be studious, in the sense in which Mr. Lincoln was studious, is to follow eagerly and fearlessly the curiosity of a mind which will not be satisfied unless it understands. That is a deep studiousness; that is the thing which lays bare the map of life and enables men to understand the circumstances in which they live, as nothing else can do.

And what commends Mr. Lincoln's studiousness to me is that the result of it was he did not have any theories at all. Life is a very complex thing. No theory that I ever heard propounded will match its varied pattern; and the men who are dangerous are the men who are not content with understanding, but go on to propound theories, things which will make a new pattern for society and a new model for the universe. Those are the men who are not to be trusted. Because, although you steer by the North Star, when you have lost the bearings of your compass, you nevertheless must steer in a pathway on the sea,—you are not bound for the North Star. The man who insists upon his theory insists that there is a way to the North Star, and I know, and every one knows, that there is not—at least none yet discovered. Lincoln was one of those delightful students who do not seek to tie you up in the meshes of any theory.

Such was Mr. Lincoln,—not a singular man; a

very normal man, but normal in gigantic proportions,—the whole character of him is on as great a
scale—and yet so delightfully informal in the way
it was put together—as was the great frame in which
he lived. That great, loose-jointed, angular frame
that Mr. Lincoln inhabited was a very fine symbol
of the big, loose-jointed, genial, angular nature that
was inside; angular, not in the sense of having sharp
corners upon which men might wound themselves,
but angular as nature is angular. Nature is not symmetrical like the Renaissance architecture. Nature
is an architect who does not, in the least, mind putting a very different thing on one side from what it
has put on the other. Your average architect wants
to balance his windows; to have consistency and balance in the parts. But nature is not interested in
that. Nature does what it pleases, and so did the
nature of Lincoln. It did what it pleased, and was
no more conventionalized and symmetrical than the
body of the man himself.

Mr. Lincoln belonged to a type which is fast disap-
pearing, the type of the frontiersman. And he belonged to a process which has almost disappeared
from this country. Mr. Lincoln seemed slow in his
development, but when you think of the really short
span of his life and the distance he traversed in the
process of maturing, you will see that it cannot be
said to have been a slow process. Mr. Lincoln was
bred in that part of the country—*this* part, though
we can hardly conceive it now—where States were
made as fast as men. Lincoln was made along with
the States that were growing as fast as men were.

States were born and came to their maturity, in that day, within the legal limit of twenty-one years, and the very pressure of that rapid change, the very imperious necessity of that quick process of maturing, was what made and moulded men with a speed and in a sort which have never since been matched. Here were the processes of civilization and of the building up of polities crowded into a single generation; and where such processes are crowded, men grow. Men could be picked out in the crude, and, if put in that crucible, could be refined out in a single generation into pure metal. That was the process which made Mr. Lincoln. We could not do it that way again, because that period has passed forever with us.

Mr. Lincoln could not have been born at any other time and he could not have been made in any other way. I took the liberty of saying in New York the other day that it was inconceivable that Mr. Lincoln could have been born in New York. I did not intend thereby any disparagement of New York, but simply to point the moral that he could not have been born in a finished community. He had to be produced in a community that was on the make, in the making. New York is on the make, but it is not in the making.

Mr. Lincoln, in other words, was produced by processes which no longer exist anywhere in America, and therefore we are solemnized by this question: Can we have other Lincolns? We cannot do without them. This country is going to have crisis after crisis. God send they may not be bloody crises, but they will be intense and acute. No body politic so abounding in life and so puzzled by problems as ours is can avoid moving from crisis to crisis. We must have the leadership of sane, genial men of universal use like Lincoln, to save us from mistakes and give us the necessary leadership in such days of struggle and of difficulty. And yet, such men will hereafter have to be produced among us by processes which are not characteristically American, but which belong to the whole world.

There was something essentially native, American, about Lincoln; and there will, no doubt, be something American about every man produced by the processes of America; but no such distinguished process as the process, unique and separate, of that early age can be repeated for us.

It seems to me serviceable, therefore, to ask ourselves what it is that we must reproduce in order not to lose the breed, the splendid breed, of men of this calibre. Mr. Lincoln we describe as "a man of the people," and he was a man of the people, essentially. But what do we mean by a "man of the people"? We mean a man, of course, who has his rootage deep in the experiences and the consciousness of the ordinary mass of his fellow-men; but we do not mean a man whose rootage is holding him at their level. We mean a man who, drawing his sap from such sources, has, nevertheless, risen above the level of the rest of mankind and has got an outlook over their heads, seeing horizons which they are too submerged to see; a man who finds and draws his inspiration from the common plane, but nevertheless has lifted himself to a new place of outlook and of insight; who has come out from the people and is their leader,

not because he speaks from their ranks, but because
he speaks for them and for their interests.

Browning has said:

> "A Nation is but the attempt of many
>   To rise to the completer life of one;
>   And they who live as models for the mass
>   Are singly of more value than they all."

Lincoln was of the mass, but he was so lifted and
big that all men could look upon him, until he became the "model for the mass" and was "singly of
more value than they all."

It was in that sense that Lincoln was "a man of
the people." His sources were where all the pure
springs are, but his streams flowed down into other
country and fertilized other plains, where men had
become sophisticated with the life of an older age.

A great nation is not led by a man who simply re-
peats the talk of the street-corners or the opinions
of the newspapers. A nation is led by a man who
hears more than those things; or who, rather, hearing those things, understands them better, unites
them, puts them into a common meaning; speaks, not
the rumors of the street, but a new principle for a
new age; a man in whose ears the voices of the nation
do not sound like the accidental and discordant notes
that come from the voice of a mob, but concurrent
and concordant like the united voices of a chorus,
whose many meanings, spoken by melodious tongues,
unite in his understanding in a single meaning and
reveal to him a single vision, so that he can speak

what no man else knows, the common meaning of the
common voice. Such is the man who leads a great,
free, democratic nation.

We must always be led by "men of the people,"
and therefore it behooves us to know them when we
see them. How shall we distinguish them? Judged
by this man, interpreted by this life, what is a "man
of the people"? How shall we know him when he
emerges to our view?

Well, in the first place, it seems to me that a man
of the people is a man who sees affairs as the people
see them, and not as a man of particular classes or
the professions sees them. You cannot afford to take
the advice of a man who has been too long submerged
in a particular profession,—not because you cannot
trust him to be honest and candid, but because he
has been too long immersed and submerged, and
through the inevitable pressure and circumstances of
his life has come to look upon the nation from a particular point of view. The man of the people is a
man who looks far and wide upon the nation, and is
not limited by a professional point of view. That
may be a hard doctrine; it may exclude some gentlemen ambitious to lead; but I am not trying to exclude them by any arbitrary dictum of my own;
I am trying to interpret so much as I understand of
human history, and if human history has excluded
them, you cannot blame me. Human history has
excluded them, as far as I understand it, and that is
the end of the matter. I am not excluding them. In
communities like ours, governed by general opinion
and not led by classes, not dictated to by special in-

terests, they are of necessity excluded. You will see
that it follows that a man of the people is not sub-
dued by any stuff of life that he has happened to
work in; that he is free to move in any direction his
spirit prompts. Are you not glad that Mr. Lincoln
did not succeed too deeply in any particular calling;
that he was sufficiently detached to be lifted to a
place of leadership and to be used by the whole country? Are you not glad that he had not narrowed his
view and understanding to any particular interest,—
did not think in the terms of interest but in the terms
of life? Are you not glad that he had a myriad of
contacts with the growing and vehement life of this
country, and that, because of that multiple contact,
he was, more than any one else of his generation, the
spokesman of the general opinion of his country?

Why was it that Mr. Lincoln was wiser than the
professional politicians? Because the professional
politicians had burrowed into particular burrows and
Mr. Lincoln walked on the surface and saw his fellow-
men.

Why could Mr. Lincoln smile at lawyers and turn
away from ministers? Because he had not had his
contact with life as a lawyer has, and he had not lectured his fellow-men as a minister has. He was detached from every point of view and therefore superior,—at any rate in a position to becoming superior,—to every point of view. You must have a
man of this detachable sort.

Moreover, you must not have a man, if he is to be
a man of the people, who is standardized and conventionalized. Look to it that your communities,

your great cities, do not impose too arbitrary standards upon the men whom you wish to use. Do not reduce men to standards. Let them be free. Do not compel them by conventions. Let them wear any clothes they please and look like anything they choose; let them do anything that a decent and an honest man may do without criticism; do not laugh at them because they do not look like you, or talk like you, or think like you. They are freer for that circumstance, because, as an English writer has said: "You may talk of the tyranny of Nero and Tiberius, but the real tyranny is the tyranny of your next-door neighbour. There is no tyranny like the tyranny of being obliged to be like him,"—of being considered a very singular person if you are not; of having men shrug their shoulders and say, "Singular young man, sir, singular young man; very gifted, but not to be trusted." Not to be trusted because unlike your own trustworthy self! You must take your leaders in every time of difficulty from among absolutely free men who are not standardized and conventionalized, who are at liberty to do what they think right and what they think true; that is the only kind of leadership you can afford to have.

And then, last and greatest characteristic of all, a man of the people is a man who has felt that unspoken, that intense, that almost terrifying struggle of humanity, that struggle whose object is, not to get forms of government, not to realize particular formulas or make for any definite goal, but simply to live and be free. He has participated in that struggle; he has felt the blood stream against the

tissue; he has known anxiety; he has felt that life
contained for him nothing but effort, effort from the
rising of the sun to the going down of it. He has,
therefore, felt beat in him, if he had any heart, a
universal sympathy for those who struggle, a universal understanding of the unutterable things that
were in their hearts and the unbearable burdens that
were upon their backs. A man who has that vision,
of how—

> "Now touching good, now backward hurled,
> Toils the indomitable world"—

a man like Lincoln—understands. His was part of
the toil; he had part and lot in the struggle; he knew
the uncertainty of the goal makind had but just
touched and from which they had been back; knew
that the price of life is blood, and that no man who
goes jauntily and complacently through the world
will ever touch the springs of human action. Such
a man with such a consciousness, such a universal
human sympathy, such a universal comprehension of
what life means, is your man of the people, and no
one else can be.

What shall we do? It always seems to me a poor
tribute to a great man who has been great in action,
to spend the hours of his praise by merely remem-
bering what he was; and there is no more futile
eulogy than attempted imitation. It is impossible to
imitate Lincoln, without being Lincoln; and then it
would not be an imitation. It is impossible to reproduce the characters, as it is impossible to reproduce

the circumstances of a past age. That ought to be a
truism; that ought to be evident. We live, and we
have no other choice, in this age, and the tasks of
this age are the only tasks to which we are asked to
address ourselves. We are not asked to apply our
belated wisdom to the problems and perplexities of an
age that is gone. We must have timely remedies,
suitable for the existing moment. If that be true,
the only way in which we can worthily celebrate a
great man is by showing to-day that we have not
lost the tradition of force which made former ages
great, that we can reproduce them continuously in a
kind of our own. You elevate the character of a
man like Lincoln for his fellow-men to gaze upon,
not as if it were an unattainable height, but as one
of those conspicuous objects which men erect to mark
the long lines of a survey, so that when they top the
next hill they shall see that mark standing there
where they have passed, not as something to daunt
them, but as a high point by which they can
lengthen and complete their measurements and make
sure of their ultimate goal and achievement. That
is the reason we erect the figures of men like this to
be admired and looked upon, not as if we were men
who walk backward and deplore the loss of such
figures and of such ages, but as men who keep such
heights in mind and walk forward, knowing that the
goal of the age is to scale new heights and to do
things of which their work was a mere foundation,
so that we shall live, like every other living thing,
by renewal. We shall not live by recollection, we
shall not live by trying to recall the strength of the

old tissue, but by producing a new tissue. The process of life is a process of growth, and the process of growth is a process of renewal; and it is only in this wise that we shall face the tasks of the future.

The tasks of the future call for men like Lincoln more audibly, more imperatively, than did the tasks of the time when civil war was brewing and the very existence of the Nation was in the scale of destiny. For the things that perplex us at this moment are the things which mark, I will not say a warfare, but a division among classes; and when a nation begins to be divided into rival and contestant interests by the score, the time is much more dangerous than when it is divided into only two perfectly distinguishable interests, which you can discriminate and deal with. If there are only two sides I can easily make up my mind which side to take, but if there are a score of sides then I must say to some man who is not immersed, not submerged, not caught in this struggle, "Where shall I go? What do you see? What is the movement of the mass? Where are we going? Where do you propose you should go?" It is then I need a man of the people, detached from this struggle yet cognizant of it all, sympathetic with it all, saturated with it all, to whom I can say, "How do you sum it up, what are the signs of the day, what does the morning say, what are the tasks that we must set our hands to?" We should pray, not only that we should be led by such men, but also that they should be men of the particular sweetness that Lincoln possessed.

The most dangerous thing you can have in an age

like this is a man who is intense and hot. We have
heat enough; what we want is light. Anybody can
stir up emotions, but who is master of men enough
to take the saddle and guide those awakened emotions? Anybody can cry a nation awake to the necessities of reform, but who shall frame the reform but
a man who is cool, who takes his time, who will draw
you aside for a jest, who will say: "Yes, but not
to-day, to-morrow; let us see the other man and see
what he has to say; let us hear everybody, let us
know what we are to do. In the meantime I have a
capital story for your private ear. Let me take the
strain off, let me unbend the steel. Don't let us settle
this thing by fire but let us settle it by those cool,
incandescent lights which show its real nature and
color."

The most valuable thing about Mr. Lincoln was
that in the midst of the strain of war, in the midst
of the crash of arms, he could sit quietly in his room
and enjoy a book that led his thoughts off from everything American, could wander in fields of dreams,
while every other man was hot with the immediate
contest. Always set your faith in a man who can
withdraw himself, because only the man who can
withdraw himself can see the stage; only the man
who can withdraw himself can see affairs as they are.

And so the lesson of this day is faith in the common product of the nation; the lesson of this day is
the future as well as the past leadership of men, wise
men, who have come from the people. We should not
be Americans deserving to call ourselves the fellow-
countrymen of Lincoln if we did not feel the com-

pulsion that his example lays upon us—the compulsion, not to heed him merely but to look to our own duty, to live every day as if that were the day upon which America was to be reborn and remade; to attack every task as if we had something here that was new and virginal and original, out of which we could make the very stuff of life, by integrity, faith in our fellow-men, wherever it is deserved, absolute ignorance of any obstacle that is insuperable, patience, indomitable courage, insight, universal sympathy,— with that programme opening our hearts to every candid suggestion, listening to all the voices of the nation, trying to bring in a new day of vision and of achievement.

THE SPIRIT OF LEARNING

ADDRESS DELIVERED BEFORE PHI BETA KAPPA CHAPTER
AT CAMBRIDGE, JULY 1, 1909. FROM THE "HARVARD
GRADUATES' MAGAZINE," SEPTEMBER, 1909, VOL. XVIII,
PP. 1-14.

WE have fallen of late into a deep discontent
with the college, with the life and the work
of the undergraduates in our universities. It is an
honorable discontent, bred in us by devotion, not
by captiousness or hostility or by an unreasonable
impatience to set the world right. We are not critics,
but anxious and thoughtful friends. We are neither
cynics nor pessimists, but honest lovers of a good
thing, of whose slightest deterioration we are jealous.
We would fain keep one of the finest instrumentalities
of our national life from falling short of its best,
and believe that by a little care and candor we can
do so.

The American college has played a unique part in
American life. So long as its aims were definite and
its processes authoritative it formed men who brought
to their tasks an incomparable morale, a capacity that
seemed more than individual, a power touched with
large ideals. The college has been the seat of ideals.
The liberal training which it sought to impart took
no thought of any particular profession or business,
but was meant to reflect in its few and simple dis-

ciplines the image of life and thought. Men were
bred by it to no skill or craft or calling: the discipline to which they were subjected had a more general object. It was meant to prepare them for the
whole of life rather than for some particular part of
it. The ideals which lay at its heart were the general
ideals of conduct, of right living, and right thinking, which made them aware of a world moralized by
principle, steadied and cleared of many an evil thing
by true and catholic reflection and just feeling, a
world, not of interests, but of ideas.

Such impressions, such challenges to a man's spirit,
such intimations of privilege and duty are not to be
found in the work and obligations of professional and
technical schools. They cannot be. Every calling
has its ethics, indeed, its standards of right conduct
and wrong, its outlook upon action and upon the
varied relationships of society. Its work is high and
honorable, grounded, it may be, in the exact knowledge which moralizes the processes of thought, and in
a skill which makes the whole man serviceable. But
it is notorious how deep and how narrow the absorp-
tions of the professional school are and how much
they are necessarily concentrated upon the methods
and interests of a particular occupation. The work
to be done in them is as exact, as definite, as exclusive as that of the office and the shop. Their atmosphere is the atmosphere of business, and should be.
It does not beget generous comradeships or any ardor
of altruistic feeling such as the college begets. It does
not contain that general air of the world of science
and of letters in which the mind seeks no special in-

terest, but feels every intimate impulse of the spirit
set free to think and observe and listen,—listen to all
the voices of the mind. The professional school differs from the college as middle age differs from youth.
It gets the spirit of the college only by imitation or
reminiscence or contagion. This is to say nothing to
its discredit. Its nature and objects are different
from those of the college,—as legitimate, as useful, as
necessary; but different. The college is the place of
orientation; the professional school is the place of
concentration. The object of the college is to liberalize and moralize; the object of the professional
school is to train the powers to a special task. And
this is true of all vocational study.

I am, of course, using the words liberalize and
moralize in their broadest significance, and I am very
well aware that I am speaking in the terms of an
ideal, a conception, rather than in the terms of realized fact. I have spoken, too, of what the college
did "so long as its aim were definite and its processes
authoritative," as if I were thinking of it wholly in
the past tense and wished to intimate that it was
once a very effective and ideal thing but had now
ceased to exist; so that one would suppose that I
thought the college lost out of our life and the present
a time when such influences were all to seek. But
that is only because I have not been able to say everything at once. Give me leave, and I will slowly write
in the phrases which will correct these impressions
and bring a true picture to light.

The college has lost its definiteness of aim, and has
now for so long a time affected to be too modest to

assert its authority over its pupils in any matter of prescribed study that it can no longer claim to be the nurturing mother it once was; but the college is neither dead nor moribund, and it has made up for its relaxed discipline and confused plans of study by many notable gains, which, if they have not improved its scholarship, have improved the health and the practical morals of the young gentlemen who resort to it, have enhanced their vigor and quickened their whole natures. A freer choice of studies has imparted to it a stir, an air of freedom and individual initiative, a wealth and variety of instruction which the old college altogether lacked. The development of athletic sports and the immoderate addiction of undergraduates to stimulating activities of all sorts, academic and unacademic, which improve their physical habits, fill their lives with interesting objects, sometimes important, and challenge their powers of organization and practical management, have unquestionably raised the tone of morals and of conduct in our colleges and have given them an interesting, perhaps valuable, connection with modern society and the broader popular interests of the day. No one need regret the breaking-up of the dead levels of the old college, the introduction and exaltation of modern studies, or the general quickening of life which has made of our youngsters more manly fellows, if less docile pupils. There had come to be something rather narrow and dull and morbid, no doubt, about the old college before its day was over. If we gain our advances by excessive reactions and changes which change too much, we at least gain them, and should be careful not to lose the advantage of them.

Nevertheless, the evident fact is, that we have now for a long generation devoted ourselves to promoting changes which have resulted in all but complete disorganization, and it is our plain and immediate duty to form our plans for reorganization. We must reëxamine the college, reconceive it, reorganize it. It is the root of our intellectual life as a nation. It is not only the instrumentality through which we must effect all the broad preliminary work which underlies sound scholarship; it is also our chief instrumentality of catholic enlightenment, our chief means for giving widespread stimulation to the whole intellectual life of the country and supplying ourselves with men who shall both comprehend their age and duty and know how to serve them supremely well. Without the American college our young men would be too exclusively shut in to the pursuit of individual interests, would lose the vital contacts and emulations which awaken them to those larger achievements and sacrifices which are the highest objects of education in a country of free citizens, where the welfare of the commonwealth springs out of the character and the informed purposes of the private citizen. The college will be found to lie somewhere very near the heart of American social training and intellectual and moral enlightenment.

The process is familiar to every one by which the disintegration was brought about which destroyed the old college with its fixed disciplines and ordered life and gave us our present problem of reorganization and recovery. It centred in the break-up of the old curriculum and the introduction of the principle that the student was to select his own studies from a great variety of courses, as great a variety as the resources of the college and the supply of teachers available made possible. But the change could not in the nature of things stop with the plan of study. It held at its heart a tremendous implication: the implication of full manhood on the part of the pupil, and all the untrammelled choices of manhood. The pupil who was mature and well informed enough to study what he chose was also by necessary implication mature enough to be left free to *do* what he pleased, to choose his own associations and ways of life outside the curriculum without restraint or suggestion; and the varied, absorbing college life of our day sprang up as the natural offspring of the free election of studies.

There went along with the relaxation of rule as to what undergraduates should study, therefore, an almost absolute divorce between the studies and the life of the college, its business and its actual daily occupations. The teacher ceased to look upon himself as related in any responsible way to the life of his pupils, to what they should be doing and thinking of between one class exercise and another, and conceived his whole duty to have been performed when he had given his lecture and afforded those who were appointed to come the opportunity to hear and heed it if they chose. The teachers of this new régime, moreover, were most of them trained for their teaching work in German universities, or in American universities in which the methods, the points of view, the spirit, and the object of the German universities were, consciously or unconsciously, reproduced. They think of their pupils, therefore, as men already disciplined by some general training such as the German gymnasium gives, and seeking in the university special acquaintance with particular studies, as an introduction to special fields of information and inquiry. They have never thought of the university as a community of teachers and pupils: they think of it, rather, as a body of teachers and investigators to whom those may resort who seriously desire specialized kinds of knowledge. They are specialists imported into an American system which has lost its old point of view and found no new one suitable to the needs and circumstances of America. They do not think of living with their pupils and affording them the contacts of culture; they are only accessible to them at stated periods and for a definite and limited service; and their teaching is an interruption to their favorite work of research.

Meanwhile, the constituency of the college has wholly changed. It is not only the bookish classes who now send their sons to college, but also the men of business and of affairs, who expect their sons to follow in their own footsteps and do work with which books have little connection. In the old days of which I have spoken most young men who went to college expected to enter one or other of the learned professions, expected to have to do with books and some of the more serious kinds of learning all their lives. Books were their proper introduction to the work that lay before them; learning was their natural discipline and preparation. But nowadays the men who are looking forward to the learned professions are in a minority at the college. Most undergraduates come out of an atmosphere of business and wish a breeding which is consonant with it. They do not wish learning. They wish only a certain freshening of their faculties for the miscellaneous contacts of life, a general acquaintance with what men are doing and saying in their own generation, a certain facility in handling themselves and in getting on with their fellows. They are much more interested in the incidental associations of college life than in the main intellectual occupations of the place. They want to be made men of, not scholars; and the life led at college is as serviceable for that as any of the tasks set in the class-room. If they want what the formal teaching offers them at all, it is for some definite and practical purpose connected with the calling they expect to follow, the business they expect to engage in. Such pupils are specially unsuitable for such teachers.

Here, then, is our situation. Here is the little world of teachers and pupils, athletic associations, musical and literary clubs, social organizations and societies for amusement, class-room and playground, of which we must make analysis, out of which we must get a new synthesis, a definite aim, and new processes of authoritative direction, losing nothing that has been gained, recovering what has been lost. All the fresh elements we have gained are valuable, many of the new points of view are those from which we must look upon the whole task and function of the college if we would see it truly; but we have fallen upon an almost hopeless confusion and an utter dispersion of energy. We must pull the whole inorganic thing together under a new conception of what the college must be and do.

The chief and characteristic mistake which the teachers and governors of our colleges have made in these latter days has been that they have devoted themselves and their plans too exclusively to the business, the very commonplace business, of instruction, to well-conceived lectures and approved classroom method, and have not enough regarded the life of the mind. The mind does not live by instruction. It is no prolix gut to be stuffed. The real intellectual life of a body of undergraduates, if there be any, manifests itself, not in the class-room, but in what they do and talk of and set before themselves as their favorite objects between classes and lectures. You will see the true life of a college in the evenings, at the dinner-table or beside the fire in the groups that gather and the men that go off eagerly to their work, where youths get together and let themselves go upon their favorite themes,—in the effect their studies have upon them when no compulsion of any kind is on them and they are not thinking to be called to a reckoning of what they know.

The effects of learning are its real tests, the real tests alike of its validity and of its efficacy. The mind can be driven, but that is not life. Life is voluntary or unconscious. It is breathed in out of a sustaining atmosphere. It is shaped by environment. It is habitual, continuous, productive. It does

not consist in tasks performed, but in powers gained
and enhanced. It cannot be communicated in class-
rooms if its aim and end is the class-room. Instruction is not its source, but only its incidental means
and medium.

Here is the key to the whole matter: the object
of the college, as we have known and used and loved
it in America, is not scholarship (except for the few,
and for them only by way of introduction and first
orientation), but the intellectual and spiritual life.
Its life and discipline are meant to be a process of
preparation, not a process of information. By the
intellectual and spiritual life I mean the life which
enables the mind to comprehend and make proper use
of the modern world and all its opportunities. The
object of a liberal training is not learning, but discipline and the enlightenment of the mind. The edu-
cated man is to be discovered by his point of view,
by the temper of his mind, by his attitude towards
life and his fair way of thinking. He can see, he
can discriminate, he can combine ideas and perceive
whither they lead; he has insight and comprehension.
His mind is a practised instrument of appreciation.
He is more apt to contribute light than heat to a discussion, and will oftener than another show the power
of uniting the elements of a difficult subject in a
whole view; he has the knowledge of the world which
no one can have who knows only his own generation
or only his own task.

What we should seek to impart in our colleges,
therefore, is not so much learning itself as the spirit
of learning. You can impart that to young men;

and you can impart it to them in the three or four years at your disposal. It consists in the power to distinguish good reasoning from bad, in the power to digest and interpret evidence, in a habit of catholic observation and a preference for the non-partisan point of view, in an addiction to clear and logical processes of thought and yet an instinctive desire to interpret rather than to stick in the letter of the reasoning, in a taste for knowledge and a deep respect for the integrity of the human mind. It is citizenship of the world of knowledge, but not ownership of it. Scholars are the owners of its varied plots, in severalty.

If we recognize and accept these ideas, this conception of the function and the possibilities of the college, there is hope of a general understanding and accommodation. At present there is a fundamental misunderstanding. The teachers in our colleges are men of learning and conceive it their duty to impart learning; but their pupils do not desire it, and the parents of their pupils do not desire it for them. They desire something else which the teacher has little thought of giving, generally thinks it no part of his function to give. Many of the parents of our modern undergraduates will frankly tell you that what they want for their sons is not so much what they will get in the class-room as something else, which they are at a loss to define, which they will get from the associations of college life: and many more would say the same thing if they were equally ingenuous. I know what they mean, and I am free to say that I sympathize with them. They under-

stand that all that their boys get in the class-room
is instruction in certain definite bodies of knowledge;
that all they are expected to bring away from their
lectures and recitations is items of learning. They
have consorted with college men, if they are not college bred themselves, and know how very soon items
of knowledge slip away from them, no matter how
faithful and diligent they may have been in accumulating them when they were students. They observe
that that part of the college acquisition is very soon
lost. College graduates will tell you without shame
or regret, within ten years of their graduation, that
they remember practically nothing of what they
learned in the class-room; and yet in the very same
breath they will tell you that they would not have
lost what they did get in college for anything in the
world; and men who did not have the chance to go
to college will everywhere be found to envy them,
perceiving that college-bred men have something
which they have not. What have they got, if learning is to be left out of the reckoning? They have got
manliness, certainly, *esprit de corps,* the training of
generous comradeships, a notable development of their
social faculties and of their powers of appreciation;
and they have lived under the influence of mental
tasks of greater or less difficulty, have got from the
class-room itself, from a quiet teacher here and there,
some intimation, some touch of the spirit.of learning.
If they have not, they have got only what could no
doubt be got from association with generous, self-
respecting young men anywhere. Attendance on the
exercises of the college was only a means of keeping

them together for four years, to work out their comradeships and their mutual infections.

I said just now that I sympathized with men who
said that what they wanted for their sons in college
was not what they got in the class-room so much as
what they got from the life and associations of the
place; but I agree with them only if what is to be
got in the class-room is nothing more than items of
knowledge likely to be quickly lost hold of. I agree
with them; but I see clearly what they are blindly
feeling after. They should desire chiefly what their
sons are to get out of the life and associations of the
place; but that life and those associations should be
freighted with things they do not now contain. The
processes of life, the contagions of association, are
the only things that have ever got any real or permanent hold on men's minds. These are the conducting media for every effect we seek to work on
the human spirit. The undergraduate should have
scholars for teachers. They should hold his attention
steadily upon great tested bodies of knowledge and
should insist that he make himself acquainted with
them, if only for the nonce. But they will give him
nothing he is likely to carry with him through life
if they stop with formal instruction, however thorough or exacting they may make it. Their permanent
effects will be wrought upon his spirit. Their teaching will follow him through life only if they reveal
to him the meaning, the significance, the essential
validity of what they are about, the motives which
prompt it, the processes which verify it. They will
rule him, not by what they know and inform him

of, but by the spirit of the things they expound. And
that spirit they cannot convey in any formal manner.
They can convey it only atmospherically, by making
their ideals tell in some way upon the whole spirit
of the place.

How shall their pupils carry their spirit away with
them, or the spirit of the things they teach, if beyond
the door of the class-room the atmosphere will not
contain it? College is a place of initiation. Its effects are atmospheric. They are wrought by impression, by association, by emulation. The voices which
do not penetrate beyond the doors of the class-room
are lost, are ineffectual, are void of consequence and
power. No thought will obtain or live there for the
transmission of which the prevailing atmosphere is a
non-conducting medium. If young gentlemen get
from their years at college only manliness, *esprit de
corps,* a release of their social gifts, a training in
give and take, a catholic taste in men, and the standards of true sportsmen, they have gained much, but
they have not gained what a college should give them.
It should give them insight into the things of the
mind and of the spirit, a sense of having lived and
formed their friendships amidst the gardens of the
mind where grows the tree of the knowledge of good
and evil, a consciousness of having taken on them
the vows of true enlightenment and of having under-
gone the discipline, never to be shaken off, of those
who seek wisdom in candor, with faithful labour and
travail of spirit.

These things they cannot get from the class-room
unless the spirit of the class-room is the spirit of the

place as well and of its life; and that will never be
until the teacher comes out of the class-room and
makes himself a part of that life. Contact, com-
panionship, familiar intercourse is the law of life for
the mind. The comradeships of undergraduates will
never breed the spirit of learning. The circle must
be widened. It must include the older men, the teachers, the men for whom life has grown more serious
and to whom it has revealed more of its meanings.
So long as instruction and life do not merge in our
colleges, so long as what the undergraduates do and
what they are taught occupy two separate, air-tight
compartments in their consciousness, so long will the
college be ineffectual.

Looked at from the point of view at which I stand
in all that I have been saying, some of the proposals
made in our day for the improvement of the college
seem very strangely conceived. It has been proposed,
for example, to shorten the period of general study
in college to (say) two years, and let the student
who has gone the distance our present sophomores
have gone enter at once upon his professional studies
or receive his certificate of graduation. I take it for
granted that those who have formulated this proposal
never really knew a sophomore in the flesh. They
say, simply, that the studies of our present sophomores are as advanced as the studies of seniors were
in the great days of our grandfathers, and that most
of our present sophomores are as old as our grandfathers were when they graduated from the pristine
college we so often boast of; and I dare say that is
all true enough. But what they do not know is, that

our sophomore is at the age of twenty no more mature
than the sophomore of that previous generation was
at the age of seventeen or eighteen. The sap of manhood is rising in him but it has not yet reached his
head. It is not what a man is studying that makes
him a sophomore or a senior: it is the stage the college process has reached in him. A college, the
American college, is not a body of studies: it is a
process of development. It takes, if our observation
can be trusted, at least four years for the completion
of that process, and all four of those years must be
college years. They cannot be school years: they
cannot be combined with school years. The school
process is an entirely different one. The college is
a process of slow evolution from the schoolboy and
the schoolboy's mental attitude into the man and his
entirely altered view of the world. It can be accomplished only in the college environment. The
environment is of the essence of the whole effect.

If you wish to create a college, therefore, and are
wise, you will seek to create a life. We have allowed ourselves to grow very anxious and to feel very
helpless about college athletics. They play too large
a part in the life of the undergraduate, we say; and
no doubt they do. There are many other things which
play too large a part in that life, to the exclusion
of intellectual interests and the dissipation of much
excellent energy: amusements of all kinds, social pre-
occupations of the most absorbing sort, a multitude
of activities which have nothing whatever to do with
the discipline and enlightenment of the mind. But
that is because they are left a free field. Life, at

college, is one thing, the work of the college another, entirely separate and distinct. The life is the field that is left free for athletics not only, but also for every other amusement and diversion. Studies are no part of that life, and there is no competition. Study is the work which interrupts the life, introduces an embarrassing and inconsistent element into it. The faculty has no part in the life; it organizes the interruption, the interference.

This is not to say that there are not a great many undergraduates seriously interested in study, or that it is impossible or even difficult to make the majority of them, the large majority, pass the tests of the examinations. It is only saying that the studies do not spring out of the life of the place and are hindered by it, must resist its influences if they would flourish. I have no jealousy of athletics: it has put wholesome spirit into both the physical and the mental life of our undergraduates. There are fewer morbid boys in the new college which we know than there were in the old college which our fathers knew; and fewer prigs, too, no doubt. Athletics are indispensable to the normal life of young men, and are in themselves wholesome and delightful, besides. In another atmosphere, the atmosphere of learning, they could be easily subordinated and assimilated. The reason they cannot be now is that there is nothing to assimilate them, nothing by which they can be digested. They make their own atmosphere unmolested. There is no direct competition.

The same thing may be said, for it is true, of all the other amusements and all the social activities of the little college world. Their name is legion: they are very interesting; most of them are in themselves quite innocent and legitimate; many of them are thoroughly worth while. They now engross the attention and absorb the energies of most of the finest, most spirited, most gifted youngsters in the undergraduate body, men fit to be scholars and masters in many fields, and for whom these small things are too trivial a preparation. They would not do so if other things which would be certain to grip these very men were in competition with them, were known and spoken of and pervasive in the life of the college outside the class-room; but they are not. The field is clear for all these little activities, as it is clear for athletics. Athletics has no serious competitor except these amusements and petty engrossments; they have no serious competitor except athletics. The scholar is not in the game. He keeps modestly to his class-room and his study and must be looked up and asked questions if you would know what he is thinking about. His influence can be set going only by the deliberate effort of the undergraduate himself who looks him up and stirs him. He deplores athletics and all the other absorbing and non-academic pursuits which he sees drawing the attention of his pupils off from study and serious preparation for life, but he will not enter into competition with them. He has never dreamed of such a thing; and, to tell the truth, the life of the place is organized in such a way as to make it hardly possible for him to do so. He is therefore withdrawn and ineffectual.

It is the duty of university authorities to make of

the college a society, of which the teacher will be as
much, and as naturally, a member as the undergraduate. When that is done other things will fall into
their natural places, their natural relations. Young
men are capable of great enthusiasms for older men
whom they have learned to know in some human,
unartificial way, whose quality they have tasted in
unconstrained conversation, the energy and beauty of
whose characters and aims they have learned to ap-
preciate by personal contact; and such enthusiasms
are often amongst the strongest and most lasting influences of their lives. You will not gain the affection
of your pupil by anything you do for him, impersonally, in the class-room. You may gain his admiration and vague appreciation, but he will tie to
you only for what you have shown him personally
or given him in intimate and friendly service.

Certain I am that it is impossible to rid our colleges of these things that compete with study and
drive out the spirit of learning by the simple device
of legislation, in which, as Americans, we have so
childish a confidence; or, at least, that, if we did succeed in driving them out, did set our home in order
and sweep and garnish it, other equally distracting
occupants would crowd in to take their places. For
the house would be empty. There must be life as well
as study. The question is, not of what are we to
empty it, but with what must we fill it? We must
fill it with the things of the mind and of the spirit;
and that we can do by introducing into it men for
whom these things are supremely interesting, the
main objects of life and endeavour, teachers who will

not seem pedagogues but friends, and who can by the gentle infection of friendliness make thought a general contagion. Do that; create the atmosphere and the contacts of a society made up of men young and old, mature and adolescent, serious and gay, and you will create an emulation, a saturation, a vital union of parts in a common life, in which all questions of subordination and proportion will solve themselves. So soon as the things which now dissipate and distract and dissolve our college life *feel* the things which should coördinate and regulate and inspire it in direct contact with them, *feel* their ardour and their competition, they will fall into their proper places, will become pleasures and cease to be occupations, will delight our undergraduate days, but not monopolize them. They are exaggerated now because they are separated and do not exchange impulses with those greater things of whose presence they are sometimes hardly conscious.

No doubt there are many ways in which this vital association may be effected, but all wise and successful ways will have this in common, that they will abate nothing of the freedom and self-government which have so quickened and purified our colleges in these recent days of change, will have no touch of school surveillance in them. You cannot force companionships upon undergraduates, if you treat them like men. You can only create the conditions, set up the organization, which will make them natural. The scholar should not need a statute behind him. The spirit of learning should not covet the support of the spirit and organization of the nursery. It will prevail of its own grace and power if you will but give it a chance, a conducting medium, an air in which it can move and breathe freely without effort of self-consciousness. If it cannot, I, for one, am willing to lend it artificial assistance. It must take its chances in the competition and win on its merits, under the ordinary rules of the game of life, where the most interesting man attracts attention, the strongest personality rules, the best organized force predominates, the most admirable thing wins allegiance. We are not seeking to force a marriage between knowledge and pleasure; we are simply trying to throw them a great deal together in the confidence that they will fall in love with one another. We are seeking to expose the undergraduate when he is most susceptible to the best and most stimulating influences of the university in the hope and belief that no sensible fellow fit for a career can resist the infection.

My plea, then, is this: that we now deliberately set ourselves to make a home for the spirit of learning: that we reorganize our colleges on the lines of this simple conception, that a college is not only a body of studies but a mode of association; that its courses are only its formal side, its contacts and contagions its realities. It must become a community of scholars and pupils,—a free community but a very real one, in which democracy may work its reasonable triumphs of accommodation, its vital processes of union. I am not suggesting that young men be dragooned into becoming scholars or tempted to become pedants, or have any artificial compulsion whatever put upon

them, but only that they be introduced into the high
society of university ideals, be exposed to the hazards
of stimulating friendships, be introduced into the
ease comradeships of the republic of letters. By this
means the class-room itself might some day come to
seem a part of life.

THE TARIFF MAKE-BELIEVE

FROM THE "NORTH AMERICAN REVIEW," OCTOBER, 1909,
VOL. CXC, PP. 535-556.

THE wrong settlement of a great public question is no settlement at all. The Payne-Aldrich tariff bill, therefore, which its authors would fain regard as a settlement of the tariff question, is no settlement at all. It is miscellaneously wrong in detail and radically wrong in principle. It disturbs more than it settles, and by its very failure to settle forces the tariff question forward into a new and much more acute stage.

It is so obviously impossible to settle the question satisfactorily in the way these gentlemen have attempted to settle it; it is so evident that men of their mind and with their attitude towards the economic interests of the country can never settle it that thinking men of every kind realize at last that new men and new principles of action must be found. These gentlemen do not know the way and cannot find it. They "revised" the tariff, indeed, but by a method which was a grand make-believe from beginning to end. They may have convinced themselves of the intelligence and integrity of the process, but they have convinced nobody else. The country must now go to the bottom of the matter and obtain what it wants.

It has gone to the bottom of it at some points already, and the process will be carried very far before it is through with it. In the first place, it is the general opinion throughout the country that this particular revision was chiefly pretense, and that it is the first time that we have had tariff legislation of this kind. The McKinley tariff bill and the Dingley tariff bill, whatever may be thought of their wisdom or of their validity as acts of statesmanship, were unquestionably frank and genuine. There was no concealment or make-believe about either their purpose or their character. No doubt many things were accomplished by them of which the public knew nothing and was intended to know nothing. Not all the advantages gained by this, that or the other industry from legislation of that kind could be explained to the public without creating inconvenient comment and startling questions that might cut very deep; but that is true of all legislation which is meant to give particular classes of citizens a special economic assistance or advantage. Private favours will inevitably creep in. But no one was deceived. The men who put those measures through had no doubt that they had the support of the country in doing so. They gave the country what they thought opinion would sustain; gave it what they honestly supposed that it wanted. But no one who is capable of assessing opinion now can possibly claim that that is what the men who were behind the Payne-Aldrich legislation did. They knew that they were not giving the country what it wanted, and the more thoughtful and statesmanlike among them deeply re-

gretted that they could not. There was a process
almost of haphazard in the construction of the House
bill, and mere false leadership and chicanery produced the bill which the Senate substituted for it and
which largely prevailed in conference.

The methods by which tariff bills are constructed
have now become all too familiar and throw a significant light on the character of the legislation involved. Debate in the Houses has little or nothing
to do with it. The process by which such a bill is
made is private, not public; because the reasons
which underlie many of the rates imposed are private.
The stronger faction of the Ways and Means Committee of the House makes up the preliminary bill,
with the assistance of "experts" whom it permits
the industries most concerned to supply for its guidance. The controlling members of the committee also
determine what amendments, if any, shall be accepted, either from the minority faction of the committee or from the House itself. It permits itself to
be dictated to, if at all, only by the imperative action
of a party caucus. The stronger faction of the
Finance Committee of the Senate, in like fashion,
frames the bill which it intends to substitute for the
one sent up from the House. It is often to be found
at work on it before any bill reaches it from the
popular chamber. The compromise between the two
measures is arranged in private conference by conferees drawn from the two committees. What takes
place in the committees and in the conference is confidential. It is considered impertinent for reporters
to inquire. It is admitted to be the business of the

manufacturers concerned, but not the business of the public, who are to pay the rates. The debates which the country is invited to hear in the open sessions of the Houses are merely formal. They determine nothing and disclose very little.

It is the policy of silence and secrecy, indeed, with regard to the whole process that makes it absolutely inconsistent with every standard of public duty and political integrity. If the newspapers published and the public read even the debates, empty of significance as they generally are, the entire country would presently realize how flagrant the whole make-believe is. The committees under whose guidance the bills are put through the House disclose nothing that is not wrung from them by members who have made investigations of their own and who insist upon having their questions answered; and there are few enough who have the audacity or take the trouble. But here and there a fact is dragged out, and before the encounters of debate are over enough has been brought to the light to make extremely instructive reading. It is devoutly to be wished,—merely to cite examples,—that every voter in the United States had read, or would yet read, the debates in the Senate on the duty on electric carbons,—the carbons used in the arc-lights in all our cities,—and on the duty on razors. Every detail is a commentary on the whole depressing business.

One extraordinary circumstance of the debates in the Senate should receive more than a passing allusion. The Republican party platform had promised that the tariff rates should be revised and that the

standard of revision should be the differences between
the cost of producing the various articles affected in
this country and in the countries with which our
manufacturers compete. One of our chief industrial
competitors is now Germany, with its extraordinary
skill in manufacture and the handicrafts and its
formidable sagacity in foreign trade; and the Department of State, in order to enable Congress the more
intelligently to fulfill the promises of the party, had,
at the suggestion of the President, requested the German Government to furnish it with as full information as possible about the rates of wages paid in the
leading industries in that country,—wages being
known, of course, to be one of the largest items in
the cost of production. The German Government of
course complied, with its usual courtesy and thoroughness, transmitting an interesting report, each
portion of which was properly authenticated and
vouched for. The Department of State placed it at
the disposal of the Finance Committee of the Senate.
But Senators tried in vain to ascertain what it contained. Mr. Aldrich spoke of it contemptuously as
"anonymous," which of course it was not, as "unof-
ficial," and even as an impertinent attempt, on the
part of the German Government, to influence our
tariff legislation. It was only too plain that the con-
tents of the report made the members of the controlling faction of the Finance Committee very uncomfortable indeed. It undoubtedly showed, what
independent private inquiries readily enough confirm, that the wages paid to skilled laborers in Germany are practically as great as those paid in the

United States, the difference in the cost of living in the two countries being taken into consideration. To have made it public would have been to upset half the arguments for the rates proposed with which the committee had been misinforming the country. It would no doubt have explained, for example, why the skilled grinders of Solingen do not think it worth their while to emigrate to America and oblige almost all razor-makers in other countries to send their blades to them to be ground,—and many another matter left studiously undebated, unexplained, about which Senators had been asking for information. It would have proved that the leaders of the party were deliberately breaking its promise to the country. It was, therefore, thrown into a pigeon-hole and disregarded. It was a private document.

In pursuance of the same policy of secrecy and private management, the bill was filled with what those who discovered them were good-natured or cynical enough to call "jokers,"—clauses whose meaning did not lie upon the surface, whose language was meant not to disclose its meaning to the members of the Houses who were to be asked to enact them into law, but only to those by whom the law was to be administered after its enactment. This was one of the uses to which the "experts" were put whom the committees encouraged to advise them. They knew the technical words under which meanings could be hidden, or the apparently harmless words which had a chance to go unnoted or unchallenged. Electric carbons had been taxed at ninety cents per hundred; the new bill taxed them at seventy cents per hundred *feet,*—an apparent reduction if the word feet went unchallenged. It came very near escaping the attention of the Senate, and did quite escape the attention of the general public, who paid no attention at all to the debates, that the addition of the word feet almost doubled the existing duty.

The hugest practical joke of the whole bill lay in the so-called maximum and minimum clause. The schedules as they were detailed in the bill and presented to the country, through the committees and the newspapers,—the schedules by which it was made believe that the promise to the country of a "downward" revision was being kept by those responsible for the bill, were only the minimum schedules. There lay at the back of the measure a maximum provision about which very little was said, but the weight of which the country may come to feel as a very serious and vexatious burden in the months to come. In the case of articles imported from countries whose tariff arrangements discriminate against the United States, the duties are to be put at a maximum which is virtually prohibitive. The clause is a huge threat. Self-respecting countries do not yield to threats or to "impertinent efforts, on the part of other Governments, to affect their tariff legislation." Where the threat is not heeded we shall pay heavier duties than ever, heavier duties than any previous Congress ever dared impose.

When it is added that not the least attempt was made to alter the duties on sugar by which every table in the country is taxed for the benefit of the Sugar Trust, but just now convicted of criminal prac-

tices in defrauding the Government in this very matter; that increased rates were laid on certain classes
of cotton goods for the benefit, chiefly, of the manufacturers of New England, from which the dominant
party always counts upon getting votes, and that the
demand of the South, from which it does not expect
to get them, for free cotton bagging was ignored;
that the rates on wool and woollen goods, a tax which
falls directly upon the clothing of the whole population of the country, were maintained unaltered; and
that relief was granted at only one or two points,—
by conceding free hides and almost free iron ore,
for example,—upon which public opinion had been
long and anxiously concentrated; and granted only
at the last moment upon the earnest solicitation of
the President,—nothing more need be said to demonstrate the insincerity, the uncandid, designing, un-
patriotic character of the whole process. It was not
intended for the public good. It was intended for
the benefit of the interests most directly and selfishly
concerned.

There was noticeable confusion in the counsels of
the dominant party. Some said this, some said that.
Many were anxious, probably a majority in the House,
to fulfill in entire good faith the promise their party
convention had given in its platform and the President had so frankly interpreted and repeated; others
were willing, some were eager, to evade it. Their
leaders led them by the way of evasion. I do not
know whether they were conscious of doing so or not.
It need make no difference to the country whether
they were or not: it is only the fact that interests it,

however the fact may affect individuals. If the leaders of the Republican party were not aware that they were seeking a way of evasion, they have an unusual capacity for deceiving themselves; if they were they did not deal honestly by the country. Either alternative proves them wholly unserviceable and untrustworthy. We need not stop, therefore, to choose between the alternatives: for we are not discussing their characters, but the present interests of the country with regard to the tariff. The question that interests us is this: How out of this confusion of counsel was an agreement reached, and why was the agreement that which the leaders of the Houses desired rather than that which the rank and file of the party would have honestly preferred? What, when its policies are in debate within its own ranks, finally determines the course the Republican party will take in a matter like this?

I know, of course, as every one does, how great the power of the Speaker of the House is, and the great and sinister hold the chairman of the Finance Committee of the Senate has upon the legislative machinery of that body, whatever signs of apparent independence it may show in the open processes of debate. It is matter of common knowledge what Mr. Cannon and Mr. Aldrich would prefer to have the House do when any question of this sort is under consideration. But these men represent forces, they do not constitute them. The forces that control the Republican party lie outside of them. They are only the spokesmen of those forces. Why do the rank and file of the Republican members still, in this day of change, find themselves unable to make an independent choice in a matter like this, of capital importance to their party and to the country? They do not mistake the signs of the times. Why, then, are they impotent?

The question can be answered very frankly, and, I hope, without partisan bias and without offense to honourable men whose principles I would not presume to call in question. The Republican party is old at the business of tariff-making and has established a business constituency. Its leaders feel that they must satisfy that constituency, and they force their followers to follow them by very concrete and practical arguments. It has come to a point where they have grown very stubborn and short-sighted in their loyalty to their constituency, but that is hardly to be wondered at. The loyalty is of long standing and has become a fundamental asset, as it seems to them, of party business.

The business of tariff-making naturally grows more and more complex, naturally comes to involve a greater and greater complexity of interests. Those who conduct it extend their clientage from generation to generation, to make sure that they have clients enough. Whatever principle may underlie tariff-making, and however valid that principle may be, however fundamental to the general development and prosperity of the country, tariff schedules arranged for "protection" are governmental favours. Those who make them, though acting for the nation, are the patrons of the industries favoured: they dispense the largess of the Government, and those who receive the favours will be their partisans and followers so long as the favours continue. The relation cannot be avoided. The only thing that can be avoided is the corrupting influence of the relationship, and that can be avoided only by very strong men. A political party cannot withstand it for many generations together: cannot, I mean, withstand the gradual corruption of its will,—the temptation to make use of the patronage it dispenses for the perpetuation of the power it derives from it, the unfailing support at the elections of the wealthiest and most influential classes of the country.

Here, in a protective tariff, are the entrenchments of Special Privilege, and every beneficiary will of course crowd into them on the day of battle, determined to keep his own. Shall a man not defend what he has?

I am not seeking to point a moral. Neither am I drawing up an indictment of the Republican party. I am merely outlining the natural history of a governmental policy whose prime object is to make particular industries safe against competition. Parties are capital epitomes of human nature; and I dare say that any other party that espoused this principle of legislation would use it for party advantage in the same way. My point is rather how it has been used than who has used it. Its uses and effects are plain,—painfully plain now. Its use is to extend to certain undertakings Government favour and assistance; its effect has been to build up special privilege. No doubt the country will have to hold those responsible who managed the business; but its real interest

will not be in punishing them, many of them honest
and public-spirited enough, but in getting rid of special privilege. That it has made up its mind to do.
It now only seeks the best and most effectual way.

It sees plainly enough, at last, that the place to
begin is the tariff. That it saw before the last Presidential election; but Mr. Cannon and Mr. Aldrich
have managed between them to make it more evident
than ever before. They have executed their purpose,
not wisely, but too well. A day of judgment is at
hand.

> "The sword of Heaven is not in haste to smite,
>   Nor yet doth linger."

The purpose of the people has much the same habit.
Perhaps it *is* the sword of Heaven!

It is not a question of schedules. It is possible that
by reasonable schedules,—by a minimum of favouritism and make-believe,—the tariff-makers of the special session might have quieted the country,—might
have induced it to let the troublesome and perplex-
ing subject drop for a decade or two. But it would
have been only a stay of judgment. The essential
wrong would still have cried out to be righted. And
the essential wrong is this: that, except for a few
men who have been fairly hynotized by a system
which they have accepted as political gospel since
their youth, it has ceased to be a matter of principle
at all and has become merely a method of granting
favours. The favours are obtained in two ways—by
"influence" and by supplication of a kind for which

there is no classical or strictly parliamentary designation. In the vulgar, it is called "the baby act."

What "influence" consists of is a very occult matter, into which the public is not often privileged to inquire. It is compounded of various things, in varying proportions: of argument based upon the facts of industry and of commercial interest, of promises of political support of campaign contributions, not explicitly given upon condition, but often spoken of by way of reminder, of personal "pressure" through the channels of old friendships and new alliances,—of things too intimate to mention,—though not, I believe, even in the minds of the most cynical and suspicious, of direct bribes. There is seldom any question of personal corruption. It is wholly a question of party corruptions, so far as it is a question of corruption at all.

The "baby act" consists in resorting to the Ways and Means Committee of the House and the Finance Committee of the Senate with pitiful tales, hard-luck stories, petitions for another chance, as the hosiery-makers did at the special sessions. It is an act very unpalatable to American pride, and yet very frequently indulged in with no appearance of shame. "Foreigners make better goods," is the burden of its cry, "pay smaller wages, and can add the ocean freights to their price and still beat us in our own markets." It often seems to mean that the foreigner has superior skill, uses better machinery, adapts his patterns more quickly to changing tastes, is more practised in economies of all sorts and is content with smaller profits. And so a handful of American gen-

tlemen go to Congress and beg to be helped to make
a living and support their operatives. Some among
them do not need the protection: they have perfected
their processes and their stuffs, can afford by better
organization and more studied economies to pay
American wages and still beat the foreigner, if need
be, in his own markets overseas. But the rest do need
it to make good their failure. American labour is
the most intelligent in the world, and when intelligently made use of is worth its extra wage, earns it
without affecting the market. But the Government
must support those who do not know how to use it
intelligently as their rivals, and the people of the
country must be made to buy the goods they make
at prices that will support them. This is indeed the
"baby act" and these are easily recognizable as "infant industries"!

And so the question comes to be, What will the
people say of this new system of the support of
favoured industries by the Government, now that
they have come to understand it? For it is a new
system. The principle upon which the system of protection was originally founded was the development
of the country, the development of the resources of
the continent and the skill of the people. That principle is intelligible and statesmanlike, particularly
in a new country, without capital and unprepared for
competition in a trading world. The principle now
proclaimed and acted upon, with show of patriotic
fervor, is that profits must be assured to those who
cannot stand competition after development, *after*
the accumulation of capital in the country, the per-

fecting of skill and the full attainment of economic
and industrial independence amidst the trading and
manufacturing nations of the world. This is indeed
a new theory and will not bear examination.

Hamilton's position, the position of those who have
intelligently and consistently followed him, is defensible enough. It is idle to bid a new nation on an
undeveloped continent to put its faith in the natural
laws of trade and production, buy in the cheapest
and sell in the dearest market, build up its wealth on
the demand for what it has and buy what it has not.
For it has not at the outset capital enough to find out
either its resources or its capacities. There must be
a waiting and a spending time at the first before it
finds out what its resources are and what it can do
with them. The farmer cannot expect a crop the first
season from unbroken prairie or uncleared land. It
costs money to put nature into shape to be profitably
used. Deposits of ore do not constitute riches until
the mines have been opened and machinery has been
installed by which the ore can be readily and economically got out. That takes time and money.
Even when the mines are opened and can be worked
at a profit they produce only ore. The nation that
cannot use its ores in manufacture is still a poor
nation, however rich its deposits. Only a few men
in it will be rich until other men in it get the capital
and the opportunity to use the ores in manufacture.
That, again, takes time and money. South Africa
was not rich because a few men owned and worked
diamond mines in it. Taking the world at large and
as a whole, how are you to know which is the cheap-

est market in which to buy or the most advantageous
in which to sell, so long as a whole continent lies undeveloped, a whole nation untrained, so long as
America or South Africa has not come into the markets with its hidden stuffs and its unschooled peoples?

This is the question for statesmen. Nobody now
doubts that the policy of Hamilton put the nation
under a great stimulation, gave it the economic independence it needed, immensely quickened the development of its resources and the powers of its
people. Protected from the direct competition of
those who had already acquired capital oversea, who
had already become masters of industry and put
hundreds of ships upon the sea, who had the stuffs
to work in and the skill to work them, things took on
a very different aspect for the enterprising spirits
of the young nation from that which they had worn
in the old colony days. Those who cared to venture
upon enterprise,—and who in America did not?—
had the markets of a growing and industrious people
to themselves. As the nation grew their trade grew,
and their wealth,—with their wealth, their independence and their spirit of enterprise. It was wise,
—in the circumstances it was more than wise, it was
necessary,—to give the country an opportunity thus
to find itself. It was necessary and wise to put it
thus economically upon its own feet and make it
worth its while to discover and develop its own resources.

It is perfectly consistent with such a policy, moreover, to give to every new enterprise, even in our
day of America's abounding wealth and resource-

fulness, such protection as it may need to get its start and come to its proper perfection of equipment and operation, provided it be an enterprise suitable to America's soil or resources or capacities. So far as the policy of protection has for its object the diversification and enrichment of American industry, it is admissible, dangerous though it be, because liable to be used in a spirit of favouritism and for party ends. The only thing not consistent with the sound original policy upon which the single defensible theory of the system rests is the encouragement and support by "protection" of industries in their very nature not natural to America, but forced and artificial. Being artificial, not indigenous from the outset, they will need artificial stimulation to the end. Those who undertake them will always have to be supported out of the public purse—by the taxes laid at the ports.

But this original basis and theory of protection, this genuine enterprise of statesmanship, was long ago abandoned or forgotten by the leaders of the party that stood for the system. Its leaders no longer talk of "infant industries" to be carefully nurtured and brought to maturity for the sake of the nation and its development. They know the sort of smile with which such talk would now be received and do not relish the thought of it. They boast, rather, of the economic supremacy of America in the money-markets, the steel-markets, the foodstuff-markets, the implement and machinery markets of the world, and naïvely insist that that supremacy should be maintained by import duties at the parts levied for the

sake of those who are conducting our successful enterprises, in order to keep their profits safely up and
make them feel that the country (which is, being interpreted, the party in power) will take care of them.
It is not a system of stimulation or development; it
is a system of patronage. Statesmen need no longer
debate it: politicians of very ordinary managing
abilities can easily keep it going. Indeed, it is no
proper job for statesmen. It is a thing of lobbies
and private interviews, not a thing of open debate
and public policy.

Even this bad system worked no radical harm
upon the country for a generation or two. The continent abounded in every kind of natural riches, individuals were greatly stimulated by the many inviting opportunities for manufacture and trade, the
population of the country was growing by leaps and
bounds, its domestic markets widening with every
decade, its diversified industries enriching one another. The country was generously big and wide
and various, its immense stretches extending into
every climate of the temperate zone, its hills and
valleys and high ascending western slopes inviting
to every development of modern civilization. Its vast
areas of free trade, trade absolutely without hin-
drance or restriction, guaranteed exemption from restraint by the interstate commerce clause of the
Constitution, made it an incomparable field for rapid
and normal development, a development about which,
it turned out, there was almost nothing that was artificial and little that was not sound and lasting.

Moreover, those who had undertaken the great industries to which the customs legislation of Congress had given leave and not yet gone into combination. Enterprise was entered upon on individual initiative, was conducted by simple partnerships and small companies. There was a very active and quickening competition within the field of each undertaking that proved profitable. Those who succeeded had no more power than their mere wit at succeeding gave them. Fortunes were made, but upon a modest scale. The rich men of the country had only their local influence and did not determine the industrial processes of a whole continent or the methods of a whole industry. The prosperity of the country wore a generous and democratic aspect and did not set classes off in sharp contrast against one another. There was favouritism in arranging the system of protection, of course, and individuals were very often thought of rather than the country as a whole. The "log-rolling" in Congress was very often spoken of in the newspapers and with a great deal of asperity. The system had its glaring faults and dangers. But it was at least a game into which almost any one could get. It did not yet wear the ugly face of monopoly or special privilege.

We look upon a very different scene now. It is no longer a scene of individual enterprise, of small bodies of capital embarked upon a thousand undertakings,—a scene of individual opportunity and individual achievement,—able men everywhere, singly or in small groups, making themselves the economic servants of communities and reaping the legitimate profit of many an enterprise their own brains had conceived. It was in that day that the industries of the country were originated and put upon a footing to succeed. In our later day those who control the great masses of capital swept together out of the multitudinous earnings of the last two or three generations have combined together and put at the head of every great industry a dominating corporation, or group of corporations, with an organization and resources which are irresistible by any individual competitor,—by any competitor not supported by a like colossal combination of brains and means. The richest of those who enjoy the favours of the Government have combined to enjoy a monopoly of those favours. Enormous fortunes are piled up for a few, for those who organize and control these great combinations; but they are relatively very few in number and all men in their field of enterprise who are not in their combination are apt to become, first their crushed rivals, and then their servants and subordinates.

It is a very different America from the old. All the recent scandals of our business history have sprung out of the discovery of the use those who directed these great combinations were making of their power: their power to crush, their power to monopolize. Their competition has not stimulated, it has destroyed. Their success has not varied industry, it has standardized it and brought it all under a single influence and regulation,—not the regulation of law, but the regulation of monopoly.

It is easy to exaggerate the iniquity of many of the things that have been done under this régime of the trust and the colossal corporation. Most of their

methods were simply the old cut-throat methods of
private individual competition on a new scale. What
made them cruel and disastrous was not their kind,
but their scope. Their kind was as old as economic
history and rivalry in industrial enterprise, but their
scale was new and ominous. The competition, the
underselling, the aggressive canvassing, the rival ex-
penditure and rapid improvement of process possible
to these men who had vast capital behind them, who
shipped so much that every railroad stood ready to
bid for their patronage with lowered rates, who could
buy a competitor out at any price and stood always
ready to buy at the moment of greatest strain and
discouragement, could not be withstood. The field
cleared before them. The power was theirs, and
smaller men, smaller concerns, went down before
them. They had "cornered" the opportunity which
the Government's favouring legislation had been intended to create.

Too much moral blame, it seems to me, has been
laid upon the men who effected these stupendous
changes. They were men of extraordinary genius,
many of them, capable of creating and organizing
States and Empires. Commercial morals had not been
adjusted, by themselves or any one else, to the new
and unprecedented scale upon which they did business. Private consciences were pooled and confused
and swallowed up in those huge combinations. Men
were excited and blinded by the vast object they
sought, and pursued it, as it were, impersonally, by
means they would not have used had they been dealing simply and face to face with persons and not

merely upon paper with complex transactions, involving the business of a continent. It was a process in which commercial morals had again to find themselves, as in the days of treasure fleets and international spoilation.

But my present object is not to assess individual responsibility. I am describing conditions, not drawing up an indictment against those who created them or framing an excuse for them. I am studying a national policy and its effects; and about that, viewed in its present aspects, some things are very plain and ought to be plainly spoken of.

In the first place, it is plain that these new masters of our industry do not need the assistance or the "protection" of the Government. They own or control a preponderant percentage of the resources of the country: of its mines, its forests, its cattle, its railways. They have brought the industries they control to a high state of perfection in equipment and organization, economizing their processes and improving their output. They have invaded foreign markets and sell to all the world, where there is no Government to assist them, where, on the contrary, there are hostile tariffs to overcome. They have made themselves entire masters of the opportunity created for them. Manufacturers engaged in the same lines of industry elsewhere copy their machinery and imitate their methods. All the world is justly jealous of their huge success. Their balance-sheets, on the one hand, and the success and skill of their processes, on the other, show how little they need protection.

In the second place, no political party can afford
to be their partners in business. It amounts to that.
In the earlier days of protection, when import duties
created opportunities for thousands of men, the political party that maintained the system of protection
had all the nation for partner. The benefits of the
system were widely distributed. Its beneficiaries
could nowhere be assembled in a single lobby. Their
names could be included in no possible list. They
were the people of the country by sample. But now,
as compared with the former thousands, they are
few. The names of most of them are known everywhere. Their influence is direct, personal, pervasive.

They are doing nothing novel through the lobby.
It is just what the beneficiaries of this dangerous system have always done. It would seem the natural
process of obtaining protection,—to ask for it and
argue its necessity with the figures of the business
in hand. But they are so few, so individually powerful, and command so many things that political
parties need, or think that they need, for their success: money, widely-extended influence, the gift and
the use of business organization national in their
scope and control! They have as powerful a machinery ready to their hand as the Government itself. It
is highly dangerous for the Government to be in
partnership with them in the great enterprise of developing the country: their grip upon it can so easily
become too direct and personal! The country cannot afford an alliance of private interest with governmental authority, for whatever purpose originally
conceived, however honourably arranged at the out-

set. No body of business men, no political party, can long withstand the demoralizing in fluences of the relationship,—particularly no body of men so compact and unified in interest as those who manage and finance the trusts.

It is not necessary for my argument to claim or to prove that high protection created the trusts and combinations of our time. I believe that it can be shown that it did, though I am ready to admit that they might, and probably would, have arisen in any case, though in a different form and with different proportions. But that is a complicated question which may for the present be put upon one side. Certainly the trusts have now cornered the opportunities created by the system of high tariffs. They no longer need the assistance of the Government; and it is highly desirable that there should be no alliance, and no appearance of an alliance, between them and either of the political parties.

That our industries are still greatly stimulated is evident enough. They are very vital and very prosperous. There is general employment; and when things go well and the money-market is not manipulated, or upset by our uncommonly bad system of currency, there is a general feeling of ease and hopefulness. But there is not general prosperity: that is a very different matter. When the great industrial and trade combinations can operate freely and without fear of disturbing prices and a frightened money-market there is always ready enough employment for those who seek it,—at wages forced up and maintained, not by prosperity or the good busi-

ness of the great corporations, but by the aggressive-
ness and determination of organized labour.   The
country is given occupation by those who have cornered the privileges to be had under the favour of
Congress, and their success is easily made to look like
the reign of unbounded opportunity for the 'rank and
file; but that does not increase the proportion of
employers to employees.   The initiative and control
are still with the few.   Their money makes the mare
go, and it is they who ride.

It does not do to think of these things with bitterness.   It is not just to think of them with bitterness.
They came about by natural process, not by deliberate or malignant plan.   But it is necessary to point
them out in plain language, to discuss them with
candour and to comprehend them, when the talk is
done, with wide-open eyes.   It is easy to fall into
exaggeration.   Not all the industry of the country is
in the hands of great trusts and combinations.   Only
its main undertakings are its largest and most lucrative enterprises.   But the picture I have drawn is,
in the rough, true and tends from decade to decade
to represent the truth more and more perfectly and
completely.   If the tendency had worked itself out to
its ultimate consequences, if it had accomplished its
perfect work, it would probably be too late for reform.   The body politic is still sound and still elastic
enough to work upon; and many of the very men who
have profited most by this new and ominous state of
affairs are ready to join in the wholesome processes
of reformation which will make opportunity general
again,—not a monopoly, but a universal stimulus.

The fact which has disclosed itself to us, in these later days of the country's awakening, is this, then. We have witnessed the partial creation, the almost complete creation, on the one hand, of a comparatively small privileged class or body of men, the men who control capital and the uses to which it is put and who have, as the representatives (as all too literally the representatives) of the business of the country, the ear of Congressional committees; and we begin to see, under them, associated with them, on the other hand, a vast unprivileged body ("class" is too definite and formal a word) which forces its way to a share in the benefits of our apparently prosperous conditions only by threats and strikes, and is steadily deprived of a large percentage of what it thus gains by rapidly rising prices which day by day increase the cost of living amongst us. And the rise of prices itself seems to be connected with the system.

There has been a rise in prices in almost all the trading countries. The large recent increase in the supply of gold has had a great deal to do with it, here as elsewhere. Gold, the world's standard of value, having become cheaper because more abundant, more of it is demanded in exchange for goods, whose value has not changed. But this universal phenomenon of the rise of prices has had its special features and vagaries in America utterly dissociated from the price of gold; and it would be easy to prove that those who have managed to get control of the greater part of the output of the mines and factories have, by combination, set the prices to please themselves. They have made the usual use of their opportunity.

While the Government has, by its high protective policy, spared them the anxiety of foreign competition, they have, by organization and agreement, spared themselves the embarrassment of any competition at all.

What, then, shall we do? Shall we adopt Thorough as our motto and sweep the whole system away, be quit of privilege and favours at once, put our industries upon their own resources and centre national legislation wholly upon the business of the nation? By no means. The system cannot be suddenly destroyed. That would bring our whole economic life into radical danger. The existing system was built up by statesmanlike and patriotic men, upon a theory upon which even the most sceptical economist must concede it possible to found a valid and effective policy. It is very likely that by slower, sounder, less artificial means the country might have worked its way up to the same extraordinary development and success, the same overwhelming material achievement and power; but that is a question no longer worth debate by practical men. As a matter of fact, the method of artificial stimulation was adopted, has been persisted in from generation to generation with a constant increase of the stimulation, and we have at last, by means of it, come to our present case. It will not do to reverse such a policy suddenly or in revolutionary fashion.

It must in some conservative way be altered from decade to decade, if possible from year to year, until we shall have put all customs legislation upon a safe, reasonable and permanent footing. A process of alternation, steadily and courageously persisted in, will not disturb the business or embarrass the industries of the country, even if tariff act follows tariff act from session to session, if it be founded upon a definite principle by which its progress may be forecast and made ready for. Such a principle must be found. And the nation must find means to insist that, whatever party is in power, that principle shall be followed with courage, intelligence and integrity. The present method and principle of legislation does not keep business equable or free from harassing anxiety. It is based upon no principle, except that of self-interest,—which is no principle at all. No calculable policy can be derived from it. Discussion gives place to intrigue, and nothing is ever fixed or settled by its application.

What, then, shall the principle of reform be which shall hold us steady to an impartial and intelligible process? The old principle of Hamilton, in a new form and application: the very principle upon which the protective policy was set up, but applied for the purpose of reforming the system and bringing it to the test of a single definite object, its original purpose and energy having been fulfilled and spent.

Hamilton's purpose was to develop America, to give her industries of her own; to make it immediately worth the while of her enterprising and energetic men to discover and use her natural resources, the richness and extent of which even he never dreamed of; to enrich and expand her trade and give her an interior economic development which should make her an infinitely various market within herself;

and to continue the stimulation until her statesmen should be sure that she had found her full vigour and capacity, was mistress of her own wealth and opportunity, and was ready to play her independent part in the competitions and achievements of the world. That object has been attained. No man not blinded by some personal interest or inveterate prepossession can doubt it. What would Hamilton do now?

In one sense, it is not a question of politics. It does not involve Hamilton's theories of Government or of constitutional interpretation. Some of us are Jeffersonians, not Hamiltonians, in political creed and principle, and would not linger long over the question, What shall we do to return safely to Hamilton? It is not a Hamiltonian question. Constitutional lawyers long ago determined that it was certainly within the choice of Congress to lay import duties, if it pleased, with a view to the incidental benefit of traders and manufacturers within the country; and, if that incidental object has in later days become the chief and only guiding object of the rates of duty, that, I take it, is only a question of more or less, not a question which cuts so deep as to affect the power of Congress or draw it seriously into debate again. As a matter of fact, the policy was entered upon and has been carried—to what lengths we know. The Hamiltonian principle, not a political, but an economic principle, was the only wise and defensible principle upon which it could have been established. It is also the only wise and safe principle upon which it can be modified and in part got rid of. For when you have the general benefit of the country

as your standard, you have a principle upon which it
is as legitimate to withdraw protection as to give it.

It may seem like a vague principle, affording room
for many varieties of contrary judgment; but it will
be found to lose its vagueness when stated in contrast
with the principle upon which Congress has acted in
recent years. In all the recent tariff legislation of
the country, in all legislation since 1828, the committees of the House and Senate, when making up
the several schedules of duties they were to propose,
have asked, not what will be good for the country,
but what will be good for the industries affected,
what can they stand, what rates of duty will assure
them abundant profits? It is true that they have assumed,—it has been the burden of innumerable weary
campaign speeches,—that the prosperity of the individual interest considered would be the prosperity
of the country; but the poor sophistry of that argument has long been commonplace. By hard, desper-
ately hard, use that assumption has been worn
through to the thread. It must be replaced by new
and sounder stuff. No doubt you can say to the
country, ''Feed and sustain these corporations and
they will employ you: feed your employers out of the
taxes and they, in turn, will give you work and feed
you.'' But no candid student of this great question
can now confidently believe that a policy which has
the profits of the manufacturers as its main object
is likely to promote the impartial, natural, wholesome, symmetrical, general development of the
country.

The men who happen to possess the field do not

constitute the nation; they do not even represent it
when they speak of their own interest. We have
taught them, by our petting, to regard their own interest as the interest of the country; but the two are
by no means necessarily identical. They may be,
they may not be. It is a question of fact to be looked
into. Their prosperity and success may or may not
benefit the country as a whole. Even if the country
be indisputably benefited, it might be still more
highly benefited by the promotion of an entirely different interest. What the fact is may depend upon
many circumstances. It is those circumstances we
are bound to look into, if we be indeed statesmen
and patriots, asking not what the protected interests
want or can prove that they need, but what it is to
the general interest of the country to do: whether
some interests have not been too much favoured,
given a dominance not at all compatible either with
honest politics or wholesome economic growth. In
brief, we are now face to face with a great question
of fact. What part of the protective system still
benefits the country and is in the general interest;
what part is unnecessary; what part is pure favouritism and the basis of dangerous and demoralizing
special privilege? These are the questions which
should underlie a tariff policy. No other questions
are pertinent or admissible.

"The benefit of the country" is a big phrase.
What do you mean by it? What do you mean by
"the country"? *Whom* do you mean by it? If you
are honest and sincere, you mean the people of the
country, its sections and varieties of climate and

population taken, not separately or by their voting strength, but together; its men and women of every rank and quality and circumstance; its bone and sinew. If any particular industry has been given its opportunity to establish itself and get its normal development, under cover of the customers, and is still unable to meet the foreign competition which is the standard of its efficiency, it is unjust to tax the people of the country any further to support it. Wherever the advantages accorded by a tariff have resulted in giving those who control the greater part of the output of a particular industry the chance, after their individual success has been achieved, to combine and "corner" the advantage, those advantages ought to be withdrawn; and the presumption is that every industry thus controlled has had the support of the Government as long as it should have it.

There is something more than the economic activities of the country to be considered. There is its moral soundness; the variety, not of employment, but of opportunity for individual initiative and action which the policy of its law creates; the standards of business its trades and manufactures observe and are gauged by; and the connection which exists between its successful business men and its Government. By these significant matters should the tariff policy of Congress be judged, as well as by the tests of successful business.

Only those undertakings should be given the protection of high duties on imports which are manifestly suited to the country and as yet undeveloped or only imperfectly developed. From all the rest protection should be withdrawn, the object of the Government being, not to support its citizens in business, but to promote the full energy and development of the country. Existing protection should not be suddenly withdrawn, but steadily and upon a fixed programme upon which every man of business can base his definite forecasts and systematic plans. For the rest, the object of customs taxation should be revenue for the Government. The Federal Government should depend for its revenue chiefly on taxes of this kind, because the greater part of the field of direct taxation must be left to the States. It must raise abundant revenue, therefore, from customs duties. But it should choose for taxation the things which are not of primary necessity to the people in their lives or their industry, things, for the most part, which they can do without without suffering or actual privation. If taxes levied upon these do not suffice, the things added should be those which it would cause them the least inconvenience or suffering to dispense with. Customs thus laid and with such objects will be found to yield more, and the people will be freer.

There is no real difficulty about finding how and where to lay such taxes when once a just principle has been agreed upon, if statesmen have the desire to find it. The only trouble is to ascertain the facts in a very complex economic system. Honest inquiry will soon find them out, and honest men will readily enough act upon them, if they be not only honest, but also courageous, true lovers of justice and of their country.

ADDRESS TO PITTSBURGH ALUMNI

DELIVERED AT PITTSBURGH BANQUET, APRIL 16, 1910.
FROM "PITTSBURGH DISPATCH," APRIL 17, 1910.

MR. WILSON said in part:
How does the nation judge Princeton? The institution is intended for the service of the country, and it is by the requirements of the country that it will be measured. I trust I may be thought among the last to blame the churches, yet I feel it my duty to say that they—at least the Protestant churches—are serving the classes and not the masses of the people. They have more regard for the pew rents than for men's souls. They are depressing the level of Christian endeavor.

It is the same with the universities. We look for the support of the wealthy and neglect our opportunities to serve the people. It is for this reason the State University is held in popular approval while the privately supported institutions to which we belong is coming to suffer a corresponding loss of esteem.

While attending a recent Lincoln celebration I asked myself if Lincoln would have been as serviceable to the people of this country had he been a college man, and I was obliged to say to myself that he would not. The process to which the college man is subjected does not render him serviceable to the country as a whole. It is for this reason that I have dedicated every power in me to a democratic regeneration.

The American college must become saturated in the same sympathies as the common people. The colleges of this country must be reconstructed from the top to the bottom. The American people will tolerate nothing that savours· of exclusiveness. Their political parties are going to pieces. They are busy with their moral regeneration and they want leaders who can help them accomplish it. Only those leaders who seem able to promise something of a moral advance are able to secure a following. The people are tired of pretense, and I ask you, as Princeton men, to heed what is going on.

* * * *

If she loses her self-possession, America will stagger like France through fields of blood before she again finds peace and prosperity under the leadership of men who know her needs.

HIDE AND SEEK POLITICS

FROM THE "NORTH AMERICAN REVIEW," MAY, 1910, VOL. CXCI, PP. 585-601.

THE political discussions of recent years concerning the reform of our political methods have carried us back to where we began. We set out upon our political adventures as a nation with one distinct object, namely, to put the control of government in the hands of the people, to set up a government by public opinion thoroughly democratic in its structure and motive. We were more interested in that than in making it efficient. Efficiency meant strength; strength might mean tyranny; and we were minded to have liberty at any cost. And now, behold! when our experiment is an hundred and thirty-odd years old, we discover that we have neither efficiency nor control. It is stated and conceded on every side that our whole representative system is in the hands of the "machine": that the people do not in reality choose their representatives any longer, and that their representatives do not serve the general interest unless dragooned into doing so by extraordinary forces of agitation, but are controlled by personal and private influences; that there is no one anywhere whom we can hold publicly responsible, and that it is hide-and-seek who shall be punished, who rewarded, who preferred, who rejected,—that the processes of government amongst us, in short, are haphazard, the processes of control obscure and ineffectual. And so we are at the beginning again. We must, if any part of this be true, at once devote ourselves again to finding means to make our governments, whether in our cities, in our States, or in the nation, representative, responsible and efficient.

Efficiency, of course, depends largely upon organization. There must be definite authority, centred in somebody in particular whom we can observe and control, and an organization built upon obedience and coöperation, an organization which acts together, with system, intelligence, and energy. We were afraid of such an organization at the outset. It seemed to mean the concentration of authority in too few hands and the setting up of a government which might be too strong for the people. Our chief thought was of control. We concluded that the best means of obtaining it was to make practically every office elective, whether great or small, superior or subordinate; to bring the structure of the government at every point into direct contact with the people. The derivation of every part of it we desired should be directly from the people. We were very shy of appointments to office. We wished only elections, frequent and direct.

As part of the system,—we supposed an indispensable part,—we defined the duties of every office, great or small, by statute and gave to every officer a definite legal independence. We wished him to take his orders only from the law,—not from any superior, but from the people themselves, whose will the law was intended to embody. No officer appointed him and no officer could remove him. The people had given him his term, short enough to keep him in mind of his responsibility to them, and would not suffer any one but themselves to displace him, unless he became himself an actual breaker of the law. In that case he might be indicted like any other law-breaker. But his indictment would be a family affair; no discipline imposed upon him by his superiors in office, but a trial and judgment by his neighbours. A district attorney elected on the same "ticket" with himself, would bring the matter to the attention of a grand jury of their neighbours, men who had in all likelihood voted for them both, and a petit jury of the same neighbourhood would hear and decide the case if a true bill were found against him. He stood or fell by their judgment of the law, not by his character or efficiency.

A sheriff in one of the States suffered a prisoner to be taken from him by a mob and hanged. He made no show or pretense even of resistance. The Governor of the State wrote him a sharp letter of rebuke for his criminal neglect of his duty. He replied in an open letter in which he bluntly requested the Governor to mind his own business. The interesting feature of the reply was not its impudence, but the fact that it could be written with perfect impunity. The fact was as he had stated it. He was not responsible to the Governor or to any other officer whatever, but only to the voters of his neighbourhood, many of whom had composed the mob which took his prisoner from him and hanged him at their leisure. He was never called to account for what he had done.

This is a sample of our direct responsibility to the people as a legal system. It was very serviceable and natural so long as our communities were themselves simple and homogeneous. The old New England town meeting, for example, was an admirable instrument of actual self-government. Where neighbourhoods are small and neighbours know one another they can make actual selection of the men they wish to put into office. Every candidate is known by everybody, and the officers of government when elected serve a constituency of whose interests and opinions they are keenly and intimately aware. Any community whose elements are homogeneous and whose interests are simple can govern itself very well in this informal fashion. The people in such a case, rather than the government, are the organism. But those simple days have gone by. The people of our present communities, from one end of the country to the other, are not homogeneous, but composite, their interests varied and extended, their life complex and intricate. The voters who make them up are largely strangers to each other. Town meetings are out of the question, except for the most formal purposes, perfunctorily served; life sweeps around a thousand centres, and the old processes of selection, the old bases of responsibility, are impossible. Officers of government used to be responsible because they were known and closely observed by neighbours of whose opinions and preferences they were familiarly aware; but now they are unknown,

the servants of a political organization, not of their
neighbours, irresponsible because obscure, or because
defended by the very complexity of the system of
which they form a part. The elective items on every
voter's programme of duty have become too numerous to be dealt with separately and are, consequently,
dealt with in the mass and by a new system, the system of political machinery against which we futilely
cry out.

I say "futilely cry out" because the machine is
both natural and indispensable in the circumstances
and cannot be abolished unless the circumstances are
changed, and very radically changed at that. We
have given the people something so vast and complicated to do in asking them to select all the officers of government that they cannot do it. It must
be done for them by professionals. There are so
many men to be named for office; it is futile to name
one or two unless you name a whole ticket; the offices
that fill a ticket are so many and so obscure that it
is impossible the thing should be done informally and
offhand by direct, unassisted popular choice. There
must be a preliminary process of selection, of nomination, of preparing the ticket as a whole, unless
there is to be hopeless confusion, names put up at
haphazard and nobody elected by a clear majority at
the end. The machine is as yet an indispensable
instrumentality of our politics.

Public opinion in the United States was never better informed, never more intelligent, never more
eager to make itself felt in the control of government
for the betterment of the nation than it is now; and

yet, I venture to say, it was never more helpless to obtain its purposes by ordinary and stated means. It has to resort to convulsive, agitated, almost revolutionary means to have its way. It knows what it wants. It wants good men in office, sensible laws adjusted to existing conditions, conscience in affairs and intelligence in their direction. But it is at a loss how to get these. It flings itself this way and that, frightens this group of politicians, pets that, hopes, protests, demands, but cannot govern.

In its impatience it exaggerates the inefficiency and bad morals of its governments very grossly and is very unfair to men who would serve it if they could, who do serve it when they can, but who are caught in the same net of complicated circumstances in which opinion itself finds itself involved. There is no just ground for believing that our legislative and administrative bodies are generally corrupt. They are not. They are made up for the most part of honest men who are without leadership and without free opportunity; who try to understand the public interest and to devise measures to advance it, but who are subordinate to a political system which they cannot dominate or ignore. The machinery of the bodies to which they belong is inorganic, as decentralized as our elective processes would lead one to expect. No one person or group of persons amongst them has been authorized by the circumstances of their election to lead them or to assume responsibility for their programme of action. They therefore parcel out initiative and responsibility in conformity with the obvious dictates of the system. They put their business in the hands of committees,—a committee for each subject they have to handle,—and give each of their members a place upon some committee. The measures proposed to them, therefore, come from the four quarters of the heaven, from members big and little, known and unknown, but never from any responsible source. There can be neither consistency nor continuity in the policies they attempt. What they do cannot be watched, and it cannot be itself organized and made a whole of. There is so much of it and it is so miscellaneous that it cannot be debated. The individual member must do the best he can amidst the confusion. He has only an occasional part and opportunity.

He is controlled, as a matter of fact, from out-of-doors,—not by the views of his constituents, but by a party organization which is intended to hold the heterogeneous elements of our extraordinary political system together.

When public opinion grows particularly restless and impatient of our present party organization, it is common to hear it defended by the argument that parties are necessary in the conduct of a popular government; and the argument can be sustained by very sound and eloquent passages out of Burke and many another public man of the English-speaking peoples who has seen below the surface of affairs and convinced us of the real philosophy of our form of government; but the argument is quite aside from the point. Of course parties are necessary. They are not only necessary, but desirable, in order that conviction upon great public questions may be organ-

ized and bodies of men of like opinion and purpose
brought together in effective and habitual coöperation. Successful, orderly popular government is impossible without them. But the argument for our
own particular organization of parties is quite another matter. That organization is undoubtedly necessary in the circumstances, but you cannot prove
its necessity out of Burke or any other man who
made permanent analysis of liberty. We could have
parties without organizing them in this particular
way. There have been parties in free governments
time out of mind and in many parts of the world,
but never anywhere else an organization of parties
like our own.

And yet that organization is for the time being
necessary. It centres, as everybody knows, in the
nominating machinery. There could be no party organization if our elective system were literally carried out as it was intended to be, by the actual direct
and informal selection of every officer of government,
not by party agents or leaders, but by the scattered
voters of the thousand neighbourhoods of a vast country. It was necessary to devise some machinery by
which these innumerable choices should be coördi-
nated and squared with party lines. It was a huge
business and called for a compact and efficient organization.

Moreover, there was more than the process of selection to be overseen and directed. Students of our
political methods have not often enough brought into
their reckoning the great diversity of social and economic interest and development which has existed

among the different sections and regions of this various country, which even yet shows every stage and variety of growth and make-up and an extraordinary mixture of races and elements of population. It has been necesssary to keep this miscellaneous body together by continual exterior pressure, to give it a common direction and consciousness of purpose by sheer force of organization, if political action was not to become hopelessly confused and disordered. It was not conscious of any immediate solidarity of interest or object. It might have broken up into a score of groups and coteries. We might have had more parties than France, as many sections of political opinion as there were distinctly marked regions of population and development. Party interest has been kept alive, party energy stimulated, by entrusting to local agents and leaders the duty of seeing to it that systematic party nominations were regularly made and urged upon the voters by organized campaigns, whether there was any natural reason or not why, in any given locality, this party or that should be preferred; and national parties have been pieced together out of these local fragments. The creation of the parts was necessary to the creation of the whole. I do not know how else co-ordinated parties could have been made out of such heterogeneous materials and such diversified interests.

The result has been that the nominating machinery has become the backbone of party organization. By it local leaders are rewarded with influence or office are kept loyal, watchful and energetic. By it national majorities are pieced together. If one goes

back to the source of this matter, therefore, it is
easy to see that the nominating machine was no
barnacle, but a natural growth, the natural fruit of
a system which made it necessary to elect every officer of government. The voter has not the leisure
and, therefore, has not the knowledge for the difficult and intricate business. He cannot organize a
government every year or two, make up its whole
personnel, apply its punishments and rewards, effect
its dismissals and promotions. Neither is there any
officer or any group of officers of the government itself who can organize it for him, for no officer has
the legal authority. The structure of the government is disintegrated by the law itself, so far as its
personnel is concerned. The constitutions and statutes by which the officers are created endeavor, of
course, to integrate their functions; but they disintegrate their personnel by making each officer the
direct choice of the voters. The only possible means
of integration lies outside governments, therefore,
and is extra-legal. It is the nominating machine.
The machine applies the necessary discipline of administration and keeps the separately elected officers
of one mind in the performance of their duties,—
loyal to an exterior organization.

The punishment it inflicts is definitely and clearly
understood. It will not renominate any man who
when in office has been disobedient to party commands. It can in effect dismiss from office. Any one
who wishes to remain in public life, at any rate in the
smaller and less conspicuous offices within the gift of
the managers, must keep in their good graces. In-

dependence offends the machine deeply, disobedience
it will not tolerate at all. Its watchfulness never
flags; its discipline is continuous and effective. It is
the chief instrument of party government under our
system of elections.

Thus have we necessitated the setting-up outside
the government of what we were afraid ourselves to
set up inside of it: concentrated power, administrative discipline, the authority to appoint and dismiss.
For the power to nominate is virtually the power to
appoint and to dismiss, as Professor Ford has pointed
out in his lucid and convincing "Rise and Growth of
American Politics." It is exercised by the bosses, instead of by responsible officers of the government,—
by the men who have charge of the nominating machinery: men who are themselves often entirely outside the government as legally constituted, hold no
office, do not ask the people for their suffrages, and
are picked out for their function by private processes
over which the people have no control whatever.
They are private citizens and exercise their powers of
oversight and management without any public invita-
tion of any kind. Just because there are innumerable offices to be filled by election, just because there
are long and elaborate tickets to be made up, just because it needs close and constant attention to the
matter to perform the duty of selection successfully,
—as careful and constant attention as the superintendent of a great business or the head of a great
government bureau has to exercise in selecting and
keeping up the personnel of his factory, his office, or
his bureau,—it cannot possibly be done by the voters

as a body. It requires too much knowledge and too much judgment, bestowed upon little offices without number as well as upon great. No officer of the government is authorized to appoint or select. Party managers must undertake it, therefore, who are not officers of the government; and their nominations are virtual appointments if they belong to the successful party. The voters only choose as between the selections, the appointees, of the one party boss or the other. It is out of the question for them to make independent selections of their own.

If this machine, thus bossed and administered, is an outside power over which the voter has no control, —which he can defeat only occasionally, when, in a fervor of reform, he prefers the candidates of some temporary amateur machine (that is, nominating apparatus) set up by some volunteer "committee of one hundred" which has undertaken a rescue,—it is the system which is to blame, not the politicians. Somebody, amateurs or professionals, must supply what they supply. We have created the situation and must either change it or abide by its results with such patience and philosophy as we can command.

Our efforts at reform have been singularly misdirected. For years we laboured at the reform of the ballot itself, as if the way we printed it and the way we voted it were at fault. We adopted the so-called Australian method of voting, for example; isolated the voter in a closed booth, made it as easy as possible in the circumstances for him to mark and alter his ballot unscrutinized and unmolested, and passed laws which gave groups of voters not formally organized as parties the right to put names in nomination on the official ballot which had not passed through the party caucus or any other part of the machine. Finally in many of the States where the ardour of non-partisan action was warmest, we forbade the placing of any party sign or symbol at the head of the list of candidates printed on the official ballot, contrived a blanket ballot on which the names of all nominees were printed in impartial alphabetical order under the names of the several offices for which they had been nominated, so that the voter,—such was our unsophisticated hope,—might choose the best man for each office without regard to who had nominated him, whether a regular party machine or a group of independent voters nominating by petition. I have seen a ballot of this kind which contained seven hundred names. It was bigger than the page of a newspaper and was printed in close columns as a newspaper would be. Of course no voter who is not a trained politician, who has not watched the whole process of nomination carefully, who does not know a great deal about the derivation and character and association of every nominee it contains, can vote a ticket like that with intelligence. In nine cases out of ten, as it has turned out, he will simply mark the first name under each office, and the candidates whose names come highest in the alphabetical order will be elected. There are cases on record where shrewd seekers of office have had their names changed to names beginning with some letter at the head of the alphabet preparatory to candidacy on such a ballot, knowing that they had no chance of election other-

wise. And of course politicians govern themselves
accordingly in choosing a winning ticket. They are
always the professionals, whatever system of choice
you oblige them to employ, and always know better
than any one else the actual results of the processes
used.

It is very desirable to have secret voting to pro-
tect the voter against scrutiny or any kind of coercion, direct or indirect; it may be very desirable to
have non-partisan nominations; but no secret or non-
partisan device can make it possible for the voter to
use such ballots intelligently or to pick out his own
candidates for office when there are a multitude of
offices to be filled. It is the size and variety of the
ballot that perplexes and baffles him, be he never so
intelligent and never so anxious to vote for the best
candidates. He cannot possibly make himself acquainted with the individual claims of the men whose
names appear on these long lists. Many of the offices
he is voting to fill are themselves as obscure as the
men who have been nominated to occupy them. He
is not interested in the list as a whole. A few conspicuous names upon it, candidates for the greater
offices, he may have heard something about, a candidate for Congress or for the Governorship of his
State, but the rest are mere names to him. It is impossible that he should discriminate. He is excusable
if he presently comes to think of the whole thing as
a farce and for feeling that, do what he will, the
politicians will take him in. He has in any event no
choice but to put himself in their hands. It is too
occult a business for him to fathom.

The result is the unchecked power of the irresponsible politician; and some of the consequences are painfully interesting. Since the choice of candidates for office is a matter of private arrangement; since nominees thus chosen are our lawmakers, and our lawmakers by the same token appointees of the nominating machine, it follows very naturally that public business loses its public character and becomes itself a matter of private arrangement. It is settled in private conferences at State capitals and at Washington, not by public discussion, and the voters are informed what was actually agreed upon after an election, not before it. The Secretary of the Treasury smilingly informed a public audience the other evening that the monetary commission of which Senator Aldrich is chairman, and which is expected to recommend to Congress well-considered measures for the reform of our banking and currency systems, would probably not make its report until after the next Congressional elections. The plain inference was that the commission thought it best, before making its report, to wait and see which party would be in control of Congress, and thought it imprudent to let their conclusions be known before the elections for fear that they might in some way affect the result. In short, they deemed it best that the people should not be given an opportunity to discuss or express an opinion upon their own affairs, upon some of the most important and far-reaching questions now awaiting their decision! Judge by the sample. Elections must be managed by the subtle alchemy of nomination, with as little regard to public questions

as possible, and then the appointees of the successful managers must decide those questions in the best
interest of the party in power.

It is thus that the public business is managed with
as careful privacy as the business of any private corporation. Corporations will, indeed, when they are
well and wisely managed, often take the public more
into their confidence than the managers of government do, in order to enhance the credit of the corporation and increase or steady the value of its
securities in the money-market, as well as the sale of
its products. But politicians are very secretive.
They have become so by the habit of the system. Debate has fallen out of fashion in our legislative assemblies because the business of those assemblies is
for the most part discussed and prepared by committees. The sittings of their committees are seldom
public, except upon extraordinary occasions. Even
when they are public few persons except those directly and privately interested attend, and the matter is too particular, too much like a mere single item
of the session, to attract the attention of the ordinary
newspaper. The business of legislation, therefore,
like that of nomination, is for the most part conducted in private by the conference of small groups
of men under party discipline. The public is not
present either in fact or in thought. Committeemen
get into the habit of being reticent and silent about
what occurred in the committee-room and soon find
themselves under the impression that it is their own
private affair, anyway.

The habit spreads to the deliberative bodies them-

selves. Boards of Aldermen will often refuse to open
their debates to reporters or to publish the names of
those who voted *Aye* or *No* in the division when the
debate was ended. And on the administrative side
much of what is to be done or proposed is agreed
upon by private conference between the executives
of our cities and States and the party managers,—
sometimes the managers who appear in public and
are known, sometimes those who keep in the background and occupy no office, but are nevertheless
omnipotent in matters of nomination and who wish
the executive business of the government to be carried on in a way which will not embarrass them.
And so, wherever we turn, we find the intimate business of government sealed up in confidences of every
kind: confidences against the people with regard to
their own affairs, confidences with regard to the way
in which their interests are to be served and safe-
guarded. Public discussions are the mere formal
dress parade of politics.

It was very amusing, when Mr. Roosevelt was
President, to notice how seasoned politicians shivered
when he spoke in public,—shivered at his terrible
indiscretions, his frank revelations, whenever he
chose, of what was going on inside political circles,
his nonchalant failure to keep any confidences whatever that he chose to make public use of. He spoke
of any inside matter he pleased, as if it were the
people's privilege to know what was going on within
their government. He may have chosen and chosen
very astutely which confidences to keep, which to
break, but he was strong and popular in proportion

as he broke them and gave the people the impression that he was really telling them all he knew about their business, about the men and the motives which were retarding the proper transaction of their business and the proper correction of the abuses under which they were suffering at the hands of men who enjoyed the confidence and protection of the managing politicians.

There is no ground for wonder that under a system under which it is constant hide-and-seek to discover who is responsible, to find out where public action originates and whither it is tending, this system of confidences should have sprung up. I do not know that any one in particular is to blame. But the situation is certainly extraordinary and makes it thoroughly worth while to inquire how the people may be reintroduced into their own affairs.

It is high time. The people must be brought into their own again. They have been excluded from free and effective participation in their own governments too long,—so long that a universal distrust of representative methods of government has sprung up, a universal suspicion that there is nowhere any candor or honesty in the administration of public business, and we are in danger of revolutionary processes, of very radical changes which might be as futile as what we have already attempted by way of reform, while all the while a remedy, a very simple remedy, is at hand. We have not fallen upon these evil ways by any one's sinister intention or machinations, but the fact is the same. The system we are under, though nobody invented it to cheat the people, has grown up and does cheat the people and must be done away with by very definite intention.

There is no reason to despair, or even to tire, of representative government. It has not failed as some suppose, because it is representative and not direct. It has come near to breaking down only because it is not representative, only because the people of this country are prevented by the system of elections in which they have become entangled from electing representatives of their own choice. The people of other countries are not prevented. They manage to get their will very directly expressed, alike in legislation and in the administration of their governments. Foreign cities, for example, succeed excellently well, as well as it is reasonable ever to expect to succeed in matters of such magnitude and complexity, in getting their affairs administered in the way a majority of their people really wish them to be administered. Most of the badly governed cities of the civilized world are on this side of the Atlantic, most of the well governed on the other side; and the reason is not accidental. It has nothing to do with differences of capacity or of virtue or of theory, nothing to do with differences of principle or of national character. It results from differences of organization of the most fundamental and important kind which cut to the very roots of the whole matter.

Let the city of Glasgow serve as an example. It is known as one of the best-governed cities in the world, is a thoroughly modern city teeming with factories and with the movements of a great commerce and handling a vast population under many a natural disadvantage, and its government is not in any essential particular peculiar to itself. It is a sample, though a favourable sample, of the way in which most European cities, great and small, are governed. Its administration is entirely in the hands of its municipal council, which has a membership of thirty-two. The mayor of the city has no independent executive powers. He is merely chairman of the council and titular head of the city when it needs a public representative on formal occasions, when it welcomes guests or undertakes a ceremonious function. There is no upper and lower chamber of the council: it is a single body. It is not a legislature. No city council is. It is an administrative body conducting the business of a great chartered corporation. Its members are elected by the voters of the city by wards, one councilman for each ward. The voter's connection with the government of the city is very simple. He votes for only one person, the councilman from his ward. That is his whole ticket.

In its simplicity lies his power. He does not need the assistance of professional politicians to pick out a single candidate for a single conspicuous office. Any group of interested or public-spirited neighbours can do that. And the simple structure of the city's government enables him to follow his representative throughout every vote and act of administration. The council divides itself into committees, a committee for each branch of the city's business. All the actual executive servants of the city are appointed and are the responsible agents of the several committees under which they serve. All business is

public, whether transacted by the council as a whole
or by its committees. Everything that is done or
agreed upon is published in full in the "Glasgow
Herald," with the votes taken and the names of
those who voted this way or that. By a mere glance
at his morning paper the voter can keep his eye upon
his own particular representative and know what he
is doing, whether in the council or in the committee
to which he has been assigned. His votes speak for
themselves. His responsibility is unmistakable. Another candidate may easily be nominated if his record
is unsatisfactory and a whole campaign centred, so
far as that ward is concerned, upon the definite question of a choice between this man and that. That is
representative government. If all the officials of the
city government, or even the chief of them, were
elected upon a common ticket it would not be. A
machine would be necessary, amateur or professional,
and the direct representative principle would, in fact,
disappear.

The same idea underlies one of the most interesting
reforms that has recently been undertaken in our
own cities. Following the example of Galveston, in
Texas, a number of our cities have obtained from the
legislatures of their States charters which authorize
them to put their administration entirely in the
hands of a small commission consisting generally of
only five or six persons. The voter's attention is concentrated upon this commission both at election-time
and throughout the course of its administration.
This ticket of five or six names is the only ticket he
is called upon to vote. The results have in several

cases been extremely satisfactory, though the experiment has nowhere been of long enough standing to justify the formation of a confident or final judgment as to its ultimate effects. The commission has felt the responsibility and has responded to it. The voters have known by whom they were being governed and the nominating machine has, of course, sunk into insignificance. It remains a question, however, whether the load imposed upon the commission is not too heavy, whether it is fair to hold so small a body of men wholly responsible for the successful administration of a modern city. Can five men, by any feasible division of labour, so long as a working day has only a limited number of hours in it and every man must take a little sleep and recreation, master the affairs committed to their charge in sufficient detail really to keep them clear of inefficiency and abuse? It will probably turn out that it requires a considerably larger body of men really to direct and control matters of such magnitude and variety. But that need not result in putting a greater burden on the voter and bringing the nominating machine again into existence as his indispensable assistant and ultimate master. He need not be made to vote for the whole body upon a common ticket. He need only vote for the representative from his own ward. The essential thing is that his task should be comprehensible and manageable, that the men he is called upon to vote for should be so few that he can select them for himself or at least easily judge the action of those who do select them.

That this is the simple and effectual solution of the

matter, the certain means of restoring to the people
a genuine choice of representatives and by the same
token a genuine representative government, is no
matter of conjecture. It has been tried in every
country but our own, until we began to set up governments by commission, and has had the desired
result. It is not a panacea. It is a conclusion of
obvious common sense. If the trouble is that we have
given the people an impossible task in asking them
to choose the whole personnel of our governments,
and have thereby put them in the hands of persons
to whom they are, by reason of its very complexity,
obliged to depute it, the obvious remedy is to make
their task simple and practicable, to make it something that they can do and can take an interest in
doing without neglecting their daily business and
turning politicians. We have been mistaken,—this
is the long and short of the matter,—in supposing
that we were giving the people control of their gov-
ments by making all offices elective. We actually,
as a matter of fact and of experience, put them in
control only when we make only the chief, the really
responsible offices elective, allow those whom we elect
to appoint all minor officials, all executive agents,
and hold them strictly responsible as the superintendents of our business. Our own experience has
been very instructive in this matter in particulars
which we have not enough observed. For example,
the Governor of New Jersey, like the Governors of
one or two other States of the Union, is entrusted
with the power of appointing all the judges of the
State, and the bench of New Jersey is famous for its

excellence, much more famous than the bench of
neighbouring States whose judges are elected. The
State has had Governors good, bad, and indifferent,
but all alike have made excellent appointments to the
bench. They could share the responsibility with no
one and it was a very conspicuous responsibility. In
that matter if in no other the eye of public opinion
was centred upon them personally, not merely upon
their party. They could not venture to do that thing
ill or in the interest of any coterie or machine. It
always operates so, though we have not always taken
note of the fact or understood the scope of the
inference.

The short ballot is the short and open way by
which we can return to representative government.
It has turned out that the methods of organization
which lead to efficiency in government are also the
methods which give the people control. The busy
owner is more effectually in control if he appoints a
capable superintendent and holds him responsible for
the conduct of the business than he would be if he
undertook himself to choose all the subordinate agents
and workmen and superintend both them and the superintendent; and the business is also better conducted,—incomparably better conducted. What the
voters of the country are now attempting is not only
impossible, but also undesirable if we desire good
government. Such a charter as that of the city of
New York, for example, is a mere system of obscurity
and of inefficiency. It disperses responsibility, multi-
plies elective offices beyond all reason or necessity,
and makes both of the government itself and of its

control by the voters a game of hide-and-seek in a
labyrinth. Nothing could have been devised better
suited to the uses of the professional politician,
nothing susceptible of being more perfectly articu-
lated with the nominating machine. As a means of
popular government, it is not worth the bother and
expense of an election.

Simplicity is necessary in government as in business, for unity, for responsibility, for efficiency, and
for control: these four are, indeed, as a matter of
experience, almost interchangeable and equivalent
words. You cannot form or execute a judgment
either in business or in politics without some such
system of coherence and simplicity.

Simplicity does not involve, in the case of government, a return to any of the abuses we have partially
corrected. We did begin at the wrong end when we
devoted the ardour and labour of years of reform
to the mere reform of the existing civil service, to
the introduction of a system of qualification for appointment to office by examination. We should have
begun by making more offices appointive and the
business of appointing so conspicuous and responsible
a thing that those who undertook it could not afford
to make appointments upon any principle of fa-
voritism, could not afford to serve their own private
objects in making them or any private interest whatever. But responsible officers need not object, will
not object, to being themselves protected and assisted
by a system of qualifying examinations for appointment. They should and probably would prefer it.
It is a sensible and serviceable system and secures

the public service against many a minor abuse which might creep in even if those who made appointments made them with full responsibility to public opinion,—in the fierce, revealing light that beats upon every act of personal power. The instrumentalities we have already created would prove more serviceable than ever.

It is a very interesting and very vital thing to have come back to our original problem, to be obliged thus to become once more thoughtful partisans of genuine democracy. The issue is nothing less. What we need is a radical reform of our electoral system, and the proper reform will be a return to democracy. It is the high duty of every lover of political liberty to become a partisan of such a reform if once he becomes convinced of it. Another great age of American politics will have dawned when men seek once more the means to establish the rights of the people and forget parties and private interests to serve a nation.

BACCALAUREATE ADDRESS

LAST ADDRESS AT PRINCETON UNIVERSITY, JUNE 12, 1910.
FROM ORIGINAL TYPEWRITTEN MANUSCRIPT BEARING
MR. WILSON'S OWN CORRECTIONS, AT THE LIBRARY
OF PRINCETON UNIVERSITY.

We look not at the things which are seen, but at the things
which are not seen; for the things which are seen are
temporal; but the things which are not seen are eternal.—
II Corinthians IV, 18.

THIS is inevitably a day of reckoning. This is
a turning point in your lives: a day of endings
and of beginnings. We cannot choose but stop and
ask what it signifies, what profit and loss there is as
we look backward, and what confidence as we look
forward. We must examine so much of life as we
have had; and as we look we realize that "we look
not at the things which are seen, but at the things
which are not seen," and perceive, as we never perceived before, that "the things which are seen are
temporal, but the things which are not seen are
eternal." It is an old and very familiar text: now
at last we are in a way to see what it means.

Your Commencement has come. Your own particular year and month in the annals of the college; and
you find it a season of singular contrasts. Everyone
else about you is gay, but you are sad. It is your particular season, the month and year and day to which

you have looked forward with hope and ambition for
four years,—it may be for longer,—it may be ever
since you formed at school the wish to go to college
and to become a son of Princeton; and yet your spirits
flag.   There is a dull ache at your heart, and no
gayety, no light ardour of enjoyment.   For the other
men who crowd the town, the graduates of other days,
it is a season of reunion, but for you it is a time of
parting.   Your mood is more like that of the old gentlemen who graduated fifty years ago than like that
of the men who graduated last year.   They miss their
old friends and are sad, knowing that they will see
them no more: you are parting friend from friend
and fear that you will see each other no more.   And
the life of these four years, the life that has bound
you together, that you know you are breaking with
forever.   This little world in which you have lived
and been happy together you now turn away from
and abandon.   You can never reconstruct it again.
It is a thing already finished.   It does not comfort
you that you will, many of you, be back again a
year hence, happy to be reunited, because you know
that you will not all be here at any time again.   You
will then be happy over nothing but fragments of
this complete and beautiful thing that you have had,
the life that was so much your own and of your own
making.

I do not have to imagine what you feel.   I know;
for I have felt it in days which will never seem to
me very long ago.   I have lived here now twenty years
as a member of the faculty and the work of Princeton has become part of the very warp and woof of

my life; but it has never in all those years been for
a single moment the same Princeton for me that it
was in the magical years that ran their cheerful course
from the exciting autumn of 1875 to the gracious
June of 1879. The four years of college life can
never be repeated or reconstructed. They stand
unique in every man's experience to whom they mean
anything at all.

But you would not turn back. Your sadness is
not the sadness of foreboding. You are not sad because you stand at the threshold of another life, but
only because you are at the end of a life you loved.
You are conscious of being readier for the things that
lie ahead of you because of the days that lie behind
you, for all you turn away from those days so re-
luctantly. You came here a body of strangers from
all parts of the country, bred in many ways, under
many influences, youngsters of every degree of raw-
ness and inexperience, and you are now a homogeneous body of classmates, men who have learned a
common lesson, comrades in a single school of experience and of principle. It is because you have all
been wrought upon alike that you share so consciously
the feeling of the day. You are keenly aware of the
influences that have formed and united you here.
They have become very familiar and very dear to
you. They seem part of your very selves. It is hard
to think of yourselves as scattered again to the four
quarters of the country, shaken apart as individuals
again, broken up into your units. You know how
the common influences have worked upon you and it
renders you uneasy, unhappy even, to be drawn out

of them as if for ever. It is the feeling you had when
you left home.

But you have never in fact left off feeling the influence of home, have you? You never can leave off.
Those impressions are indelible. So are also the impressions you have received here. I wonder if you
have taken stock of them. You think that it is your
friendships that have governed and formed you here,
the daily experiences of the campus life, the four
years together in a various comradeship. But you
cannot dissect the facts in that way. It is the whole
Princeton that has gripped you and grappled you
thus. That is the reason this cannot be a day of
endings for you, why it is in reality a day fuller of
what is to come than of what has gone by. What is
shaking you to-day is in reality the throb of this
puissant place as a whole: the throb of what Princeton has put into you.

Princeton does not consist, has never consisted, of
you and your classmates. Here men come and go,
the men of her faculty and trustees as well as the
men of her classes, but her force is not abated. She
fails not of the impressions she makes. Her men are
formed from generation to generation as if by a spirit
that survives all persons and all circumstances.
There is a sense, a very real sense, not mystical but
plain fact of experience, in which the spirit of truth,
of knowledge, of hope, of revelation, dwells in a place
like this, as it were inevitably, unless it be wholly
decayed or demoralized. It has made some things
certain for you, permanently and beyond conjecture.
It has not left your minds fluid, volatile, escaping all

mould and form. There must be very few of you,
if there be any, who have failed to get a definite
undoubting grasp of some things that have here become certitudes for you. How could you feel at home
here, else? How could you love a place that had
left you groping and in the dark, the puzzled play-
thing of conjecture and blank surmise? Mere comradeships and pleasures cannot have satisfied you.
You must have been fed upon something and been
nourished.

I am not now thinking of knowledge so much as
of what certainly underlies all knowledge. I do not
mean merely that you have acquired certain definite
information here which may serve you always as the
material upon which your thought will feed. Information is no great matter. It changes from age
to age, is often altered, and can be made to take a
thousand shapes. I am thinking, rather, of what
lies behind all knowledge, gives it colour, significance,
variety. Science, for example, alters its allegations
of fact from decade to decade, alters even its theories
and hypotheses, but it does not alter its method. You
feel that solid under your feet, do you not, as you
have traversed it in the classroom and in the laboratory? It has made the world for you not a place for
children and for ignorant guesses, but a place of
definite ascertainable phenomena to be candidly and
discerningly sought out and rationally explained by
careful and clarified processes of reason. You know
that the mind can be used as an instrument of precision and also as an instrument of definition when
once it has mastered that thing of enlightenment, the

method of science. There is one certitude for you.
The physical world need not remain the realm of conjecture.

You are certain also, are you not, that there are
definite comprehensible practices, immutable principles of government and of right conduct in the
dealing of men with one another. The narratives,
whether of history or of biography, are faulty, no
doubt full of errors and of circumstances misappre-
hended, but you cannot doubt that the main lines
are drawn with substantial accuracy and truth; you
cannot be uncertain how it is that men come by happiness or failure; you are sure that there is such a
thing as justice and a noble force in men who are
righteous and love the truth; you perceive that some
governments are free, some tyrannous and cruel, that
there is a way of freedom and of peace and a way
of certitude and strife in the affairs of men, and that
it is all a rewarding study of human life in its
realities, in its actual habit as it lives,—that you have
looked in the face of life, very noble, very tragical,
full at once of pathos and of hope.

And the literature you have studied and the
philosophy you have read under wise masters. Have
they not yielded you something that you will not
henceforth doubt? All the great books of any language are records of the human spirit, the voices of
men like yourselves who speak to you the secrets of
your own souls as well as theirs. You enter a wide
comradeship when you read them. You are made
free of the company of all men everywhere; as you
are also in your study of philosophy, where is the

same thing unfolded in orderly and formal fashion, with the insight of interpretation, as if life were read for you by men of science.

Surely you cannot be bewildered now. The world can no longer be to you a place of vague conjectures and childish ifs and buts, a play whose rules are guesses. And yet this is not information. This is not knowledge. You know very little. You are a good deal at sea in respect of your facts. You are glad your definite examinations are behind you. You have been made certain only of what sort of world it is you live in and how you should handle yourselves in it. The things you have been rendered certain of are intangible, but more actual, authentic, infallible than facts themselves. They represent the human spirit in command of the facts. They are the laws and masteries of the mind. They are the spiritual processes and realities by which we are made sure of life. Life is made definite and manageable by masteries and convictions, and these are what you have acquired, if you have acquired anything.

But what is the ultimate certainty? Is your certainty piecemeal and fragmentary? Have you learned only in disconnected segments? Education is a method of enlightenment concerning your relations to the material universe and to your fellowmen: has this brought you no confidence with regard to your relations to the God and Father of us all? Are you not more certain than ever that God is in his Heaven? Is your spirit awakened to all these other perceptions of life and reality without being vouchsafed a glimpse of the Father of Spirits? To

know these other things that only implied Him is life,
to know Him is life eternal,—eternal because perfect,
stripped of its last doubt and uncertainty, given the
very spirit of vision.

I have read in your hearing this morning the 103rd
Psalm. Did it seem to you unreal and fanciful? Had
it not, on the contrary, a reality which you would
be at a loss to find anywhere else in the whole body
of great songs men have conceived, unless perhaps in
some other Psalm which speaks the same confident
meaning with the same supreme conviction? When
Paul stood upon Mars Hill facing that Athenian
crowd gathered about him in skeptical curiosity, did
he tell them anything that seems to you incredible,
a tale of mere credulity and superstition? He did
not hesitate to call the ignorance of the Athenians
religion; was his religion not the religion of certitude,
of knowledge? "I perceive," he said, "that in all
things you are very religious. For as I passed by,
and beheld your devotions, I found an altar with this
inscription, TO AN UNKNOWN GOD. Whom therefore you ignorantly worship, Him declare I unto
you, God that made the world and all things therein,
seeing that he is Lord of heaven and earth, dwelleth
not in temples made with hands; neither is worshipped with man's hands, as though he needed anything, seeing he giveth to all life, and breath, and
all things; and hath made of one blood all the nations of men for to dwell on all the face of the earth,
and hath determined the times before appointed, and
the bounds of their habitation; that they should seek
the Lord, if haply they might feel after Him, and

find Him, though He be not far from every one of us: for in Him we live, and move, and have our being; as certain of your own poets have said, For we are also his offspring.''

We have an instinctive sympathy with and comprehension of Paul as he stands there. His voice of expostulation and interpretation seems our own. He is very natural, very inevitable. ''We look not at the things which are seen, but at the things which are not seen.'' And we see deeper than did the Athenians who once stood about Mars Hill and listened to the great apostle. We do not spend our time ''in nothing else, but either to tell, or to hear some new thing.'' In all our studies we have seen this to be a world of law, not dead but quick with forces of which the phenomena about us are not the reality but the mere temporary embodiment. At every turn it has been life that we have studied, whether the life of nature or the life of men; only in life have we been interested. We perceive now that it is not knowledge that we have been getting, but understanding, comprehension, insight, and that what we chiefly desire to understand are ourselves and our fellowmen. And so we have seen Scripture become mere plain philosophy, the words of Christ the words of a teacher who has seen the ultimate realities and speaks them very simply, with the simplicity of utter authority.

It is plain enough to us that ''man's life does not consist in the abundance of the things which he possesseth,'' but in his mastery of himself, of circumstance, of physical forces and of human relationships, of the spirit that is within him: that man "doth not live by bread alone," but by every word of truth, every word that proceedeth out of the mouth of God, the author of truth, however spoken. Our thought cannot stop short of these ultimate realities, is not content without them. Mysteries become plain facts, the things which are seen appear thin to our gaze like mere masks, and the things which are not seen become real.

Our experience here, as well as our formal study, becomes part of the explanation as our thought dwells upon it. The things we have been most conscious of are our comradeships, our companionships, the commerce we have had with one another, and we have become conscious, as we never were before, that life is a thing that links spirit with spirit, that it is itself personal, not abstract, and yet intangible, not material; a thing too of law, but not of law imposed, of law accepted, rather, not made up of what we must so much as of what we will. We are drawn into it by impulse and affection as well as by interest. It is a thing by which we live and move and have our conscious being. And so we are drawn on to Paul's conclusion. If life be thus personal, if it be of law, if the law of highest compulsion be the law of our own spirits, how shall we dispense with the knowledge of him who is the Father of Spirits; and yet how can we know Him whom we have not seen,— how can we know him except in the person of Christ, the express image of the Father, the Word that became flesh and "dwelt among us, full of grace and truth?"

I have heard this called an age of science, in which individual choice counts for less and less and law for more than ever before. I have heard it said, by men who claimed to base their statements upon observation, that this is an age in which individual men of necessity fall into the background, an age of machinery, of combinations of individuals, of massed and aggregate power; and I marvel that the obvious facts should be so ignored. Perhaps not so many individuals are of significance as formerly, but the individuals who do tell more tremendously, wield a greater individual choice, command a power such as kings and conquerors never dreamed of in the simpler days gone by. Their sway is the sway of destiny over millions upon millions of their fellow-countrymen, over the policy and fortunes of nations. There never was a time when the spirit and character of individual men was of more imperial import and consequence than now. The whole scale of action is altered; but with the scale are magnified also the essential elements themselves.

And so the type and symbol is magnified,—Christ, the embodiment of great motive, of divine sympathy, of that perfect justice which sees into the hearts of men, and that sweet grace of love which takes the sting out of every judgment. ''We look not at the things which are seen, but at the things which are not seen'': we do not, we cannot, see Christ, but there he stands, the most indubitable fact of history, with a sway over the hearts and lives of men which has not been broken or interrupted these nineteen hundred years. No man can ever think of him as dead, unreal, a thing of books, a creature of theology. "The things which are seen are temporal," but He, He is the embodiment of those things which, not seen, are eternal,—the eternal force and grace and majesty, not of character, but of that which lies back of character, obedience to the informing will of the Father of our spirits.

The force and beauty of Christ seem not to have been his own, as if original. He spoke always of his father, and of himself only as doing his father's will and speaking his father's words. There dwelt in him a spirit, great and universal, as that of the round world itself, compact of law and truth, a spirit greater than the world, conveying life and vision from the source from which all worlds and existence itself must have taken origin. He is our revelation. In him is our life explained and our knowledge made comprehensible. He is the perfect elder brother of our spirits. In him we are made known to ourselves,—in him because he is God, and God is the end of our philosophy; the revelation of the thought which, if we will but obey it, shall make us free, lifting us to the planes where duty shall seem happiness, obedience liberty, life the fulfillment of the law. Science is our intimation; literature is the imperfect voice of our fellow-men, seeking, like ourselves, an exit for their hopes; philosophy is what we would fain convince ourselves of but cannot see: in all of these the things which are unseen and real lurk, but elude us. In Christ, in the God whom he reveals, the veil is torn away. Look! Look there and have your fill of what you have sought most. You must ever

seek in vain until you raise your eyes to the Christ
where he is lifted up. "As Moses lifted up the ser-
pent in the wilderness, even so must the Son of Man
be lifted up: that whosoever believeth in him should
not perish but have eternal life,"—that life which
subsisteth upon the things which are not seen.

GENTLEMEN OF THE GRADUATING CLASS: The real
question for every one of you to-day as you turn
away from the University to take up the tasks which
may lead to your final achievements, is What sort
of life the University has bred in you. Universities
deal with the spirits, not with the fortunes, of men.
They are of an unserviceable sort when men may
come and buy knowledge in them, purchase what
store of information they may need for their business,
as one would buy commodities in a mart, as if learning were merchandise; and you may fairly enough
judge a university by the love men have for it,—or
the indifference. You would not love this place if
you felt that it were a mere market. You have not
dealt in learning here. You have not been formed
by the facts you have gathered in the classroom and
the laboratory. These things would stir no affection
in you, and without affection or repulsion there is no
life. If your minds have been awakened here, it has
been by contact with other minds, with that vital
stuff, the minds of your teachers or of your comrades,—best of all, of those of your teachers who
have also been your comrades. Fire has kindled fire,
life life. You have been quickened to see new things,
to comprehend realities, or else this has been no university to you, but only a place of dull or playful

sojourn where you made believe to do what you were not really doing. Men love only the places where they have been stirred, to which the deeper experiences of life have attached them.

What sort of life has the University bred in you that you should love her? Four years has seemed a long time to you, but a very short time to us who have sought to lead and teach you. Perhaps you think that to us you are only so many more in the indistinguishable mass of youngsters who pass before us in annual procession, the years through; but you are deeply mistaken. If that were true, you would have taken nothing from us. You have been the comrades of our thoughts, and we watch you with very wistful eyes as you turn away and leave us. To-day we part, not to forget and be strangers again, for with a common heritage are we bound in a perpetual partnership. We can be partners only in that which we have inherited, that precious stuff in which we have traded,—in the things of the spirit, in the things which are not seen but which are eternal. May God bless you and keep you, and confirm you in the vision of these things. This in you will be Princeton's immortality.

THE BIBLE AND PROGRESS

ADDRESS IN THE AUDITORIUM, DENVER, AT THE TERCEN-
TENARY CELEBRATION OF THE TRANSLATION OF THE
BIBLE INTO THE ENGLISH LANGUAGE, MAY 7, 1911.
FROM "CONGRESSIONAL RECORD," 62D CONGRESS, 2D
SESSION, VOL. XLVIII, APPENDIX 499-502.

MR. PRESIDENT, ladies and gentlemen, the
thought that entered my mind first as I came
into this great room this evening framed itself in a
question, Why should this great body of people have
come together upon this solemn night? There is
nothing here to be seen. There is nothing delectable
here to be heard. Why should you run together in
a great host when all that is to be spoken of is the
history of a familiar book?

But as I have sat and looked upon this great body
of people I have thought of the very suitable circumstance that here upon the platform sat a little group
of ministers of the gospel lost in this great throng.

I say the "suitable circumstance," for I come here
to-night to speak of the Bible as the book of the
people, not the book of the minister of the gospel,
not the special book of the priest from which to set
forth some occult, unknown doctrine withheld from
the common understanding of men, but a great book
of revelation—the people's book of revelation. For
it seems to me that the Bible has revealed the people
to themselves. I wonder how many persons in this

great audience realize the significance for English-speaking peoples of the translation of the Bible into the English tongue. Up to the time of the translation of the Bible into English, it was a book for long ages withheld from the perusal of the peoples of other languages and of other tongues, and not a little of the history of liberty lies in the circumstance that the moving sentences of this book were made familiar to the ears and the understandings of those peoples who have led mankind in exhibiting the forms of government and the impulses of reform which have made for freedom and for self-government among mankind.

For this is a book which reveals men unto themselves, not as creatures in bondage, not as men under human authority, not as those bidden to take counsel and command of any human source. It reveals every man to himself as a distinct moral agent, responsible not to men, not even to those men whom he has put over him in authority, but responsible through his own conscience to his Lord and Maker. Whenever a man sees this vision he stands up a free man, whatever may be the government under which he lives, if he sees beyond the circumstances of his own life.

I heard a very eloquent sermon to-day from an honoured gentleman who is with us to-night. He was speaking upon the effect of a knowledge of the future life upon our conduct in this life. And it seemed to me that as I listened to him I saw the flames of those fires rekindled at which the martyrs died—died forgetful of their pain, with praise and thanksgiving upon their lips, that they had the opportunity to render their testimony that this was not the life for which they had lived, but that there was a house builded in the heavens, not built of men, but built of God, to the vision of which they had lifted their eyes as they passed through the world, which gave them courage to fear no man, but to serve God. And I thought that all the records of heroism, of the great things that had illustrated human life, were summed up in the power of men to see that vision.

Our present life, ladies and gentlemen, is a very imperfect and disappointing thing. We do not judge our own conduct in the privacy of our own closets by the standard of expediency by which we are daily and hourly governed. We know that there is a standard set for us in the heavens, a standard revealed to us in this book which is the fixed and eternal standard by which we judge ourselves, and as we read this book it seems to us that the pages of our own hearts are laid open before us for our own perusal. This is the people's book of revelation, revelation of themselves not alone, but revelation of life and of peace. You know that human life is a constant struggle. For a man who has lost the sense of struggle life has ceased.

I believe that my confidence in the judgment of the people in matters political is based upon my knowledge that the men who are struggling are the men who know; that the men who are in the midst of the great effort to keep themselves steady in the pressure and rush of life are the men who know the significance of the pressure and the rush of life, and that they, the men on the make, are the men to whom to go for your judgments of what life is and what its problems are. And in this book there is peace simply because we read here the object of the struggle. No man is satisfied with himself as the object of the struggle.

There is a very interesting phrase that constantly comes to our lips which we perhaps do not often enough interpret in its true meaning. We see many a young man start out in life with apparently only this object in view—to make name and fame and power for himself, and there comes a time of maturity and reflection when we say of him, "He has come to himself." When may I say that I have come to myself? Only when I have come to recognize my true relations with the rest of the world. We speak of a man losing himself in a desert. If you reflect a moment you will see that is the only thing he has not lost. He himself is there. What he means when he says that he has lost himself is that he has lost all the rest of the world. He has nothing to steer by. He does not know where any human habitation lies. He does not know where any beaten path and highway is. If he could establish his relationship with anything else in the world he would have found himself. Let it serve as a picture.

A man has found himself when he has found his relation to the rest of the universe, and here is the book in which those relations are set forth. And so when you see a man going along the highways of life with his gaze lifted above the road, lifted to the sloping ways in front of him, then be careful of that

man and get out of his way. He knows the kingdom
for which he is bound. He has seen the revelation
of himself and of his relations to mankind. He has
seen the revelations of his relation to God and his
Maker, and therefore he has seen his responsibility
in the world. This is the revelation of life and of
peace. I do not know that peace lies in constant
accommodation. I was once asked if I would take
part in a great peace conference, and I said, "Yes;
if I may speak in favour of war"—not the war which
we seek to avoid, not the senseless and useless and
passionate shedding of human blood, but the only
war that brings peace, the war with human passions
and the war with human wrong—the war which is
that untiring and unending process of reform from
which no man can refrain and get peace.

No man can sit down and withhold his hands from
the warfare against wrong and get peace out of his
acquiescence. The most solid and satisfying peace
is that which comes from this constant spiritual warfare, and there are times in the history of nations
when they must take up the crude instruments of
bloodshed in order to vindicate spiritual conceptions.
For liberty is a spiritual conception, and when men
take up arms to set other men free, there is something
sacred and holy in the warfare. I will not cry
"peace" so long as there is sin and wrong in the
world. And this great book does not teach any doctrine of peace so long as there is sin to be combated
and overcome in one's own heart and in the great
moving force of human society.

And so it seems to me that we must look upon the

Bible as the great charter of the human soul—as the "Magna Charta" of the human soul. You know the interesting circumstances which gave rise to the Magna Charta. You know the moving scene that was enacted upon the heath at Runnymede. You know how the barons of England, representing the people of England—for they consciously represented the people of England—met upon that historic spot and parleyed with John, the King. They said, "We will come to terms with you here." They said, "There are certain inalienable rights of English-speaking men which you must observe. They are not given by you, they cannot be taken away by you. Sign your name here to this parchment upon which these rights are written and we are your subjects. Refuse to put your name to this document and we are your sworn enemies. Here are our swords to prove it."

The franchise of human liberty made the basis of a bargain with a king. There are kings upon the pages of Scripture, but do you think of any king in Scripture as anything else than a mere man? There was the great King David, of a line blessed because the line from which should spring our Lord and Saviour, a man marked in the history of mankind as the chosen instrument of God to do justice and exalt righteousness in the people.

But what does this Bible do for David? Does it utter eulogies upon him? Does it conceal his faults and magnify his virtues? Does it set him up as a great statesman would be set up in a modern biography? No; the book in which his annals are written strips the mask from David, strips every shred of counterfeit and concealment from him and shows him as indeed an instrument of God, but a sinful and selfish man, and the verdict of the Bible is that David, like other men, was one day to stand naked before the judgment seat of God and be judged not as a king but as a man. Is not this the book of the people? Is there any man in this Holy Scripture who is exempted from the common standard and judgment? How these pages teem with the masses of mankind. Are these the annals of the great? These are the annals of the people—of the common run of men.

The New Testament is the history of the life and the testimony of common men who rallied to the fellowship of Jesus Christ and who by their faith and preaching remade a world that was under the thrall of the Roman army. This is the history of the triumph of the human spirit, in the persons of humble men. And how many sorts of men march across the pages, how infinite is the variety of human circumstance and of human dealings and of human heroism and love! Is this a picture of extraordinary things? This is a picture of the common life of mankind. It is a mirror held up for men's hearts, and it is in this mirror that we marvel to see ourselves portrayed.

How like to the Scripture is all great literature! What is it that entrances us when we read or witness a play of Shakespeare? It is the consciousness that this man, this all-observing mind, saw men of every cast and kind as they were in their habits, as

they lived. And as passage succeeds passage we
seem to see the characters of ourselves and our
friends portrayed by this ancient writer, and a play
of Shakespeare is just as modern to-day as upon the
day it was penned and first enacted. And the Bible
is without age or date or time. It is a picture of the
human heart displayed for all ages and for all sorts
and conditions of men. Moreover, the Bible does
what is so invaluable in human life—it classifies
moral values. It apprises us that men are not judged
according to their wits, but according to their characters—that the last of every man's reputation is
his truthfulness, his squaring his conduct with the
standards that he knew to be the standards of purity
and rectitude.

How many a man we appraise, ladies and gentlemen, as great to-day whom we do not admire as
noble! A man may have great power and small
character. And the sweet praise of mankind lies not
in their admiration of the smartness with which the
thing was accomplished, but in that lingering love
which apprises men that one of their fellows has gone
out of life to his own reckoning, where he is sure
of the blessed verdict, "Well done, good and faithful
servant."

Did you ever look about you in any great city, in
any great capital, at the statues which have been
erected in it? To whom are these statues erected?
Are they erected to the men who have piled fortunes
about them? I do not know of any such statue anywhere, unless after he had accumulated his fortune
the man bestowed in it beneficence upon his fellow-

men, and alongside of him will stand a statue of
another meaning, for it is easy to give money away.
I heard a friend of mine say that the standard of
generosity was not the amount you gave away, but
the amount you had left. It is easy to give away
of your abundance; but look at the next statue, the
next statue, and the next in the market place of great
cities, and whom will you see? You will see here a
soldier who gave his life to serve, not his own ends,
but the interests and the purposes of his country.

I would be the last, ladies and gentlemen, to dis-
parage any of the ordinary occupations of life, but
I want to ask you this question: Did you ever see
anybody who had lost a son hang up his yardstick
over the mantelpiece? Have you not seen many families who had lost their sons hang up their muskets
and their swords over the mantelpiece? What is the
difference between the yardstick and the musket?
There is nothing but perfect honour in the use of the
yardstick, but the yardstick was used for the man's
own interest, for his own self-support. It was used
merely to fulfill the necessary exigencies of life,
whereas the musket was used to serve no possible
purpose of his own. He took every risk without any
possibility of profit. The musket is the symbol of
self-sacrifice and the yardstick is not. A man will
instinctively elevate the one as the symbol of honour
and never dream of using the other as a symbol of
distinction.

Doesn't that cut pretty deep, and don't you know
why the soldier has his monument as against the
civilian's? The civilian may have served his State—

he also—and here and there you may see a statesman's statue, but the civilian has generally served his
country—has often served his country, at any rate—
with some idea of promoting his own interests,
whereas the soldier has everything to lose and nothing
but the gratitude of his fellow-men to win.

Let every man pray that he may in some true
sense be a soldier of fortune, that he may have the
good fortune to spend his energies and his life in
the service of his fellow-men in order that he may
die to be recorded upon the rolls of those who have
not thought of themselves but have thought of those
whom they served. Isn't this the lesson of our Lord
and Saviour Jesus Christ? Am I not reminding you
of these common judgments of our life, simply ex-
pounding to you this book of revelation, this book
which reveals the common man to himself, which
strips life of its disguises and its pretenses and ele-
vates those standards by which alone true greatness
and true strength and true valour are assessed?

Do you wonder, therefore, that when I was asked
what my theme this evening would be I said it would
be "The Bible and Progress"? We do not judge
progress by material standards. America is not
ahead of the other nations of the world because she
is rich. Nothing makes America great except her
thoughts, except her ideals, except her acceptance of
those standards of judgment which are written large
upon these pages of revelation. America has all
along claimed the distinction of setting this example
to the civilized world—that men were to think of
one another, that governments were to be set up for

the service of the people, that men were to be judged by these moral standards which pay no regard to rank or birth or conditions, but which assess every man according to his single and individual value. This is the meaning of this charter of the human soul. This is the standard by which men and nations have more and more come to be judged. And so the form has consisted in nothing more nor less than this— in trying to conform actual conditions, in trying to square actual laws with the right judgments of human conduct and more than liberty.

That is the reason that the Bible has stood at the back of progress. That is the reason that reform has come not from the top but from the bottom. If you are ever tempted to let a government reform itself, I ask you to look back in the pages of history and find me a government that reformed itself. If you are ever tempted to let a party attempt to reform itself, I ask you to find a party that ever reformed itself.

A tree is not nourished by its bloom and by its fruit. It is nourished by its roots, which are down deep in the common and hidden soil, and every process of purification and rectification comes from the bottom—not from the top. It comes from the masses of struggling human beings. It comes from the instinctive efforts of millions of human hearts trying to beat their way up into the light and into the hope of the future.

Parties are reformed and governments are corrected by the impulses coming out of the hearts of those who never exercised authority and never organized parties. Those are the sources of strength, and I pray God that these sources may never cease to be spiritualized by the immortal subjections of these words of inspiration of the Bible.

If any statesman sunk in the practices which debase a nation will but read this single book, he will go to his prayers abashed. Do you not realize, ladies and gentlemen, that there is a whole literature in the Bible? It is not one book, but a score of books. Do you realize what literature is? I am sometimes sorry to see the great classics of our English literature used in the schools as textbooks, because I am afraid that little children may gain the impression that these are formal lessons to be learned. There is no great book in any language, ladies and gentlemen, that is not the spontaneous outpouring of some great mind on the cry of some great heart. And the reason that poetry moves us more than prose does is that it is the rhythmic and passionate voice of some great spirit that has seen more than his fellowmen can see.

I have found more true politics in the poets of the English-speaking race than I have ever found in all the formal treatises on political science. There is more of the spirit of our own institutions in a few lines of Tennyson than in all the textbooks on governments put together:

> A nation still, the rulers and the ruled,
> Some sense of duty, something of a faith,
> Some reverence for the laws ourselves have made,
> Some patient force to change them when we will,
> Some civic manhood firm against the crowd.

Can you find summed up the manly, self-helping spirit of Saxon liberty anywhere better than in those few lines? Men afraid of nobody, afraid of nothing but their own passions, on guard against being caught unaware by their own sudden impulses and so getting their grapple upon life in firm-set institutions, some reverence for the laws themselves have made, some patience, not passionate force, to change them when they will, some civic manhood firm against the crowd. Literature, ladies and gentlemen, is revelation of the human spirit, and within the covers of this one book is a whole lot of literature, prose and poetry, history and rhapsody, the sober narration of the ecstasy of human excitement—things that ring in one's ears like songs never to be forgotten. And so I say let us never forget that these deep sources, these wells of inspiration, must always be our sources of refreshment and of renewal. Then no man can put unjust power upon us. We shall live in that chartered liberty in which a man sees the things unseen, in which he knows that he is bound for a country in which there are no questions mooted any longer of right or wrong.

Can you imagine a man who did not believe these words, who did not believe in the future life, standing up and doing what has been the heart and center of liberty always—standing up before the king himself and saying, "Sir, you have sinned and done wrong in the sight of God, and I am His messenger of judgment to pronounce upon you the condemnation of Almighty God. You may silence me, you may send me to my reckoning with my Maker, but you cannot silence or reverse the judgment.'' That is what a man feels whose faith is rooted in the Bible. And the man whose faith is rooted in the Bible knows that reform cannot be stayed, that the finger of God that moves upon the face of the nations is against every man that plots the nation's downfall or the people's deceit; that these men are simply groping and staggering in their ignorance to a fearful day of judgment; and that whether one generation witnesses it or not the glad day of revelation and of freedom will come in which men will sing by the host of the coming of the Lord in His glory, and all of those will be forgotten—those little, scheming, contemptible creatures that forgot the image of God and tried to frame men according to the image of the evil one.

You may remember that allegorical narrative in the Old Testament of those who searched through one cavern after another, cutting the holes in the walls and going into the secret places where all sorts of noisome things were worshipped. Men do not dare to let the sun shine in upon such things and upon such occupations and worships. And so I say there will be no halt to the great movement of the armies of reform until men forget their God, until they forget this charter of their liberty. Let no man suppose that progress can be divorced from religion or that there is any other platform for the ministers of reform than the platform written in the utterances of our Lord and Saviour.

America was born a Christian nation. America was born to exemplify that devotion to the elements of righteousness which are derived from the revelations of Holy Scripture.

Ladies and gentlemen, I have a very simple thing to ask of you. I ask of every man and woman in this audience that from this night on they will realize that part of the destiny of America lies in their daily perusal of this great book of revelations—that if they would see America free and pure they will make their own spirits free and pure by this baptism of the Holy Scripture.

THE LAWYER IN POLITICS

ADDRESS BEFORE THE KENTUCKY BAR ASSOCIATION AT
LEXINGTON, KENTUCKY, JULY 12, 1911. FROM "THE
CONGRESSIONAL RECORD," 62D CONGRESS, 2D SESSION,
VOL. XLVIII, APPENDIX, 498-499.

MR. PRESIDENT, ladies and gentlemen, the
lawyer is, by very definition, an expert in
the law; and society lives by law. Without it its
life is vague, inchoate, disordered, vexed with a hopeless instability. At every turn of its experience
society tries to express its life, therefore, in law—
to make the rules of its action universal and imperative. This is the whole process of politics.
Politics is the struggle for law, for an institutional
expression of the changing life of society.

Of course, this is the deeper view of politics. It
is not the view of the mere party man or of the professional politician. He thinks chiefly, no doubt, of
the offices and their emoluments; of the tenure of
power; of the choice of policy from day to day in
the administration of the various departments of
government; of the hundred advantages, both personal and partisan, which can be obtained in a successful contest for the control of the instruments of
politics; but even he cannot escape the deeper view
at last. He must express the policy of his party
or the advantage gained by his occupation of office

in statutes, in rules of law, imposed in the interest of some class or group, if not in the interest of society at large. He is really, in the last analysis, struggling to control law and the development and use of institutions. He needs as much as the statesman does the assistance of the legal expert, the skill of the technical guide; the lawyer must be at his elbow to see that he plays the game according to the nominal rules.

The lawyer, therefore, has always been indispensable, whether he merely guided the leaders or was himself the leader, and nowhere has the lawyer played a more prominent part in politics than in England and America, where the rules of law have always been the chief instruments of contest and regulation, of liberty and efficient organization, and the chief means of lifting society from one stage to the next of its slow development.

The lawyer's ideal part in this unending struggle is easy to conceive. There is long experience stored up in the history of law. He, above all other men, should have a quick perception of what is feasible, of the new things that will fit into the old, of the experiences which should be heeded, the wrongs that should be remedied, and the rights that should be more completely realized. He knows out of his own practice how pitiful, oftentimes, against how many obstacles, amidst how many impediments, often interposed by the law itself, sometimes interposed by the ignorance of society or by the malevolence of designing men, the men about him make their daily effort to live free from the unnecessary interference

or the selfish stupidity or the organized opposition
of their neighbours and rivals. He knows what
forces gather and work their will in the field of industry, of commerce, of all enterprise. He, if any
man, knows where justice breaks down, where law
needs amplification or amendment or radical change,
what the alterations are that must be effected before
the right will come into action easily and certainly
and with genuine energy. He should at every turn
be the mediator between groups of men, between all
contending and contesting interests. He should show
how differences are to be moderated, and antagonisms
adjusted and society given peace and ease of movement.

He can play this ideal part, however, only if he
has the right insight and sympathy. If he regards
his practice as a mere means of livelihood, if he is
satisfied to put his expert advice at the service of
any interest or enterprise, if he does not regard
himself as an officer of the State, but only as an
agent of private interest, if, above all, he does not
really see the wrongs that are accumulating, the mischief that is being wrought, the hearts that are being
broken and the lives that are being wrecked, the
hopes that are being snuffed out and the energies
that are being sapped, he cannot play the part of
guide or moderator or adviser in the large sense
that will make him a statesman and a benefactor.

It is a hard thing to exact of him, no doubt, that
he should have a non-professional attitude toward
law, that he should be more constantly conscious of
his duties as a citizen than of his interests as a prac-

titioner, but nothing less than that will fit him to play the really great rôle intended for his profession in the great plot of affairs. He must breed himself in the true philosophy of his calling. It is his duty to see from the point of view of all sorts and conditions of men, of the men whom he is not directly serving as well as of those whom he is directly serving.

This is a matter of character, of disposition, and of training outside the schools of law, in the broader schools of duty and of citizenship and of patriotism. It is a great conception when once a lawyer has filled himself with it. It lifts him oftentimes to a very high place of vision and of inspiration. It makes of him the custodian of the honour and integrity of a great social order, an instrument of humanity, because an instrument of justice and fair dealing and of all those right adjustments of life that make the world fit to live in.

If I contrast with this ideal conception of the function of the lawyer in society what I may be excused for calling his actual rôle in the struggle for law and progress and the renovation of affairs, I hope that I will not be interpreted as suggesting a view of our great profession which is in any wise touched with cynicism or even with the spirit of harsh criticism. The facts do not justify a cynical view of the profession or even a fear that it may be permanently losing the spirit which has ruled the action of the greater members of the bar and of the immortal judges who have presided at the birth and given strength and fibre to the growth and lib-

erty and human right. I wish to submit what I
have to say in all fairness and without colour even
or discouragement.

The truth is that the technical training of the
modern American lawyer, his professional prepossessions and his business involvements, impose limitations upon him and subject him to temptations
which seriously stand in the way of his rendering
the ideal service to society which is demanded by
the true standards and canons of his profession.
Modern business, in particular, with its huge and
complicated processes, has tended to subordinate
him, to make of him a servant, an instrument instead of a free adviser and a master of justice. My
professional life has afforded me a rather close view
of the training of the modern lawyer in schools, and
I must say that it seems to me an intensely technical
training. Even the greater and broader principles
of which the elder lawyers used to discourse with a
touch of broad philosophy, those principles which
used to afford writers like Blackstone occasion for
incidental disquisitions on the character and history
of society, now wear in our teaching so technical an
aspect, are seen through the medium of so many
wire-drawn decisions, are covered with so thick a
gloss of explanation and ingenious interpretation,
that they do not wear an open and genial and human
aspect, but seem to belong to some recondite and
private science.

Moreover, the prepossessions of the modern lawyer
are all in favour of his close identification with his
clients. The lawyer deems himself in conscience

bound to be contentious, to manœuvre for every advantage, to contribute to his clients' benefit his skill in a difficult and hazardous game. He seldom thinks of himself as the advocate of society. His very feeling that he is the advocate now of this, now of that, and again of another special individual interest separates him from broader conceptions. He moves in the atmosphere of private rather than public service. Moreover, he is absorbed now more than ever before into the great industrial organism. His business becomes more and more complicated and specialized. His studies and his services are apt to become more and more confined to some special field of law. He grows more and more a mere expert in the legal side of a certain class of great industrial or financial undertakings. The newspapers and the public in general speak of "corporation lawyers," and of course the most lucrative business of our time is derived from the need that the great business combinations we call corporations have at every turn of their affairs of an expert legal adviser. It is apt to happen with the most successful, and by that test the most eminent, lawyers of our American communities that by the time they reach middle life their thoughts have become fixed in very hard and definite moulds. Though they have thought honestly, they are apt to have thought narrowly; they have not made themselves men of wide sympathies or discernment.

It is evident what must happen in such circumstances. The bench must be filled from the bar, and it is growing increasingly difficult to supply the bench with disinterested, unspoiled lawyers, capable

of being the free instruments of society, the friends
and guides of statesmen, the interpreters of the common life of the people, the mediators of the great
process by which justice is led from one enlightenment and liberalization to another.

For the notable, I had almost said fundamental,
circumstance of our political life is that our courts
are, under our constitutional system, the means of
our political development. Every change in our law,
every modification of political practice, must sooner
or later pass under their scrutiny. We can go only
as fast as the legal habit of mind of our lawyers will
permit. Our politics are bound up in the mental
character and attitude and in the intellectual vigour
and vision of our lawyers. Ours is so intensely and
characteristically a legal polity that our politics depend upon our lawyers. They are the ultimate instruments of our life.

There are two present and immediate tests of the
serviceability of the legal profession to the Nation,
which I think will at once be recognized as tests
which it is fair to apply. In the first place, there
is the critical matter of reform of legal procedure—
the almost invariable theme, if I am not mistaken,
of all speakers upon this question from the President
of the United States down. America lags far behind
other countries in the essential matter of putting the
whole emphasis in our courts upon the substance of
right and justice. If the bar associations of this
country were to devote themselves, with the great
knowledge and ability at their command, to the utter
simplification of judicial procedure, to the abolition

of technical difficulties and pitfalls, to the removal
of every unnecessary form, to the absolute subordination of method to the object sought, they would do
a great patriotic service, which, if they will not address themselves to it, must be undertaken by laymen
and novices. The actual miscarriages of justice, because of nothing more than a mere slip in a phrase
or a mere error in an immaterial form, are nothing
less than shocking. Their number is incalculable,
but much more incalculable than their number is the
damage they do to the reputation of the profession
and to the majesty and integrity of the law. Any
one bar association which would show the way to
radical reform in these matters would insure a universal reconsideration of the matter from one end
of the country to the other and would by that means
redeem the reputation of a great profession and set
American society forward a whole generation in its
struggle for an equitable adjustment of its difficulties.

The second and more fundamental immediate test
of the profession is its attitude toward the regulation
of modern business, particularly of the powers and
action of modern corporations. It is absolutely necessary that society should command its instruments
and not be dominated by them. The lawyer, not the
layman, has the best access to the means by which
the reforms of our economic life can be best and
most fairly acomplished. Never before in our history did those who guide affairs more seriously need
the assistance of those who can claim an expert familiarity with the legal processes by which reforms

may be effectually accomplished. It is in this matter
more than in any other that our profession may now
be said to be on trial. It will gain or lose the confidence of the country as it proves equal to the test
or unequal.

As one looks about him at the infinite complexities
of the modern problems of life, at the great tasks to
be accomplished by law, at the issues of life and
happiness and prosperity involved, one cannot but
realize how much depends upon the part the lawyer
is to play in the future politics of the country. If
he will not assume the rôle of patriot and of statesman, if he will not lend all his learning to the service
of the common life of the country, if he will not open
his sympathies to common men and enlist his en-
thusiasm in those policies which will bring regeneration to the business of the country, less expert hands
than his must attempt the difficult and perilous business. It will be clumsily done. It will be done at
the risk of reaction against the law itself. It will
be done perhaps with brutal disregard of the niceties
of justice, with clumsiness instead of with skill.

The tendencies of the profession, therefore, its
sympathies, its inclinations, its prepossessions, its
training, its point of view, its motives, are part of
the stuff and substance of the destiny of the country.
It is these matters rather than any others that bar
associations should consider; for an association is
greater than the individual lawyer. It should embody not the individual ambition of the practitioner,
but the point of view of society with regard to the
profession. It should hold the corporate conscience

and consciousness of the profession. It is inspiring to think what might happen if but one great State bar association were to make up its mind and move toward these great objects with intelligence, determination, and indomitable perseverance.

THE RIGHTS OF THE JEWS

ADDRESS AT CARNEGIE HALL, NEW YORK, DECEMBER 6, 1911. FROM "THE CONGRESSIONAL RECORD," 62D CONGRESS, 2D SESSION, VOL. XLVIII, APPENDIX, 497-498.

MR. CHAIRMAN and gentlemen, the object of this meeting is not agitation, it is the statement of a plain case in such terms as may serve to arrest the attention of the Nation with regard to a matter which is of no mere local importance, which does not merely affect the rights and essential privileges of our Jewish fellow-citizens as freemen and Americans, but which touches the dignity of our Government and the maintenance of those rights of manhood which that Government was set up to vindicate.

The facts are these: For some 80 years a treaty has existed between this country and Russia in which it is explicitly covenanted and agreed that the inhabitants of the two nations shall have the liberty of entering any part of the territory of either that is open to foreign commerce; that they shall be at liberty to sojourn and reside in all parts whatsoever of the territory thus opened to commerce, in order to attend to their affairs; and that they shall enjoy the same security and protection as inhabitants of the country in which they are sojourning, on condition, of course, that they submit to the laws and ordinances there prevailing, and particularly to the regulations there in force concerning commerce. For some 40 years the obligations of this treaty have been disregarded by Russia in respect of our Jewish fellow-citizens. Our Government has protested, but has never gone beyond protest. After 40 years of more correspondence the Russian Government naturally does not expect the matter to be carried beyond protest to action, and so continues to act as it pleases in this matter, in the confidence that our Government does not seriously mean to include our Jewish fellow-citizens among those upon whose rights it will insist.

It is not necessary to conjecture the reasons. The treaty thus disregarded by Russia is a treaty of commerce and navigation. Its main object is trade, the sort of economic intercourse between the two nations that will promote the material interests of both. Important commercial and industrial relations have been established under it. Large American undertakings, we are informed, would be put in serious peril were those relations broken off. We must concede something, even at the expense of a certain number of our fellow-citizens, in order not to risk a loss greater than the object which would seem to justify.

I for one do not fear any loss. The economic relations of two great nations are not based upon sentiment; they are based upon interest. It is safe to say that in this instance they are not based upon mutual respect, for Russia cannot respect us when she sees us for 40 years together preferring our interests to our rights. Whatever our feeling may be with regard to Russia, whatever our respect for her statesmen or our sympathy with the great future in store for her people, she would certainly be justified in acting upon the expectation that we would follow our calculations of expediency rather than our convictions of right and justice. Only once or twice, it would seem, has she ever thought our Government in earnest. Should she ever deem it in earnest, respect would take the place of covert indifference and the treaty would be lived up to. If it was ever advantageous to her, it is doubly and trebly advantageous now, and her advantage would be her guide, as has been ours, in the maintenance of a treaty of trade and navigation.

If the Russian Government has felt through all these years that it could ignore the protest of American ministers and Secretaries of State, it has been because the American Government spoke for special interests or from some special point of view and not for the American people. It is the fact that the attention of the American people has now been drawn to this matter that is altering the whole aspect of it.

We are a practical people. Like the rest of the world we establish our trade relations upon grounds of interest, not sentiment. The feeling of the American people toward the people of Russia has always been one of deep sympathy, and I believe of ready comprehension, and we have dealt with their Government in frankness and honour, wherever it appears that the interests of both nations could be

served. We have not held off from cordial intercourse or withheld our respect because her political
policy was so sharply contrasted with ours. Our desire is to be her friend and to make her relations
with her closer and closer.

But there lies a principle back of our life. America is not a mere body of traders; it is a body of
free men. Our greatness is built upon our freedom—is moral, not material. We have a great
ardour for gain; but we have a deep passion for
the rights of man. Principles lie back of our action.
America would be inconceivable without them.
These principles are not incompatible with great material prosperity. On the contrary, unless we are
deeply mistaken, they are indispensable to it. We
are not willing to have prosperity, however, if our
fellow-citizens must suffer contempt for it, or lose
the rights that belong to every American in order
that we may enjoy it. The price is too great.

Here is a great body of our Jewish fellow-citizens,
from whom have sprung men of genius in every
walk of our varied life, men who have become part
of the very stuff of America, who have conceived its
ideals with singular clearness and led its enterprise
with spirit and sagacity. They are playing a particularly conspicuous part in building up the very
prosperity of which our Government has so great a
stake in its dealings with the Russian Government
with regard to the rights of men. They are not Jews
in America; they are American citizens. In this
great matter with which we deal to-night, we speak
for them as for representatives and champions of

principles which underlie the very structure of our Government. They have suddenly become representatives of us all. By our action for them shall be tested our sincerity, our genuineness, the reality of principle among us.

I am glad this question has been thus brought into the open. There is here a greater stake than any other upon which we could set our hearts. Here is the final test of our ability to square our politics with our principles. We may now enjoy the exhilaration of matching our professions with handsome performance. We are not here to express our sympathy with our Jewish fellow-citizens, but to make evident our sense of identity with them. This is not their cause; it is America's. It is the cause of all who love justice and do right.

The means by which the wrongs we complain of may be set right are plain. There is no hostility in what we do toward the Russian Government. No man who takes counsel of principle will have in his thought anything but purposes of peace. There need be for us in this great matter no touch of anger. But the conquests of peace are based upon mutual respect. The plain fact of the matter is that for some 40 years we have observed the obligations of our treaty with Russia and she has not. That can go on no longer. So soon as Russia fully understands that it can go on no longer, that we must, with whatever regret, break off the intercourse between our people and our merchants, unless the agreements upon which it is based can be observed in letter and in spirit, the air will clear. There is every reason why our intercourse should be maintained and extended, but it cannot be upon such terms as at present. If the explicit provisions of our present agreement cannot be maintained, we must reconsider the matter in the light of the altered circumstances and see upon what terms, if any, of mutual honour our intercourse may be reëstablished. We have advantages to offer her merchants, her mine owners, her manufacturers, which her Government will not despise. We are not suppliants. We come with gifts in our hands. Her statesmen see as clearly as ours. An intolerable situation will be remedied just as soon as Russia is convinced that for us it is indeed intolerable.

RICHMOND ADDRESS

ADDRESS DELIVERED BEFORE THE GENERAL ASSEMBLY
OF VIRGINIA AND THE CITY COUNCIL OF RICHMOND
ON FEBRUARY 1, 1912. FROM "THE CONGRESSIONAL
RECORD," 62D CONGRESS, 2D SESSION, VOL. XLVIII,
PP. 3919-3922.

YOUR Excellency, Mr. Speaker, Your Honour,
Gentlemen of the General Assembly of Virginia, and of the Council of the City of Richmond,
Ladies and Gentlemen:

I face this great audience to-night with a mixture
of emotions. I am glad to feel like a boy who has
come home to report in some degree to his neighbours, not about myself, but about the things that I
have seen, or tried to see clearly, happening in the
great communities of which we constitute a part.

I am not going to hold the distinguished gentlemen who have introduced me responsible for the
terms in which they have presented me to you. I
am ready to believe, if anything should happen to
me that is untoward, that they have uttered not a
critical judgment, but have spoken according to the
dictates of their hearts. They have been welcoming
me home—they have not been telling you exactly
what I am.

And yet, the voice of a friend melts the heart, and
I, for my part, feel it very difficult here to-night to
make an address from which the sentimental emo-

tions that rise in me are left out. I have on my lapel a badge which, if I followed the dictates of good taste, perhaps I should not wear, for it bears my own name; but it was pinned on my coat by one of the delegation from Staunton—my native place—(applause)—and I know that you indulge me in the sentiment which has led me to leave it there, not as a token of egotism, but as a token of my appreciation of the welcome which has been extended me.

You have been told to-night that the eyes of the nation were centred upon me. I hope not. That is very awkward. (Laughter.) I do not like to believe that the eyes of the nation are centred upon me. I do like to believe that the thoughts of the nation are centred upon the great questions which I, among many others, have tried honestly and fearlessly to expound—(applause)—because we are just now seeking to show our devotion, not to persons, but to a cause—a fundamental cause, a cause to which the whole history of America has been a commendatory example.

I could not stand before this audience of my one-time neighbours—for there are a great many men behind me at any rate, if not in front of me, who have known me ever since I was a boy—and try to pose myself as an important figure. They would see through it. (Laughter.) I remember the story of an innocent old woman who went into the side-show of a circus and saw, or supposed that she saw, a man read a newspaper through a two-inch board. She got up in great excitement and said, "Here, let me out of here; this is no place for me to be with these

thin things on." (Laughter and applause.) I fear
that the disguise of greatness would be too transparent; and yet I do feel that every man should, who believes in the great ideals of this country and in their
translation into action, stand up in every company
and proclaim the faith that is in him, so that by
common counsel and by common action we may
achieve something for this great nation.

I have heard men complain of the changes of the
times. I have heard men counsel that we stand still
and do nothing. How futile the counsel is! Do you
remember the quaint story of the Scottish highlander
who went into the market of Edinburgh, followed by
his dog? He went to a fishmonger's stall and the
dog incautiously dropped his tail into a basket of
lobsters, and one of the lobsters nipped his tail.
Whereupon the dog went yelping down the street,
with the lobster bouncing after. The fishmonger
said, "Hoot, mon: whussle to your dog!" "Hoot!"
said the Scotchman, "whussle to your lobster."
(Laughter and applause.)

Now if you think some of your leaders are going
too fast a pace, don't whistle to them. Whistle to
the spirit of the age. Whistle to the questions that
have whipped their consciences and dominated their
understandings. They cannot stop if they are going
to keep up with the great transmutations of affairs.
For, gentlemen, whether we have realized it or not,
we have entered a new age, and I have comforted
myself with the thought as I journeyed towards
Virginia again, that Virginia had never been daunted
by a new age; with however debonair and young and

confident a genius, Virginia led a great nation and
helped to create a great nation in a new age. (Applause.)

I have heard men say that it was un-American to
criticise the institutions we are living under. I wonder if they remember the significance of the American flag—the first insurgent flag that was flung to
the breeze—the flag that represented the most colossal "kick" that was ever taken in political transactions; a flag that I cannot look at without imag-
ining that it consists of alternate strips of parchment upon which are written the fundamental rights
of man, alternating with the streams of blood by
which those rights had been vindicated and vali-
dated. (Applause.) In the blue sky of the corner
there are swung star after star of commonwealths
of free men who were setting up their own homes
upon the principles of those vindicated rights.

Do you suppose that I will believe, or that any
one knowing the history of America or the history
of Virginia will believe, that it is inconsistent with
being an American and a Virginian to propose that
you construct liberty for each successive age, and
that if necessary you reconstruct liberty for each
successive age? If I had happened to get that
breath out of my lungs in my absence from the Old
Dominion, it would enter them again as I came back
to her. (Applause.) I have not lost it elsewhere.
The handsome contagion has infected the whole of
the great nation. Do not suppose that the people of
New Jersey have not seen visions, and dreamed
dreams. Some gentlemen in some initial quarters

wanted to suppress the dreams. (Laughter and applause.) It made the sleep of some men, in some
quarters, uneasy that they should be haunted by
those visions, but they never went out of the thought
or the sleepless eyes of those great multitudes of men
for whom happiness depends upon freedom, for
whom self-respect depends upon freedom and principle, and in New Jersey as everywhere else they
have drunk of those fountains which first began to
flow in Virginia, those fountains by which we constantly renew our youth, and devote ourselves generation after generation to the preservation of the
institutions of America.

I want, if possible, to explain to this great body
of thinking persons the age in which we live, as it
seems to me to present itself. Why, ladies and
gentlemen, in our age every question is new. Every
question that faces America is just as new now as
were the questions that faced America in 1776. I do
not mean that we are upon the verge of a revolution.
I do not mean that passion is stirring which will upset
the ancient foundations of our political order; but
I do mean that life has changed under our very
eye, so that what we do will have to be adjusted to
almost absolutely new conditions, and I want that
you will bear with me to point out just what I mean.

You know that one of the great questions that
faces this great country is the question of conservation. Now just what do you mean by conservation?
Do you mean the big thing, or do you mean the little
thing? The little thing, though big in itself, but
little by comparison, is the renewal of our forests,

the protection of our great water powers against further depletion, the safe-guarding of our mineral resources against waste and extravagance, the keeping in store as long as may be of those things which cannot be renewed, and may even within a generation, some of them, come to the point of exhaustion.

That is the question of conservation as most men discuss it; but is that all? It seems to me that the fundamental question of conservation in America is the conservation of the energy, the elasticity, the hope of the American people. (Applause.) I deal a great deal with friends, for I have had such friends all my life, who are engaged in manufacturing in this country, and almost every one of them will admit that while he studies his machinery, and will dismiss a man who overtaxes the machinery so that its bearings get heated, so that the stress of work is too much for it, so that it is racked and over done, not a man of them dismisses a superintendent because he puts too great strain upon the souls and hearts of his employees. (Applause.) We rack and exhaust and reject the man machine, and we honestly, economically, thoughtfully preserve the steel machine; for we can get more men—we have only to beckon to them; the streets are full of them waiting for employment; but we cannot, without cost, get a new machine.

Now that kind of conservation is a great deal more than the question of overstraining the factories. If I knew my business and were a manufacturer, what would I do? I would create such conditions of sanitation, such conditions of life and comfort and health as would keep my employees in the best physical condition, and I would establish such a relationship with them as would make them believe that I was a fellow human being, with a heart under my jacket, and that they were not my tools, but my partners.

Then you would see the gleam in the eye, then you would see that human energy spring into expression which is the only energy which differentiates America from the rest of the world. (Applause.) Men are used everywhere, men are driven under all climes and flags, but we have boasted in America that every man was a free unit of whom we had to be as careful as we would be of ourselves. America's economic supremacy depends upon the moral character and the resilient hopefulness of our workmen. So I say, when you are studying questions of conservation, realize what you have been wasting, the forests, water, minerals and the hearts and bodies of men. That is the new question of conservation. I say new, because only in our day has the crowding gotten so close and hot that there is no free outlet for men. Don't you remember that until the year 1890, every ten years when we took the census, we were able to draw a frontier in this country? It is true that in what is called the golden age, 1849, when gold was discovered in California, we sent outposts to the Pacific and settled the further slope of the Rocky Mountains. But between us and that slope, until 1890, there intervened an unoccupied space where the census map makers could draw a frontier. But when we reached the year 1890 there was no frontier discoverable in America.

What did that mean? That meant that men who found conditions intolerable in crowded America no longer had a place free where they could take up land of their own and start a new hope. That is what that meant, and as America turns upon herself her seething millions and the cauldron grows hotter and hotter, is it not the great duty of America to see that her men remain free and happy under the conditions that have now sprung up? It is true that we needed a frontier so much that after the Spanish war we annexed a new frontier some seven thousand miles off in the Pacific. But that is a long cry, and it takes the energy of a very young man to seek that outlet in the somewhat depressing climate of the Philippines.

So we now realize that Americans are not free to release themselves. We have got to live together and be happy in the family. I remember an old judge who was absolutely opposed to divorce, because he said that a man will be restless as long as he knows he can get loose—(laughter)—but that so soon as it is firmly settled in his mind that he has got to make the best of it, he finds a sudden current of peace and contentment. Now there is no divorce for us in our American life. We have got to put up with one another, and we have got to see to it that we so regulate and assuage one another that we will not be intolerable to each other. We have got to get a *modus vivendi* in America for happiness, and that is our new problem. And I call you to witness it *is* a new problem. America never had to finish anything before; she has been at liberty to do

the thing with a broad hand, quickly improvise
something and go on to the next thing; leave all sorts
of waste behind her, push on, blaze trails through
the forest, beat paths across the prairie. But now
we have even to top and pave our streets, we are just
finding that out. I suppose it was good for the
digestion to bump over the old cobble stones, but
it was not good for trade, and we have got to pull
up the cobble stones and make real sidewalks that
won't jolt the life out of us. Let these somewhat
whimsical comparisons serve to illustrate what I am
talking about.

Now there is another new thing in America, and
that is trade. Will you laugh at me and say, "Why,
America has been supreme in trade ever since she
was created." Has she? We have traded with one
another, but we have traded with nobody else in
proportions worth mentioning. Yes, we have in
grain, in the great foodstuffs, but do you know what
is happening? Our foodstuff exports, our grain exports are falling, falling, not because we produce
less, but because we need more ourselves. We are
getting nearer and nearer to the point where we will
ourselves consume all that our farms produce. Then
we will not have anything with which to pay our balance, will we? Yes, we will, because while our exports of grain have been falling, our exports of manufactured articles have been increasing by leaps and
bounds.

But under what circumstances? Long ago, after
we had forgotten the excellent things that the first
generation of statesmen had done for us in America,

we deliberately throttled the merchant marine of
the United States, and now it is so completely throttled that you are more likely to see the flag of the
little kingdom of Greece upon the seas than the flag
of the United States. And you know that the Nation that wants foreign commerce must have the
arms of commerce. If she has the ships, her sailors
will see to it that her merchants have the markets.
I am not arguing this to you, I am telling you, for
the facts if we look but a little ways for them, will
absolutely demonstrate this circumstance, that we
have more to fear in the competition of England,
Germany and France, because of the multitude of
English, French and German carriers upon the sea
than we have to fear from the ingenuity of the English manufacturers or the enterprise of the German
merchants.

Anybody who has dealt with railroads knows what
I am talking about. Railroads in America have
made and unmade cities and communities, have they
not? They would do it now if they were not watched
by the Interstate Commerce Commission. We are
obliging them to work without discrimination now,
but they at one time discriminated as they pleased,
and they determined where cities were to grow and
where cities were to decay.

Very well. The same thing is happening upon the
high seas. The foreign carrier can tell you where you
can go and where you cannot go. He can discriminate against you and in favour of his own merchants
and manufacturers, and he will, because he does.

And while all this is going on, and we lack the

means, we are fairly bursting our own jacket. We
are making more manufactured goods than we can
consume ourselves, and every manufacturer is wak-
ing up to the fact that if we do not let anybody climb
over our tariff wall to get in, he has got to climb to
get out; that we have deliberately domesticated ourselves; that we have deliberately cut ourselves off
from the currents of trade; that we have deliberately
divorced ourselves from world commerce; and now,
if we are not going to stifle economically, we have
got to find our way out into the great international
exchanges of the world. There is a new question.

I was speaking in Boston the other evening at a
real estate exchange, and I asked those gentlemen
what is going to keep real estate values in Boston
steady? I asked them if they realized what was
likely to happen after the year 1915. You know
that in that year it is likely that the great ditch
in the Isthmus will be open for commerce. We are
not opening it for America, by the way, because we
haven't any ships to send through it; we are opening it for England and Germany. (Applause.) We
are pouring out American millions in order that German exporters, English exporters and French exporters may profit by our enterprise; and when that
is done, of course something is going to happen to
America. I asked those gentlemen in Boston if,
after that was done, the arteries of trade in this
country would continue to run east and west. Some
great arteries are going to open north and south.
The great valley of the Mississippi is to be the home
of teeming industries and of a ceaseless commerce.

And then I wonder sometimes if it will not be colder still in the northeastern section of this country where Boston is situated. Those east winds, of which they are fond, will not bring them increasing commerce, perhaps, but they will hear the throb of that great heart in the centre of the continent, which is shifting the centre of gravity, which is throwing into different arteries the course of the blood of the great commercial world. Does that strike you as something happening in America that you cannot sit still and neglect? Hadn't you better "whussle to the lobster"? Don't whistle to the dog, but whistle to the lobster, if you think it will do any good, but I have never enticed a lobster by whistling.

There is another new question in America, and that is the question of business. Business is in a situation in America that it was never in before; it is in a situation to which we have not adjusted our laws. Our laws are still meant for business done by *individuals;* they have not been satisfactorily adjusted to business done by great *combinations,* and we have got to adjust them. I do not say we may or may not, I say we have got to, there is no choice. If your laws do not fit your facts, the facts are not injured, the law is damaged; so much the worse for the law, because the law, unless I have studied it amiss, is the expression of the facts in legal regulation. Laws have never altered the facts; laws have always necessarily expressed the facts, adjusted interests as they have arisen, and changed to one another.

When before, in the history of America, were the

Congress of the United States and the Legislature of every State called upon in every session to intervene in the regulation of business? Never before our own age.

Now why is all this happening? Why has business taken on a new aspect in America? Why does it wear a face with which we are only by degrees becoming familiar? For a very interesting reason. An ever diminishing circle of men exercise a control in America with which only the Government itself can compete.

I am not one of those, ladies and gentlemen, who speak of the interests in big letters as if they were enemies of mankind. I know the natural history of the interests, and they grew just as naturally as an oak grows; some of them grew just as naturally as a weed grows. (Laughter.)

I am not here to enter an indictment against business. No man indicts natural history. No man undertakes to say that the things that have happened by operation of irresistible forces are immoral things, though some men may have made deeply immoral use of them. I am not here to suggest that the automobile be destroyed because some fools take joy rides in it. I want to catch the fools. I am not here, in other words, to suggest that the things that have happened to us must be reversed, and the scroll of time rolled back on itself. To attempt that would be futile and ridiculous. I am here to point out as clearly as I can what I believe to be the facts, and what most of you *know* to be the facts, because some of you have been considering these things longer than I have, and I have no doubt that you have seen things clearer in twenty years than I have seen them in twenty months. I am not talking about things distant; I am talking about things that I have seen with my eyes and handled with my hands.

Now these things, if you will allow me to express them briefly—and to express them briefly means to express them imperfectly—these things amount to this, that a comparatively small number of men control the raw material of this country; that a comparatively small number of men control the water powers that can be made useful for the economical production of the power to drive our machinery almost entirely; that that same small number of men, by agreements handed around among themselves, control prices, and that that same group of men control the larger credits of the country.

Do you know that nobody can undertake the larger kind of undertakings without their approval and consent? There are very few men who can afford to stand up and tell you that, because there are very few men in my happy condition. I haven't any note in bank. (Applause.) I live within my income and I cannot be punished for what I say. (Applause.) But I know perfectly well, and I have been told by men who dared not speak above their breaths with regard to it for fear they would be punished, that I could not start a great enterprise in this country that needed a million or more of money to start it unless I made an agreement and combination with certain gentlemen who control the great credits of the country.

Now I am not hot in my mind against these gentlemen. They used the opportunities which we accorded them, and they have got us. Some of them
are just as patriotic, just as public spirited, just
as honest as any man in America. But when you
have got the market in your hand, does honesty
oblige you to turn the palm upside down and empty
it? If you have got the market in your hand and
believe that you understand the interest of the
country better than anybody else, is it patriotic to
let it go?

I was trying to analyze the other day what a Republican is. (Laughter.) I do not want to say
anything about that great body of my fellow-countrymen in various parts of America who have formed
the bad habit of voting the Republican ticket. They
are not the men I am talking about, but the Republican leaders, the men who establish the ideals and
policies of that party, how would you describe them?
Why, I would say that they are men who actually
believe that the only men whose advice it is safe to
take with regard to the happiness and prosperity of
America are the men who have the biggest material
stake in the enterprises of America. They believe,
therefore, that America ought to be governed by
trustees—(applause)—and that those trustees are
the managers of the oldest and greatest "vested interests" of the country. That is a workable theory,
that is a theory that has obtained time out of mind.
It happens, though these gentlemen have forgotten
it, that America was established to get rid of it, but,
having forgotten that, reading only the older books,

I dare say, reading back of the birth of America,
they say that there are only a few men with grasp
enough of affairs and knowledge enough of what are
the bases of prosperity to run a big, complicated
government like this.

Now, as a Democrat—(applause)—I define myself
by absolutely protesting against that view of public
affairs. I will not live under trustees if I can help
it. (Applause.) No group of men less than the
majority has a right to tell me how I have got to
live in America. I will submit to the majority, because I have been trained to do it, though I may have
my private opinion even of the majority; but, being
a dyed-in-the-wool Democrat, I am proud to submit
my judgment to that majority of my fellow-citizens.

I know that there are some gum-shoe politicians
in both camps who do not agree with that theory at
all. They say, "You need not say much about it out
loud, but we have got to run these people; this enterprise of free government has to be personally conducted"—(applause)—"that the people want this
or that we do not deny, but they do not know what
is good for them."

So there are two theories of trusteeship, a trusteeship of the big interests and a trusteeship of the
machine. I do not see my way to subscribe to either
kind of trusteeship. Not that I am an insurgent,
because I believe in organization; I believe that
party success is impossible without organization;
but I make this distinction between organization and the machine—organization is a systematic coöperation of men for a common purpose,

while the machine is a systematic coöperation of
men for a private purpose. (Great applause.) I
know what I am talking about, because we have a
perfect specimen in New Jersey.

Now I know what supports the machine, because
I have seen them eat out of a spoon. It is a golden
spoon, and I have seen the nurse that fed them,
and I have seen that nurse absolutely impartial as
between the Republican machine and the Democratic
machine—(laughter and applause)—and the price
of the food, the price of the nutrition, is that the
machine will be good, that it will see that nothing is
done that will hurt the nurse, that nothing is done
which will interfere with the private understanding
that is established in the nursery.

Now this is our problem. We have got to set to
work now systematically to conserve every resource
and every energy of America. We have got to
realize that an absolute readjustment of trade is necessary, and that that is an irresistible battering-ram
that is battering at the wall of the tariff.

The tariff is not the question it was a generation
ago. I hear gentlemen make speeches now who do
not know that, but it is not. They talk as if it was
a question of protecting us from external competition, while internal competition keeps prices down;
and I happen to know that there is not any internal
competition. (Applause.) And I happen to know
that this great, irresistible energy of America is doing more than it can keep within its own shops and
limits, and therefore it has got to be released for
the commercial conquest of the world. Say what

you will, whether you are abstractly for protection or against it, you have got to legislate for the release of the energies of America.

Then, in the next place, there is the whole matter of business adjustment. Our laws are just about a generation belated, as compared with economic conditions not only, but as compared with what other advanced nations have done to bring about adjustment. Progressive America is belated, has lost its leadership in the handsome competition to show the world the way out of its difficulties.

That is the problem, and that is the reason I say that the twentieth century is better worth living in than any century that has turned up in our recollection, and that is the reason I return with confidence to Virginia and say: "You remember that your men saw such an age when this government was set up; is she daunted now to see another age that calls for constructive statesmanship; has she less vision now; has she lost courage now; has she lost the indomitable integrity now that she had then?" I wonder what will happen when Virginia sees these things with the veil withdrawn from her eyes. She will rejoice as a bridegroom coming out of his chamber; she will say, "Here is an age fit for Virginia again."

Now, what are we going to do about it?

A VOICE—Elect Wilson. (Applause.)

MR. WILSON—I hoped that you would not hear that. What is our problem? First of all, in order to move carefully, we have got to move by standard, have we not? You cannot launch out and trust to the currents. You have got to have something to steer by. You have got to know whither you are bound.

You know that curious expression, that very erroneous expression we have, when a man has lost his way in a forest or a desert. We say he has lost himself. Did you ever reflect that that is the only thing he has not lost? He is there, but what is lost is all the rest of the world. If he knew any fixed thing in his neighbourhood and knew whether it was east of him, or north of him, or south of him, or west of him, he could steer; but he has lost even the points of the compass. He does not know how he is related to the universe. Now unless you have a standard to steer by, you are lost; how would you know in which direction to steer, and where you are going? If I want to go in that direction, this way is not my road. I have got to know whither I am bound and what landmarks to guide myself by.

Do we lack landmarks in America after all those ancient principles which we have set up like secret temples in which to go and worship and compose our spirits?

In the first place, we have the standards of liberty and equal opportunity. In the second place we have this standard that the people are entitled to a government which represents them—(applause)—and in the third place they are entitled to government by that government which is in the common interest and not in the interest of special privilege.

Are not these the temples of liberty in which we have worshipped? Will any man be charged justly with trying to upset the institutions of America who works in the spirit of the worship of those principles?

What is liberty? You say of a great locomotive engine that it runs free. What do you mean? You mean that its parts are so assembled and adjusted that friction is reduced to a minimum, and that it has perfect adjustment. What do you mean by saying that a boat sails free? Do you mean that she is independent of the great breath that is in the heavens? Do you not mean that she has accommodated herself with graceful obeisance with the winds? Throw her up in the wind and see her shiver in every stick and stitch of her, while, as a seaman would say, she is held in irons. But let her fall off, let her bow to the majesty of nature, and then she is free in her adjustment. Let these serve as images.

Human freedom consists in perfect adjustment of human interests to one another. The whole problem is a problem of adjustment, reducing the friction; not reducing it by mere lubrication—(applause)—not reducing it by merely pouring in the oil of money and persuasion and flattery, but by so adjusting the parts that they love to coöperate, that they never buckle up, that they never grow so hot that we cannot move the machine at all without danger. And unless there is this perfect adjustment there will not be given that opportunity without which men cannot draw a full breath or live a day without despair. Let any group of men have the right to say to others, "You must come to us

before you can do anything," and see how long
America will be considered a place worth living in
by free men.

Our standards, therefore, are these, and we must
fearlessly use them—we must say to ourselves, "We
are going to reject everything that does not square
with those things."

Now, what is the fact? I am happy to believe
that Virginia has so far been spared the mortifying
experience that has come upon some other States.
A great many of the States of this Union, ladies
and gentlemen, have been privately controlled.
There has not been an adjustment, there has not been
free opportunity, there has not been government
that represented the people, there has not been government in the common interests. When changes
are proposed in those commonwealths, do not fall
upon those who propose them and say they are
changing the character of our government; or, if
you do, admit they are changing it back from what
it has become to what it was originally intended to
be. (Applause.) No man that I know of and trust,
no man that I will consent to consort with, is trying
to change anything fundamental in America. But
what means have we of change? Suppose that every
time you try to change your government, you have
the experience that the enterprising people of New
Jersey had for sixteen years together, when to choose
between one ticket and another ticket was to choose
between tweedledum and tweedledee. Suppose
that every time public opinion unmistakably expressed itself, something invisible, something intang-

ible, something that you could not get at, intervened between you and the action upon which you had determined, then what image would arise in your mind? That you are disappointed in your institutions as they were established? No. That you are mortified because of the change that has come over your institutions by the extent to which they have been debased.

Now you have got to choose between one of two things. I never saw this as I see it now until I came into actual, practical contact with the administration of a great State. I thank God that I have learned something in the last eighteen months, and what I have learned is this—that you have got to choose between two courses, either constructive leadership which you will stand behind to the limit, or else a resort direct to the people themselves. There are no other ways.

What does it mean, ladies and gentlemen, that all over the United States people are demanding of their Governors and of their President that they take the affairs of those people in their own hands, demanding of them leadership, not satisfied that they are honest, merely, not satisfied with their good intentions, merely, but demanding of them that they shall translate their intentions into such persuasive government that nothing can withstand them as spokesmen of the people? That is what America is demanding.

I want to tell a story, if you will allow me; I have told it very often, but most of you probably have not heard it. While Mr. Roosevelt was President, I boarded a train near my home one day and I found one of the gentlemen who were then Senators from New Jersey on the train. I dropped into the seat beside him. I found him in a very bad humor. I said, "Senator, what is the matter?" "Oh," he said, "I wish the Constitution had not given the President the right to send messages to Congress." "Why," I said, "Senator, you are barking up the wrong tree. That is not what is the matter. The trouble is that the President publishes his messages, and if the country happens to agree with him it does not stop to hear what you have to say." The President is the only member of the government of the United States elected by the whole people of the United States; he is the only one whose utterances go into all the newspapers of the United States; and inasmuch as he has a universal audience and nobody else has, nobody can answer him; and if he happens to speak the opinion of the country nobody can resist him. (Applause.) America has got the zest for that in its imagination, and it is unquiet if it does not get a President that will do that sort of thing; and I will tell you, having ridden a restive State myself, that the people in most of the States are very uncomfortable, and full of protest if their Governors do not do it. They do not want their Governors to exercise any unconstitutional power; but what is a more constitutional power than the power of public opinion? What is more persuasive and irresistible than the voice of universal conviction? That is the force that can bring back representative government in America where it has been lost. Thank God there are a great many places where it has not been lost. It is a local question, it is a question which each community can settle for itself.

But if you cannot get constructive leadership, then what? If, every time you try it, somebody defeats the purpose which your leader expresses, what are you going to do about it?

I want to read you a passage from the Virginia Bill of Rights, that immortal document which has been a model for declarations of liberty throughout the rest of the continent.

"That all power is vested in and consequently derived from the people; that magistrates are their trustees and servants, and at all times amenable to them."

Did you ever hear the doctrine put more flatly?

"That government is, or ought to be, instituted for the common benefit, protection and security of the people of the nation or community; of all the various modes and forms of government, that is the best which is capable of producing the greatest degree of happiness and safety and is the most effectually secured against the danger of maladministration; and, when any government shall be found inadequate or contrary to these purposes, a majority of the community hath an indubitable, inalienable and indefeasible right to reform, alter or abolish it, in such manner as shall be judged most conducive to the public weal."

I have heard that read a score of times on the Fourth of July, but I never heard it read where ac-

tual measures were being debated. (Applause.)
Now I am willing to come back to Virginia and
stand with George Mason on the Bill of Rights.
When I do that, I have got native soil under my feet,
soil more fertile for the growth of liberty than any
soil that can be compounded. (Applause.) And I
say that if we cannot get constructive leadership,
and we can if we will, then we have our solution in
the Bill of Rights, "A majority of the community
hath an indubitable, inalienable and indefeasible
right to reform, alter or abolish it as may be judged
most conducive to the public weal." I do not propose anything of that sort, I do not believe it is
necessary, but I do like a gun behind the door. (Applause.) I do like to say to people, "Well, if you
can't bring the game down any other way, go and
get your gun."

There are wise and unwise ways of shooting. I
had rather pepper the animal than kill him, I had
rather touch him once than deprive him of vitality.
But you can load your gun according to your own
taste; you do not have to put buckshot in it, you
can put the smallest birdshot in it that you can find,
and then at your leisure afterwards pick it out of
the hide. But always remember that behind you
like a bulwark is that Bill of Rights, that you have
the right to any kind of government you please to
have. That is the kind of insurgent I am, because
all the while I remember the temper of America. I
honestly believe that a better nation, more long
enduring, more patiently suffering, more conservative people does not exist upon God's planet. I am

not afraid of the American people getting up and humping themselves; I am only afraid they will not; and when I hear of popular vote spoken of as mob government, I feel like telling the man who utters that that he has no right to call himself an American. (Applause.) Just picture to yourselves, ladies and gentlemen, the great voting population of Virginia, from the sea to the far borders in the mountains, going calmly, man by man, to the polls, expressing their judgment about public affairs, and ask yourselves if that is your image of a mob.

What is a mob? A mob is a body of men in hot contact with one another, moved by a single, ungovernable passion upon doing a hasty thing that they will regret the next day. Do you see anything resembling a mob in that voting population of the countryside, men tramping over the mountainside, men going to the general store up in the village, men going in little conversing groups to cast their ballots—is that your notion of a mob, or is that your picture of free self-governing people?

I am not afraid of the judgments so expressed, if you give men time to think, if you give them a clear conception of the things they are to vote for; because the deepest conviction and passion of my heart is that the common people, by which I mean all of us, are to be absolutely trusted. (Applause.) The peculiarity of some representatives, particularly of the Republican party, is that when they talk about the people, they obviously do not include themselves. Now if, when you think of the people, you are not thinking about yourself, then you do not belong in

America. I, on the other hand, am liberal and generous enough, when I speak of the people, to include them. (Applause.) They do not deserve it, but then I cannot, if I am true to my principles, exclude them, they have got to come in. You know that delightful expression of Horace Greeley, who was one of the general advocates of a general amnesty to the Southern people, made use of in an eager argument one day. He said, "You know we have got to forgive them, damn them." (Laughter and applause.) That is the only working program. You cannot have the people unless you include everybody, and therefore I am ready to admit everybody.

When I look back at the processes of history, when I look back at the genesis of America, I see this written over every page, that the nations are renewed from the bottom, not from the top; that the genius which springs up from the ranks of unknown men is the genius which renews the youth and energy of the people; and in every age of the world, where you stop the courses of the blood from the roots, you injure the great, useful structure to the extent that atrophy, death and decay are sure to ensue. That is the reason that an hereditary monarchy does not work; that is the reason that an hereditary aristocracy does not work; that is the reason that everything of that sort is full of corruption and ready to decay.

So I say that our challenge of to-day is to include in the partnership all those great bodies of unnamed men who are going to produce our future leaders and renew the future energies of America. And as

I confess that, as I confess my belief in the common man, I know what I am saying. The man who is swimming against the stream knows the strength of it. The man who is in the mêlée knows what blows are being struck and what blood is being drawn. The man who is on the make is a judge of what is happening in America, not the man who has made; not the man who has emerged from the flood, not the man who is standing on the bank looking on, but the man who is struggling for his life and for the lives of those who are dearer to him than himself. That is the man whose judgment will tell you what is going on in America, and that is the man by whose judgment I for one wish to be guided—(applause)— so that as the tasks multiply and the days come when all will seem confusion and dismay, we may lift up our eyes to the hills out of these dark valleys where the crags of special privilege overshadow and darken our path, to where the sun gleams through the great passage in the broken cliffs, the sun of God, the sun meant to regenerate men, the sun meant to liberate them from their passion and despair and to lift us to those uplands which are the promised land of every man who desires liberty and achievement.